Austerlitz

Austerlitz

Napoleon and the Eagles of Europe

Ian Castle

Pen & Sword
MILITARY

First published in Great Britain in 2005
and reprinted in this format in 2018 and 2019 by
Pen & Sword MILITARY
An imprint of Pen & Sword Books Ltd
Yorkshire – Philadelphia

Copyright © Ian Castle, 2005, 2018, 2019
ISBN: 978 1 52675 252 9

Typeset in 11/13pt Plantin by Mac Style Ltd, Scarborough, N. Yorkshire
Printed and bound in the UK by 4edge Ltd, Essex SS5 4AD

Pen & Sword Books Limited incorporates the imprints of Atlas, Archaeology,
Aviation, Discovery, Family History, Fiction, History, Maritime, Military, Military
Classics, Politics, Select, Transport, True Crime, Air World, Frontline Publishing, Leo
Cooper, Remember When, Seaforth Publishing, The Praetorian Press, Wharncliffe
Local History, Wharncliffe Transport, Wharncliffe True Crime and White Owl.

For a complete list of Pen & Sword titles please contact
PEN & SWORD BOOKS LIMITED
47 Church Street, Barnsley, South Yorkshire, S70 2AS, England
E-mail: enquiries@pen-and-sword.co.uk • Website: www.pen-and-sword.co.uk
Or
PEN AND SWORD BOOKS
1950 Lawrence Rd, Havertown, PA 19083, USA
E-mail: Uspen-and-sword@casematepublishers.com
Website: www.penandswordbooks.com

Contents

For Nicola,
Who actively indulges my passion for times long ago
and willingly accompanies me on the historical path that I tread.

List of Maps

Author's Note

While researching this book I spent much time working with German, French and Russian language texts. In an attempt to retain some of the flavour of a multi-national war, I have decided to retain the ranks of army officers in their relevant languages, when naming individuals. I have occasionally used abbreviations for some senior officer ranks. A table is given below detailing these rank definitions and abbreviations for the reader's convenience.

English	French	Austrian	Russian
Lieutenant	Lieutenant	Leutnant	Porudchik
Captain	Capitaine	Hauptmann	Kapitan
Major	Chef de Bataillon (inf.) or de Escadron (cav.)	Major	Maior
Lieutenant Colonel	Major	Oberstleutnant	Podpolkovnik (PP)
Colonel	Colonel	Oberst	Polkovnik
Brigadier General	Général de Brigade (GB)	Generalmajor (GM)	Brigadir
Major General	Général de Division (GD)	Feldmarschal-leutnant (FML)	General Maior (GM)
Lieutenant General	No equivalent	Feldzeugmeister (FZM – infantry) or General de Kavallerie (GdK – cavalry)	General Leitenant (GL)

In a similar vein, I also intended giving regimental titles in their respective languages. This has been relatively straightforward for the French and Austrian armies, examples of which are given below:

French Army	English Comparable Version
2ème Régiment de Hussards (abbreviated in text to 2ème Hussards)	2nd Hussar Regiment
12ème Régiment de Dragons (abbreviated in text to 12ème Dragons)	12th Dragoon Regiment
4ème Régiment d'Infanterie de Ligne (abbreviated in text to 4ème Ligne)	4th Line Infantry Regiment
26ème Régiment d'Infanterie de Légère (abbreviated in text to 26ème Légère)	26th Light Infantry Regiment

N.B. In addition to the above infantry abbreviations I have also used 1/4ème Ligne and 2/26ème Légère to indicate 1st and 2nd battalions of particular regiments.

Austrian Army	English Comparable Version
Infanterieregiment 4. Deutschmeister (abbreviated in text to IR4 Deutschmeister)	4th Infantry Regiment Deutschmeister
4. Hessen-Homburg-Husaren	4th Hessen-Homburg Hussars
1. Erzherzog Johann-Dragoner	1st Archduke John Dragoons

I hoped to operate a similar system for the Russian army (see examples below), but on reflection, it has been decided to use English translations of regimental titles, in order to simplify understanding of their roles.

Russian Army	English Comparable Version
Novgorod Mushketyorskii Polk	Novgorod Musketeer Regiment
Phanagoria Grenaderskii Polk	Phanagoria Grenadier Regiment
6. Egerskii Polk	6th Jäger Regiment
Mariupol Gusarskii Polk	Mariupol Hussar Regiment

Another anomaly in the Russian army is the occasional use of numerals after officers' names. This system was introduced because a great number of officers serving in the army had the same surname. For instance, there were three officers with the name 'Essen' on active service in 1805 and they were known as Essen I, Essen II and Essen III.

The spelling of Russian officers' names varies considerably in primary sources, and in Napoleonic literature in general. For the sake of consistency, I have followed the spellings given in Alexander Mikaberidze's authoritative *The Russian Officer Corps in the Revolutionary and Napoleonic Wars, 1792–1815*. This source has also been relied upon for regimental names.

Preface

I first visited the battlefield of Austerlitz in 1989 in the company of some 100 members of the Napoleonic Association, including in our number the late Dr David Chandler. Back then Czechoslovakia formed a Communist state and I remember our coaches being held at the border for five long hours while our paperwork was rejected and 'correct paperwork' processed in its place. Later that year massive anti-government demonstrations led to the 'Velvet Revolution' and the abandoning of former ties with the Soviet Union. Now Austerlitz lies in the Czech Republic (Czechia), member state of NATO and the European Union. When I visited Austerlitz again in 2000 it took less than five minutes to cross the border.

The battlefield is a rewarding place to visit as there has been little dramatic change to the terrain in the intervening 200 years. It is as simple to explore all the key geographical features of the battle today as it is to imagine the armies of France, Russia and Austria marching across them in 1805. This is made even easier on each anniversary of the battle, when Napoleonic re-enactors from all over Europe congregate in bleak, cold, December weather, to recreate this momentous battle: the hills and fields echoing once more to the blast of musketry and cannon fire. The battlefield has survived into the twenty-first century without any significant intrusive development destroying our link with one of the most famous battles of the Napoleonic era. It must therefore be hoped that increasing international opposition will defeat NATO's current plan to impose a highly visible radar station on the Pratzen Plateau, the key feature in Napoleon's battle plan.

My first trip to Austerlitz and Dr Chandler's on-site lecture fuelled my interest in the battle and set me on a research path that has finally led to this book, some sixteen years later, published appropriately to mark the 200th anniversary.

In completing this work I have been amazed by the enthusiasm and generosity I have encountered from people all over the world, many of whom I know only through the medium of email. Without their willing responses to my regular requests for information and help this book would have taken a very different form. I therefore wish to extend my thanks to John Sloan, Steve Smith and Mark Conrad in the USA, who offered me sound advice on Russian sources. I received similar help from Alexander Mikaberidze and have used his excellent book, *The Russian Officer Corps in the Revolutionary and Napoleonic Wars, 1792–1815*, as my source for the spelling of Russian names. Also in America, Kevin Kiley gave up much time to search for a copy of an elusive battle account for me. Special thanks go to Robert Goetz, with whom I have exchanged many long emails, as we bounced ideas off each other while exploring some of the less well-defined stages of the battle. From Russia I received more advice on primary Russian sources from Igor Popov and Vitali Bogdanov, and I am most grateful to Alexander Orlov, who sent me copies of many of these important documents. In the Czech Republic, Ondřej Tupy provided me with a modern map of the Austerlitz battlefield and surrounding area, and also volunteered a number of translations for me. I gained access to many first-hand accounts through Robert Ouvrard in Austria. Also in Austria, I extend my thanks to my good friend Martin Worel, with whom I have spent many hours exploring the battlefields of Dürnstein and Austerlitz, and who also painstakingly produced a number of translations from German language material for me. On the subject of translation work, a very special acknowledgement is due to Anastasia Skoybedo in America, who cheerfully translated all my Russian documents, and without whose help this project would never have got off the ground. I also extend my thanks to Emma Golby in England, for her help with French translations. Elsewhere, here in England, I would like to thank Laurence Spring of the Russian Army Study Group for his help, and also Terry Crowdy, for his assistance on questions relating to the French army. As ever, Colin Ablett has been generous in granting extended access to books from his extensive library, and Dave Hollins has continued his long-term support for this project, pointing me in the direction of German language source material, answering questions relating to the Austrian army, and offering translations when needed. Rupert Harding, from my publisher, Pen & Sword, has been very supportive throughout the project – even at times when I was less than positive about meeting my deadlines – and has allowed the project to grow beyond its original confines. And finally, very special thanks go to Nicola, my partner. She has encouraged me and remained positive through all the ups and downs of this work. She has even been interested enough to read the manuscript and produce some translations too! To everyone: *merci, danke, spasibo, děkuji*, thank you.

The Battle of Austerlitz is sometimes called the Battle of the Three Emperors, so called due to the presence on the battlefield of Napoleon, Alexander of Russia and Francis of Austria. To avoid confusion in the text I have referred throughout to Napoleon as emperor, Alexander as tsar and

Francis as kaiser. In the text I have retained the names of towns as they were in 1805. Since then many of these have changed: should any reader wish to follow the ebb and flow of the campaign on modern maps, I have compiled a list detailing old and new versions in Appendix I. An Order of Battle for Austerlitz may be found in Appendix II, which I have supplied for the reader's convenience.

Ian Castle
London, February 2005

Chapter One

War and Peace

'Eternal peace lasts only until the next year.'*

On 17 December 1805 a breathless courier arrived in London bearing urgent despatches for the British government. His most trying journey from the ancient fortified town of Olmütz in Moravia had taken him fourteen days. Written by Sir Arthur Paget, Britain's special envoy to the Habsburg court in Vienna, the despatch contained shocking news. It told of a great battle that had taken place on 2 December between a combined Russian–Austrian army and Napoleon's Grande Armée. Vast financial subsidies approved by the British government of William Pitt had enabled the Russian and Austrian armies to march against Napoleon in 1805: the news contained in the despatch stunned Pitt and his cabinet. Paget's letter explained that 'after an obstinate resistance' the centre of the Allied army was 'completely put to rout'. The rest of Paget's information was patchy, but of the Allied right wing he wrote, 'it is probable that they have suffered considerably,' and as to the fate of the left wing, he could offer 'no satisfactory intelligence'. He concluded: 'the army is retreating … and I fear for the present nothing more is to be hoped than that they have made a safe and effectual retreat.'[1]

This information shocked Pitt deeply. The great opponent of French expansion, who was in his second term as prime minister was already in ill-health. Having pored over the contents of the despatch, Government officials released an ambiguous statement to the Press later that same day. Within twenty-four hours *The Times* had converted Paget's account of a crushing defeat into a victory:

'A general battle took place on the 2nd [December], between the French and Austro-Russian armies, at Wischau [Paget did not mention Austerlitz in his despatch as he only got as far as Wischau before encountering retreating Russian soldiers]. The centre of the

* Russian proverb.

latter seems to have met with great resistance, and to have been repulsed, but the left wing of the enemy was defeated with some considerable loss, by the right wing of the Allies under the command of the Princes Liechtenstein and Bagration. The Emperor Alexander commanded his troops in person, and displayed the utmost bravery. The conflict seems to have been of the most obstinate kind, and to have been sustained by the Allies in the most exemplary manner. The loss of the French was immense.'[2]

The Times remained adamant their interpretation stood true and the government did nothing to correct them. On 19 December the newspaper printed a letter from Amsterdam, dated 11 December, which claimed a French victory. But *The Times* contemptuously dismissed its veracity by stating the pro-French Batavian Government 'will no more sanction the rumour of a defeat than the Government of Paris'.[3]

Again, on 20 December, *The Times* expanded on the battle. New information arriving from Europe told of a great battle lasting three days, 'fought with a vigour and obstinacy unparalleled in the annals of modern warfare, and terminated at length in favour of the Allied army'.[4]

By now, however, contradictory statements were appearing in Continental newspapers, some of which managed to find their way to England. Amongst these accounts was Napoleon's proclamation of 2 December, written on the battlefield of Austerlitz. It described a French victory of incredible enormity, of the Allies crushed, many thousands of prisoners taken, whole batteries seized, and numerous colours and standards captured and paraded before the emperor of the French. On 21 December, undaunted, the editor of *The Times* blasted the 'extravagance of this intelligence', writing:

'Who is there that can believe that an army of 100,000 men [inflated figure given by Napoleon in the proclamation], and most of those Russian too, could be so completely annihilated in the course of four short hours? What could have so unnerved and paralysed the arms of such a multitude of hardy warriors, fighting under the eyes of their respective Sovereigns, as to make them surrender their throats to the swords, or their limbs to the chains of the enemy, without almost striking a blow? Was there ever a precedent of a battle, in which 100,000 men were drawn up on one side, being terminated in so short a space of time? … we cannot bring ourselves to attach to it the smallest degree of credit whatsoever.'[5]

But – the exaggerated body-count notwithstanding – Bonaparte's account was true. Ten days later, on 31 December 1805, *The Times* finally accepted 'this disastrous intelligence'. Napoleon had crushed the Allies with devastating effect. On the last day of the year – a year that had promised to see the old powers of Europe returned to pre-eminence – the editor, shocked by this turn of events wrote: 'Incredible as this sudden termination of the war is, we are compelled to give it reluctant credit.'

So ended the Third Coalition formed against France. The main protagonists – Britain, Russia and Austria – had each played an active role in attempting to restrict the advance of France's borders since the wars first began in 1792. Each previous attempt had also met with defeat.

William Pitt ('the Younger') served two terms in office as prime minister of Great Britain: the first in 1783 at the extraordinarily young age of twenty-four. At that time he did much to restore Britain's confidence and prosperity in the years following the American Revolution. With the outbreak of the French Revolution, he determined to oppose the expansion of French power and influence. His preferred method was to attack French trade and colonies, while offering financial subsidies to Britain's Continental allies, enabling them to speed their armies into the field. A small British army fought in Europe in 1794 and 1795 as part of the First Coalition, while another landed briefly in 1799 in support of the campaigns of Second Coalition. But Britain's real strength lay in her navy. In 1798 a French-backed rebellion in Ireland caused Pitt to seek a solution to the government's problems there. In January 1801 the resulting Act of Union brought Ireland into a United Kingdom with Great Britain, but Pitt's move to complete the process, by granting voting rights to Roman Catholics, was blocked by his staunchest opponent, King George III. Feeling honour bound to deliver emancipation to the Catholics, Pitt resigned as prime minister in February 1801. His resignation ushered in the weak administration of Henry Addington.

While Pitt held office, the French made a number of unofficial attempts to open peace discussions in 1800, as the War of the Second Coalition drew to a close, but they were rebuffed. However, with Addington installed as prime minister, it was Britain's turn to seek peace between the two nations. In March 1801 Britain sent its first formal overture to Napoleon Bonaparte, first consul of France. So began a tortuous round of proposals and counter proposals, which encompassed British and French possessions around the globe. With the Treaty of Amiens finally concluded in March 1802, all France and Britain rejoiced. Church bells rang out across the Continent announcing peace. For the first time in ten years the guns of Europe fell silent. But the politicians could see beyond the rejoicing. Addington's negotiators were outmanoeuvred and made to look naïve. As one British agent reporting back from Paris put it: 'they say everywhere that, after having gloriously sailed past the rocks that Bonaparte's cunning had placed in its tracks, the British Ministry has completely foundered at the mouth of the harbour.' France regained many of her colonies captured by the British in the recent wars and remained under arms in Holland, renamed the Batavian Republic. But if the British government hoped her concessions would bring an end to France's territorial ambitions they were sadly mistaken.

On the far side of Europe, in Russia, great changes were taking place too. Tsar Paul I succeeded his mother, Catherine the Great in 1796. Paul's bouts of mental illness and instability, combined with his violent mood swings, made many doubt his ability to lead Russia at this difficult time (Catherine herself had favoured Alexander, Paul's eldest son, to follow her). In 1799 Paul took Russia into the Second Coalition due to his concerns regarding increasing French influence in the Mediterranean, epitomised by the occupation of Malta. Home to the ancient Order of the Knights of St John since 1530, the Knights turned to Paul for help, making him Grand Master of the Order.

Despite early success in the campaign, fighting alongside Austria, tensions grew between the two allies and Paul withdrew from the coalition late in 1799. Just over a year later, in March 1801, Tsar Paul I was dead, assassinated in a palace coup. Paul's increasing irrational and sometimes bizarre behaviour had led to this plot against his life. His son and heir, Alexander, was aware of a conspiracy to depose his father, but seems not to have appreciated that the plotters – army officers and courtiers – intended murder. Alexander collapsed with grief when he heard the news. The attempt to soften the blow by explaining that Paul had suffered an apoplectic fit at the threat of detention and died, disguised a far more grisly end. The conspirators broke into his bedroom at the Mikhailovsky Palace during the night, and in the ensuing scuffle, a heavy blow to the head with a weighty snuffbox felled him. As he lay stunned on the floor, one of his assailants attempted to strangle him with a silk scarf while another crushed his windpipe with a paperweight. Against this murderous background the 23-year-old Alexander became tsar. He was destined to take a leading role in creating a Third Coalition against France.

In the meantime, to assist him in his political deliberations, Alexander formed his 'Secret Committee', an informal group of four close, liberal-minded friends, including Prince Adam Czartoryski, a member of an influential Polish family who had been sent to Russia in 1795 as a guarantee of his family's future fidelity. The committee met regularly with Alexander, their principal task to 'discover the wisest policy for an enlightened autocrat to pursue'.[6] Czartoryski would ride beside the tsar at Austerlitz. In many ways Alexander used the meetings as a think-tank, in which he could develop ideas in private. As he gained in confidence, his reluctance to delegate became more marked, as did his emerging desire to occupy a position as the great arbiter of Europe.

Initially, Alexander looked with interest at First Consul Bonaparte's achievements in France. As long as he harboured no interests in the Balkans or eastern Mediterranean, Alexander saw no reason for future problems between the two nations: especially after France lost Malta to the British, with the final fate of the island to be settled later at Amiens. And so, in October 1801, the two countries declared a formal peace. France recognised Russia's interest in the eastern Mediterranean and agreed to consult Alexander on the subject of realigning the boundaries of the German states, where French involvement was significant.

Alexander, however, had been discussing this very topic for months with Frederick William III, king of Prussia. These discussions were conducted in private: the diplomats had not been invited.

Prussia had entered into the War of the First Coalition half-heartedly, eventually concluding a separate peace with France in April 1795 and maintained neutrality during the War of the Second Coalition. Alexander and Frederick then met in June 1802 and discussed a favourable settlement of Europe: each encouraging the other's bloated and mistaken belief that they could influence Bonaparte's foreign policy. While king and tsar cemented their new found friendship, the French leader negotiated directly with the German princes, ignoring Prussian or Russian sensibilities, and merely invited Russia to approve the *fait accompli*. Gradually Alexander's admiration for Bonaparte waned.

The other great European power of the Third Coalition was Austria. The Habsburg Empire, presided over by the kaiser, Francis II, was a vast multi-national entity and a great opponent of French expansion. Francis came to the throne as 'Holy Roman emperor and king of Bohemia and Hungary' in 1792: the same year that Revolutionary France first looked beyond her own borders. For the first twenty-three turbulent years of his reign, Francis' empire was either actively at war with France or preparing for it. In 1792 Austria and Prussia formed the First Coalition against France. Britain, Sardinia, Naples, Spain, Holland, Portugal, and the minor German States joined them. But by April 1796, after many reverses, only Austria remained active in the field. A year later, although they had pushed the French back in Germany, the advance of Bonaparte's army through Italy – and within 80 miles of Vienna – forced Francis to accept an armistice. This culminated in the Treaty of Campo Formio, signed in October 1797. By this treaty, Vienna lost the Austrian Netherlands (Belgium) and Lombardy, agreed to the French occupation of the left bank of the Rhine, and recognised the establishment of the French satellite state, the Cisalpine Republic in Italy. However, in compensation for these losses, Austria gained Dalmatia, Friol, and Venetian territory east of the River Adige.

No sooner had the war of the First Coalition officially ended than moves to create a Second Coalition were underway. Britain, Austria, Russia, Naples, Portugal and the Ottoman Empire joined the coalition, but the bulk of the fighting fell to the Austrians once more, aided by the Russians. From the start, relations between Austria and Russia were tense. Austria doubted Tsar Paul's stability and harboured concerns over her own isolation while awaiting Russian support. War broke out in March 1799 and with Bonaparte out of the way in Egypt (having captured Malta en route), the Austrians met with success: pushing the French back in Bavaria and – with Russian troops fighting alongside – also in Italy. But Austro-Russian relations continued to suffer, and later, in Switzerland, a particularly turbulent meeting between Archduke Charles and Field Marshal Suvorov, the respective Austrian and Russian commanders, spelt the end of Austro-Russian co-operation. By the end of the year Tsar Paul withdrew Russia from the coalition, and such Allied success as there had been now ended.

In October 1799 Bonaparte returned from Egypt, overthrew the French government the following month in a coup d'état, and by the end of the year securely held the reins of power as first consul. Reinvigorated by this change in command the French army resumed the war in 1800.

The Austrians – minus Russian support – attacked again in Italy and pushed the French back, but in Germany the French gained the upper hand. Then, in May 1800, Bonaparte led an army over the Alps, captured Milan, and defeated the Austrians at Marengo in June. Initial peace negotiations dragged on and in November Austria reopened the war. Only after suffering defeat at the Bavarian village of Hohenlinden in December, did the War of the Second Coalition finally come to an end. The ensuing Peace of Luneville, signed in February 1801, confirmed the agreements made at Campo Formio four years earlier.

Britain now stood alone, leaving her new prime minister, Addington, with no choice but to open peace discussions, paving the way to the signing of the Treaty of Amiens in March 1802.

The great ruling dynasties of Britain, Austria, Russia, had all now faced the emerging French nation on the field of battle and across the negotiating table. At Amiens, ten years of conflict ended. An extended peace promised time for the nations of Europe, ravaged by war, to rebuild their shattered economies. For France, with First Consul Bonaparte at the helm, it offered the opportunity to consolidate the stronger, more robust nation that had emerged from the chaos of the Revolution. But although his civil and legal achievements were remarkable, Bonaparte continued his expansionist polices: in August 1802 he annexed the island of Elba, followed swiftly by Piedmont and Parma. Then, in October, a large French force marched into and reoccupied Switzerland – a country they had evacuated but a few months earlier – thus creating buffer states along the country's south-eastern border.

Thus, the Treaty of Amiens did not curb First Consul Bonaparte's ambition: rather, it encouraged him to extend it further. And the great powers, drawn like moths to a flame, edged inevitably towards a return to hostilities. It was no longer a question of if war would resume, but when. The answer, 1805, was the year of Austerlitz: one of the greatest battles of the Napoleonic era.

Chapter 2

'Woe To Those Who Do Not Respect Treaties'*

The months that followed the signing of the Treaty of Amiens were a tense time. Britain and France continued to eye each other suspiciously, trying to fathom the other's intentions, while Britain reluctantly began relinquishing her overseas conquests as stipulated in the treaty. But when the subject of Malta was raised, Britain balked. After Bonaparte's failed Egyptian expedition, which threatened Britain's possessions in the East, the island took on a great strategic importance, almost a first line of defence against further attempts in this region. Amiens decreed that neither Britain nor France should occupy the island. Russian guardianship was projected but Britain grew wary of an apparent improvement in relations between Tsar Alexander and the first consul. Other suggestions also met with British doubts, and so her garrison remained firmly rooted on the island.

Other issues gnawed at the stability of Europe. French troops still occupied Holland (the Batavian Republic) and Switzerland. The Treaty of Luneville, signed in 1801, stipulated that French troops would evacuate Holland once peace with Britain was declared. The British negotiators presumed these clauses were still in place and so failed to restate them in the Treaty of Amiens. Bonaparte, therefore, exploited this oversight and remained firmly in occupation. In response, Britain slowed down the process of handing back her overseas conquests.

Bonaparte did not disguise his animosity towards Britain. Her constant funding of his enemies in Europe, the personal attacks against him in the British press and the safe refuge she provided for Royalist *émigrés* who plotted and schemed for a restoration of the deposed Bourbons, incensed him.

Meanwhile, in Britain itself, the anticipated benefits to trade following the declaration of peace failed to materialise. Merchants hoping to forge new markets for their goods on the Continent were disappointed, as Bonaparte had no intention of allowing Britain to profit from trade with France, and

---

* Napoleon Bonaparte to Lord Whitworth, British Ambassador in Paris, 13 March 1803.

successfully obstructed the renewal of commerce. The British government complained without result and the citizens of both countries snarled at each other across the English Channel.

In Russia, Tsar Alexander prepared to embark on a programme of domestic reform. Since the conclusion of peace with France in October 1801 Russia had been shown little respect. Bonaparte did involve Alexander in the final settlement of the German states but only because his support helped Kaiser Francis accept Habsburg losses. But Alexander's views on the interests of Sardinia and the French occupation of Switzerland were ignored. However, early accord over the determination that Britain should evacuate Malta eroded early in 1803, as reports spread of French intrigues in the Balkans, the Middle East and Egypt. The suggestion that Bonaparte may be looking to extend his influence over the decaying body of the Ottoman Empire was certain to trigger Russia's fears and further intensify questions over the Mediterranean. The subsequent French occupation of Piedmont and Parma did little to ease Russian concerns. Thus, when the first consul attempted to draw Russia into his plans, he was rejected. Increasingly, Alexander turned away from France, and alerted to Bonaparte's desire to push his territorial boundaries even further afield, changed his view on the Malta question. As tension mounted between Britain and France, Russia supported the British government's determination to stay in occupation.

In Austria too, a period of reorganisation was underway. The end of the War of the Second Coalition in 1800 had left the country seriously weakened. Public confidence in the government was at an extremely low ebb, the economy was devastated, and the administration of the empire bordering on chaos. Having borne the brunt of the fighting for the last ten years, Austria now anticipated an extended period of peace, in which to repair the damage. In consequence, she voiced no public condemnation of France's resistance to fulfil her obligations to Holland as detailed in the Treaty of Luneville.

As Austria looked to streamline her archaic bureaucracy, one man came to prominence: Archduke Charles, brother of the kaiser, and one of the few senior military men to emerge from the campaign of 1798–1800 with his reputation intact. On his recommendation, the failing State Council (*Staatsrat*) was abolished. In its place a new 'Staats und Konferenz Ministerium', with three separate ministries, dealing with internal, foreign, and military affairs, came into being. Charles headed up the third ministry but his declared interest in the wider political picture aroused suspicions in his brother the kaiser. Political intrigue was never far from the surface in the Habsburg court. Charles then commenced a major overhaul of the armed forces, his intention to 'return the army to a respectable posture so as to enable the emperor to assert his position among the powers of Europe'. His earnest efforts encountered many obstacles on the way, placed there by those wary of his ambition.

While Archduke Charles occupied himself unravelling years of maladministration in the army, the growing tensions in Europe were clearly evident. In Austria's current condition the Foreign Ministry recommended a new alliance with Russia in 1803 to safeguard Habsburg lands from Bonaparte's ambitions. It was a move rejected by both the kaiser and Charles.

Back in Paris and London, political sniping increased. In January 1803 Bonaparte openly published a report on a mission to Egypt, commenting on the decrepit state of the defences and the ease with which it could be recaptured. Britain made an official protest, demanding an explanation. In retort, Bonaparte railed against the presence of the British garrison still maintained in the Egyptian port of Alexandria, despite the fact that it was about to be removed. Then, in February, Bonaparte informed the Corps Législatif that it was necessary to bring 480,000 men under arms to defend France's interests.

In the meantime, Bonaparte authorised a number of 'commercial commissioners' to visit Britain and secretly examine harbours, fortifications and landing places for a possible future invasion.

In response to this activity and Bonaparte's statements, George III requested that parliament vote to embody the militia and increase the navy in strength by 10,000 men. The first consul reacted angrily. Lord Whitworth, Britain's ambassador in Paris, experienced his reaction first hand at a reception at the Tuileries in March 1803:

> "'So you are determined to go to war." "No, First Consul." I replied, "we are too sensible of the advantage of peace." "Why, then, these armaments? I have not a ship of the line in the French ports, but if you wish to arm I will arm also: if you wish to fight, I will fight also. You may perhaps kill France, but will never intimidate her." "We wish," said I, "neither the one nor the other. We wish to live on good terms with her." "You must respect treaties then," replied he; "woe to those who do not respect treaties. They shall answer for it to all Europe."'[1]

In his despatch to the British government the following day, Whitworth reported this encounter, concluding with: 'He was too agitated to make it advisable to prolong the conversation.'

A few days later Bonaparte apologised to the ambassador for his outburst, which clearly referred to the refusal of the British to evacuate Malta. Perhaps the apology was an acceptance that he too was failing to honour a treaty, or maybe the whole conversation had merely been a carefully placed barb to sting Britain in the political sparring that epitomised the descent from peace to war. In Britain the report caused anger and indignation.

Proposals and counter proposals over the future of Malta continued. In February, the British evacuated the Cape of Good Hope, captured from the

Dutch in 1795, in accordance with the conditions of Amiens. At the tip of southern Africa, the Cape provided a major staging post on the seaborne route to India. Malta was now considered the only bastion for the overland route to British possessions in the East. Important though it was, Britain offered to give up her interest if the French government offered some other 'equivalent security' that would achieve the same purpose. Unofficially, French negotiators suggested handing over Corfu or Crete but Bonaparte vehemently opposed them.

British concerns for the security of India were well-founded. In March 1803 Bonaparte authorised an expedition to sail for India under Général Decaen, carrying 1,800 troops. Once there, Decaen was 'to communicate with the peoples or princes who are most impatient under the yoke of the English [East India] Company'. Yet it seems clear at this point that Bonaparte did not anticipate so rapid a rupture with Britain. Ten days after the fleet departed from Brest, the rapidly deteriorating situation in Europe forced Bonaparte to send a ship in pursuit, cancelling Decaen's orders and instructing him to fall back on Mauritius.

With Britain unwilling to abandon her foothold in the Mediterranean and France unwilling to evacuate Holland – a posture that suggested an implicit threat of invasion – the eventual outcome was inevitable. Britain made a fresh proposal for a settlement at the end of April 1803 that was short and to the point: Britain to maintain a garrison in Malta for ten years and French troops to evacuate Holland and Switzerland. In response Bonaparte planned to unleash another passionate diatribe against Lord Whitworth at a reception on 1 May, but the ambassador chose to absent himself. Instead, Bonaparte wrote to Talleyrand, his foreign minister, informing him how he should manage his meeting with Whitworth:

> 'I desire that your conference shall not degenerate into a conversation. Show yourself cold, reserved, and even somewhat proud. If the [British] note contains the word ultimatum make him feel that this word implies war; if it does not contain the word, make him insert it, remarking to him that we must know where we are, that we are tired of this state of anxiety.'[2]

France responded with proposals of her own on 7 May as Whitworth, already ordered home by his government, was preparing to leave Paris. These proved unacceptable. Britain fired back a counter proposal, France rejected it on 11 May. The next day Whitworth commenced his journey to Calais. He received a final offer en route but dismissed it as a mere delaying tactic. On 17 May he crossed the English Channel, unaware that two days earlier Bonaparte had ordered an embargo on all British ships anchored in French ports. On 18 May Britain declared war on France, capturing two French merchant ships off

the Breton coast later that day. In angry response, Bonaparte lashed o
ordered that all Britons in France between the ages of eighteen and sixty were
to be apprehended and detained as prisoners of war. After ten years of war,
peace had lasted a mere fourteen months.

Although Bonaparte may not have wanted war with Britain in 1803, once it
arrived he wasted no time in beginning military preparations. On 1 June
French troops marched into Hanover, the hereditary British territory in
Germany, while others occupied the Kingdom of Naples in southern Italy. All
shipyards in Holland, France and northern Italy were tasked to step up naval
production, while orders were issued for an army, 160,000-strong, to assemble
in large camps along the Channel coast. Meanwhile, another army – of
shipwrights and boat builders – plied their trade on the great rivers of Europe,
constructing a vast armada of flat-bottom barges to transport the army across
the Channel and land them on England's shores.

In Britain, the country was alert to the danger. The regular army was not
large – perhaps 90,000-strong – but, augmented by 80,000 men of the militia,
they mustered, drilled, and rehearsed the evolutions of war. Meanwhile, some
400,000 civilians enthusiastically flocked to join the Volunteers: although
perhaps as many as 120,000 of these were armed with nothing more potent
than pikes. All along the threatened coast Martello towers sprung up: castles in
miniature, designed to delay any French landing. And all the while Britain's
powerful navy prowled menacingly up and down the Channel, blockading the
French ships in port.

Although a state of war now existed again between Britain and France,
Britain's former coalition allies did not rush forward in support of her stance.
Austria, focused on repairing the damage caused by the first two coalitions
offered little encouragement, while Prussia, holding on to its neutrality, had too
much to lose with France already gnawing away at the independent German
territories along the Rhine. In Russia, the strength of French ambition, driven
by Bonaparte at the head of her armies, had already demonstrated little regard
for the established boundaries of Europe. A half-hearted return to war by
Russia, without adequate preparation, could easily enhance Bonaparte's
dominant position. In fact, Alexander initially held Britain responsible for the
collapse of peace and maintained frosty relations with the British ambassador
in St Petersburg. Then in June 1803 Alexander was invited by Bonaparte to
mediate between the two adversaries, in a move seen in Britain as one designed
to gain time for strengthening French naval power, which lagged someway
behind that of Britain. Alexander was delighted. He envisaged it as an
opportunity to make his mark on Europe, to pronounce wise counsel and
emerge as the great arbiter, a role that fuelled his personal ambition.

Yet he misunderstood the mission. The two protagonists saw him only as a
mediator. Therefore, when Alexander presented proposals for a settlement in July,

neither party found them acceptable. Britain was to hand Malta over to Russia, while being granted Lampedusa, a tiny speck of land about 100 miles west of Malta, in compensation. France would remain secure behind her natural boundaries, but the creation of a corridor of neutral states, running through Holland, the German territories, Switzerland, and into Italy would bring security to Europe. Bonaparte listened incredulously as Alexander suggested confiscating the rewards of French martial success. Bonaparte rejected Alexander's proposal out of hand in August, while Britain was now prepared to entrust Malta to no one. These developments marked a distinct change in French–Russian relationships, which did not improve in September, when Bonaparte launched a public verbal attack on Count Morkov, the Russian ambassador in Paris. Angered by this humiliation, Alexander immediately recalled Morkov to St Petersburg.

The tsar now came under the influence of his deputy minister for foreign affairs, Adam Czartoryski, one of his friends from the 'Secret Committee', and one who had long cast a wary eye in the direction of France. In November, Russia initiated discussions with the British government on the subject of a new alliance, as reports circulated of increased activity by French agents in the Balkans, the Adriatic, and Constantinople. Britain made a positive response and dialogue between the two powers opened. But Czartoryski felt unable to push the scheme ahead without the support of Austria and an insight into Prussia's attitude. However, Sweden's ambassador to Vienna felt Austria's policy was now 'one of fear and hope – fear of the power of France, and hope to obtain favours from her'. Prussia raised objections to the French occupation of Hanover – a territory that had long attracted her own covetous glances as a means of strengthening her dominance in northern Germany – but would push matters no further.

Before the year of 1803 drew to a close, increasing pressure by Bonaparte on Spain bore fruit. Faced with the threat of an advance by 80,000 French troops into their country, the government of Spain agreed to make an annual payment of 72 million francs to the French exchequer. Portugal purchased her own neutrality by a payment of 1 million francs per month.

But attempts to draw Sweden into an alliance against Britain met with bold defiance. Instead, King Gustavus IV, a great opponent of the Revolution, turned to Britain in December 1803, seeking financial support for the protection of his European mainland province of Pomerania.

Meanwhile, as the ruling families of Europe grew more and more disturbed by Bonaparte's ambitions, a deposed dynasty proposed to take action to remove the root of the evil …

The first Bourbon-inspired plot to assassinate Bonaparte took place in Paris, in 1800, when a bomb – known to history as the 'infernal machine' – exploded: failing to kill its target, but claiming the lives of a number of innocent bystanders.

Early in 1803 Bonaparte approached the comte de Provence, exiled heir to the Bourbon throne, offering him a vast pension for life if he would renounce, on behalf of himself and future Bourbon claimants, all rights to the throne of France. The future Louis XVIII rejected Bonaparte's advance with the dignified retort: 'We have lost everything but honour.' His response met with the approval of his brother, the comte d'Artois (the future King Charles X) and amongst others, the duc d'Enghein, a Royalist *émigré* of the Bourbon Condé line. The comte de Provence showed little enthusiasm for plots and intrigues, believing a return to the throne would follow in the wake of a future conflict between France and powers of Europe.

However, in London, where a hotbed of Royalist intrigue flourished, ideas of a more direct action were fermented. At the centre, the comte d'Artois, gathered a determined group of supporters to the cause. Amongst them, two men stood out: Georges Cadoudal, a staunch opponent of the Revolution and leading light of the insurrection in the Vendée, in western France; and Charles Pichegru, a former general in the Revolutionary army. Following a coup in 1797 Pichegru had been arrested and exiled to South America, but having made good his escape, he made his way to London. The British government provided clandestine financial support for these Royalist conspirators both in London and on the Continent. Napoleon despatched Méhée de la Touche, a former assassin and spy, to London with instructions to work his way into *émigré* circles and expose the plotters. De la Touche was successful and consequently departed for the Continent, where he inveigled his way into the confidence of Britain's envoy at Munich, who was completely taken in by his plausibility as an agent of the Royalist plotters. The envoy, Drake, handed over money and a codebook, with which de la Touche immediately returned to Paris, from which place he proceeded to ply Drake with false information. Thus, Bonaparte's agents kept a close eye on developments as the plot gained momentum.

In August 1803 the plotters were ready to advance their plans and so Georges Cadoudal slipped into France. He made his way to Paris to recruit conspirators to the cause. Although elusive, his activities were monitored, and Bonaparte waited. He wanted evidence to incriminate Général Jean Moreau in the plot. Moreau, the victor of Hohenlinden in 1800, openly displayed a sullen resentment of Bonaparte's rapid rise. The first consul was uneasy, aware that many saw in Moreau a military rival to himself.

Meanwhile, Pichegru followed Cadoudal to Paris, where he held the first of three meetings with Moreau in January 1804. However, while Moreau was happy to support the removal of Bonaparte, he refused to be drawn into a plot that aimed to restore the Bourbons. But on 14 February Bonaparte was ready to move. Under interrogation, a Royalist supporter had revealed that a number of conspirators, amongst them a French prince, was about to land on the French coast at Biville near Dieppe. The following day Moreau was arrested.

On 28 February Pichegru was taken too, but Cadoudal, despite an intensive house-to-house search, evaded capture until 9 March. Other conspirators were quickly netted.

While these searches were bringing results, Bonaparte ordered Général de division Savary, a trusted aide with a great aptitude for intelligence work and who commanded the Gendarmerie d'Élite, to intercept the landing of the French prince, presumed to be the comte d'Artois. From a cliff top at Biville, Savary employed lantern signals in an attempt to lure the British vessel to discharge her cargo, but despite his best efforts, the captain grew suspicious and returned to England.

During his communications with the British envoy in Munich, Méhée de la Touche learnt of the plans of the duc d'Enghien, who, it was suggested, planned to lead an *émigré* force into France when war returned to Europe. At the time, the duke had settled just beyond the borders of eastern France, at Ettenheim in Baden, roughly 35 miles south of Strasbourg and close to the Rhine. This news reached the first consul on 1 March, prompting an investigation. The subsequent intelligence revealed that the duke was in league with another French general, Charles Dumouriez, considered a traitor since his desertion from the army, following his defeat at Neerwinden in 1793, and subsequent sojourn in England. Bonaparte's fury knew no bounds when he suddenly discovered enemies on his very borders and determined to end these constant intrigues against him once and for all.

But the first consul's spy network had let him down. Dumouriez was still in London and had never returned to France. The duc d'Enghien's companion was an innocent *émigré*, the Marquis de Thuméry, whose name – unfortunately for him – when spoken with a German accent was mistaken for 'Dumouriez'. The interrogation of one of Cadoudal's servants had provided the flimsiest scraps of intelligence: but they were enough to lead Bonaparte to the erroneous conclusion that the duc d'Enghien and Dumouriez were masterminding the plot against him, while Cadoudal was merely their weapon of execution. Ignoring the fact that these two men resided in neutral Baden, the first consul demanded their arrest and trial. What was more, he wanted to set an example to all would-be plotters. He would strike a blow, both swift and deadly, to instil fear into all who opposed him. He discussed the situation with his supporting consuls and ministers – some of whom raised doubts about the implications – but Bonaparte was determined to have his way, and ordered the seizure of d'Enghien and 'Dumouriez'.

On the evening of 14 March, under cover of darkness, a detachment of French cavalry crossed the border between France and Baden. At dawn they surrounded the house where the duke was living. There is a suggestion he received a warning of the danger and resolved to leave Ettenheim and join his grandfather. This journey required him to travel through Austrian territory, and it was while he awaited the appropriate travel documents he that was seized.[3] The duke, Thuméry, and a secretary – along with a batch of papers – were bundled out of the house and escorted speedily back to France, where they were held outside Paris at the Château de Vincennes.

The first consul authorised a trial by court martial, which would allow for a swift judgement and sentence. The recently appointed governor of Paris, the dashing cavalryman Joachim Murat, received instructions from Bonaparte to select the officers to form the court martial, a task he found repugnant. One of those selected, Général Hulin, claimed that the seven officers had not, 'the least idea about trials; and, worst of all, the reporter and clerk had scarcely more experience'.[4] GD Savary, back in Paris after his failed mission to Biville, received orders to proceed immediately to Vincennes to carry out the sentence of the court martial. Two days after the seizure, Bonaparte learnt of the error concerning Thuméry: he brushed the matter aside and concentrated on the duke. The papers taken with the duke confirmed his communications with the British government and of his hope to lead a force in a future European war, but in no way did they suggest his involvement with Cadoudal: the reason for his arrest.

The court martial went ahead on 20 March. The direction of the trial now changed, following the intelligence gleaned from the duke's papers, his complicity in the Cadoudal plot reduced to a minor charge in the prosecution. When questioned, he admitted bearing arms against France, accepting payments from Britain, and his desire to fight against the current French government. He requested an interview with the first consul, which the court was prepared to assent to, but Savary, observing proceedings and well aware of his master's wishes for a swift resolution, advised Général Hulin against it. Although showing reluctance to pass sentence immediately, the court eventually proceeded, finding the duc d'Enghien guilty of conspiracy against the State and sentencing him to death. The whole process had taken but a few hours and was completed early the following morning. With sentencing concluded, Savary lead the prisoner directly out into the dry moat of Vincennes. Denied a priest, the duke bowed his head in prayer as Savary's gendarmes formed a firing squad, the poignancy of the moment and the enormity of the deed framed in the light of a few flickering lanterns. Standing with his back to the chateau wall just a few feet from his grave, the duc d'Enghein faced the firing squad. On Savary's order, the guns fired and the duke collapsed to the ground, shot through the heart.

When the news emerged there was widespread shock in France. Many awakened for the first time to the ruthless side of the first consul's nature. Even Bonaparte's mother criticised him for what he had done: but there were no more Bourbon plots against his life.

For the main conspirators in the Cadoudal plot there was to be no reprise. On 6 April, just over two weeks later, Pichegru was discovered dead in his prison cell. Initially rumours circulated that he had been murdered, but later these were discredited and it appears more likely that he took his own life. Moreau, Cadoudal, and the other Royalist conspirators taken in February and March were put on trial. Despite a determined cross-examination of a number of witnesses, the prosecution was not able to indict Moreau directly in the plot, other than ascertain that he had met with Pichegru and was aware of the plot but did not report it to the authorities. He was sentenced to two years' imprisonment, which, with a pretence of clemency, Bonaparte commuted to banishment to America. Of the others, twenty were sentenced to death, although eight of noble birth later had their sentences commuted to imprisonment. For Cadoudal and the remaining eleven there was no reprieve: they were executed on 10 June 1804.

The enormity of his decision regarding the duc d'Enghien stayed with Bonaparte all his life. Even in his Last Will and Testament he remembered it and continued to defend his actions:

> 'I caused the duc d'Enghien to be arrested and tried, because that step was essential to the safety, interest, and honour of the French people, when the comte d'Artois was maintaining, by his own confession, sixty assassins at Paris. Under similar circumstances, I should act in the same way.'[5]

To Fouché, recently removed from the post of minister of police, and now a senator, the decision was a bad one. To him is attributed the condemnation: 'It is more than a crime; it is a mistake'.

To the crowned heads of Europe, Bonaparte simply became an unrestrained monster and murderer. Their fury knew no bounds. It was the spark that ignited the flames of war.

Chapter 3

The Eagles of Europe

'Eagles don't breed doves.'*

The shock waves created by the arrest and execution of the duc d'Enghien reverberated around Europe. The dynastic heads, as one, condemned what they considered an act of murder and territorial violation. Nowhere was this response more pronounced and more damning than in Russia: when the news reached Alexander his sense of outrage was unbounded. To the tsar, not only was Bonaparte guilty of murder, but he also directly insulted Russia: for when French troops seized the duke they violated territory ruled by the venerable margrave of Baden, father of Alexander's wife, the Tsarina Elizabeth. The king of Sweden shared the tsar's indignation: he was married to another of the margrave's daughters. Alexander declared a period of mourning at the Russian court and issued a note of protest to Paris. The carefully chosen response wounded the tsar deeply, hinting as it did, at Alexander's own complicity in the murder of his father, Paul I, as well as suggesting British involvement.[1] Unwilling to respond, Alexander called a meeting of the State Council in April 1804, when a decision was taken to issue a series of demands to France. It was August before Bonaparte bothered to issue a repudiation.

Russia put aside her plans for domestic reform and focused attention on drawing together a powerful alliance against France. Talks began with Sweden and Prussia, and discussions with Britain reopened too. There, the resumption of a state of war with France in 1803 had led to mounting pressure on Prime Minister Addington, until, with his support fading away, he resigned in April 1804. William Pitt swept back into office after an absence of three years and resumed his more belligerent stance. Pitt was determined to counter the threat of French invasion, and welcomed this new dialogue with Russia.

In Paris, the plot against Bonaparte's life focused attention on the vulnerability of his position and created an opportunity for open discussion on

---

* Dutch proverb.

the question of hereditary rule. The argument that its introduction would negate the benefits of Bonaparte's assassination to any conspirators and provide an effective block to any Bourbon return gained much support, and within two months of d'Enghien's death, the Senate conferred the title of 'emperor of the French' on Bonaparte. The date of 2 December 1804 was set for a magnificent coronation, and First Consul Bonaparte became Emperor Napoleon. On the streets of Paris the failure of the Bourbon conspirators gave rise to the witty adage: 'They came to France to give her a king, and instead gave her an emperor.' The old established rulers of Europe looked on with heightened disdain.

Russia's overtures to Prussia in May 1804 brought about a secret declaration of support if France attempted new inroads into German territory. The following month government ministers in London and St Petersburg were in the early stages of discussing a grand alliance involving Russia, Britain, Austria, Sweden, and if negotiations went well, with Prussia too. But when talks began in earnest, in September, it soon became clear that British and Russian aims were divergent. Russia looked to the establishment of lasting European peace based on a balance of power, secured by Britain and Russia on either flank. But her views on the redrawing of national boundaries on the natural lines of rivers, mountains, and seas were strongly opposed by Britain, which demanded the return of France to her pre-Revolutionary boundaries. And while Russia hoped France would respond positively to a final chance for reconciliation, Pitt remained adamant that only a victorious war would bring peace to Europe: one, of course, that deflected the weight of a threatened French invasion away from Britain's shores.

During the course of these difficult negotiations Czartoryski confided: 'We had to make England understand that the wish to fight Napoleon was not in itself sufficient to establish an indissoluble bond between her government and that of St Petersburg.' Yet Russia did give ground to Britain, aware that without her essential financial subsidies the armies of Europe could never uphold the threat of military action. After weeks of discussion, Britain presented a written response to Russia's recommendation, which, with elegant diplomatic chicanery, purported to agree with the principles of the Russian proposal, before proceeding to amend them. It arrived at St Petersburg in February 1805.

While these discussions slowly progressed, other diplomatic moves saw Sweden terminate friendly relations with France in September 1804 and sign an agreement with Britain in December. Austria and Russia moved closer together too. In a letter to Kaiser Francis, Alexander excited Austrian fears when he wrote of France gaining strength from the isolation of the great powers, adding that: 'Bonaparte has no other rule of conduct than an unquenchable thirst of power, coupled with a desire for universal dominion.' With the Austrian army still lacking the cohesion, organisation, and manpower to present a determined defence against French aggression, Francis agreed a treaty with Russia in November that provided for mutual support against French aggression. Three months earlier he had taken the opportunity to strengthen his own position by relinquishing the fading dignity of the crumbling Holy Roman Empire. This dated assemblage of German territories, owing limited allegiance to the Habsburg monarchy, no longer held its former strength and inroads by France along the Rhine further threatened its 900-year existence. Already, some fifty years earlier, the eighteenth century French philosopher Voltaire had condemned it as 'neither holy, nor Roman, nor an empire'. Therefore, Francis II of the Holy Roman Empire loosened his ties and consolidated his realm by assuming the title 'Kaiser Francis I of Austria'.

After his coronation, Napoleon continued to extend his influence in Italy and on 26 May 1805, he crowned himself 'king of all Italy' in Milan. Nine days later, he annexed the Ligurian Republic, with it's all-important port of Genoa – fertile recruiting ground for the under strength French navy. Europe saw the move as confirmation that Napoleon had not curbed his territorial ambitions …

Anglo-Russian negotiations now reached an impasse. A treaty drawn up in St Petersburg in April 1805 was despatched to London for Pitt's approval, before providing the basis of an ultimatum to Napoleon. But the Russian understanding of Britain's position, even after months of discussion, was flawed. There were a number of clauses that angered Pitt, but amongst them there was one that stated Britain would hand over Malta to a Russian garrison. The Russians had not raised this point in discussions and Pitt refused to ratify the treaty. When the news reached St Petersburg, Czartoryski reported that he had never seen the tsar, 'more dissatisfied and more out of control'.[2] Determined to bring matters to a head, Alexander decided to send the ultimatum to Napoleon anyway, assuring Pitt that Britain would not be committed to any agreement without her assent. But within a few days of its despatch came news of Napoleon's annexation of Genoa. Alexander recalled the document immediately, exclaiming: 'This man is insatiable, his ambition knows no bounds; he is a scourge of the world; he wants war; well he shall have it, and the sooner the better.'[3]

The tsar signed the treaty with Britain, excluding the contentious clauses, and on 28 July 1805 the act of ratification was finally complete. On 9 August Austria signed too, reassured of her own security by Napoleon's apparent preoccupation with an invasion of Britain. The foundations of the Third Coalition were in place, strengthened by the commitment of Sweden and Naples to the cause. But despite Russia's best efforts, Prussia could not be drawn in. By careful diplomacy Talleyrand lured King Frederick William III away from the coalition, with the prospect of the coveted prize of Hanover as reward for his neutrality.

Allied war plans had long been the subject for discussion while the diplomatic wranglings of the coalition dragged on. Now the alliance was officially in place, preparations for war were pressed forward with some urgency, the intention being to gain the advantage while the French army was arrayed along the Channel coast. Grandiose schemes involving half a million Allied soldiers marching in a vast Europe-wide sweep, entranced the protagonists. Although vastly impressive on paper, these plans were, in practice, to prove far beyond the capabilities of the coalition's commanders.

Napoleon left Milan early in July 1805 and returned to France. After a pause at Saint-Cloud he continued on to Boulogne, where he arrived in the bosom of his army on 3 August. By now any realistic hopes he held for a successful invasion of Britain had long since faded, but to his enemies, his presence at the coast would no doubt cast shadows over his intentions.

A year had passed since his last visit, at a time when he genuinely hoped to launch an invasion. Then, his senior army commanders had been warned to be ready, their soldiers already well-rehearsed in rapid embarkation. However, in order for the vast flotilla of invasion barges to cross the Channel safely, they needed the protection of French warships, but these were all bottled up in port by the British Royal Navy. Undeterred, Napoleon had ordered Admiral Latouche-Tréville to prepare to break out of Toulon, release ships from other blockaded ports, and clear the Channel for the invasion to begin. Fortunately for the soldiers of this flotilla of unseaworthy barges, the admiral died of disease on 20 August, forcing Napoleon to abandon the plan.

Other grand naval schemes formulated in September 1804 failed to disperse the superior British navy. But French naval power soon received a welcome boost. In October British ships had attacked four Spanish treasure ships sailing from Peru. In response, Spain declared war on Britain, leading inevitably to an alliance between France and Spain. In place of the former financial settlement, Spain now offered France her warships.

After a false start, a final plan to draw off the British navy got under way at the end of March 1805. Admiral Villeneuve, Latouche-Tréville's replacement, broke out of Toulon with orders to pick up a squadron of Spanish ships at Cadiz before heading westwards across the Atlantic. At Martinique he was to rendezvous with the Brest fleet under Admiral Gantheaume, augmented by more Spanish ships. Napoleon felt sure a threat to the West Indies must lure the British navy to follow; then his fleets would double back and make all speed for Europe, arrive in the Channel by mid June/mid July and gain ascendancy long enough for the invasion of Britain to be launched. The plan met with partial success. Vice-Admiral Lord Nelson, after some delay, sailed in hot pursuit of Villeneuve but Gantheaume failed to break out of Brest. Having drawn Nelson westwards, Villeneuve then turned back, heading for Ferrol on Spain's north-west coast, to pick up a Spanish squadron there before sailing for Brest and the Channel. With Nelson misdirected back towards Gibraltar there was a chance of success, but an encounter with a British fleet under Admiral Calder off the Spanish coast, although inconclusive, forced Villeneuve back to

Vigo. Unsettled by this engagement and needing to make repairs and disembark his sick, Villeneuve picked up the Ferrol squadron and sailed southwards to Cadiz. The last remote chance of a successful invasion now disappeared as Nelson, sailing northwards, joined the rest of the navy guarding the approaches to the Channel.

Now back on the French coast again, Napoleon gazed half-heartedly down the Channel for any indication of the safe arrival of Villeneuve's fleet, but his earlier determination to march on London had faded. Yet to abandon the idea suggested failure, an option Napoleon was unprepared to accept. However, the continuing negotiations between Britain, Russia and Austria offered him a way out. Perhaps his annexation of Genoa aimed to force their hand; he knew well that Austria would find it difficult to ignore the move. If Austria and Russia took aggressive steps he could abandon his failing invasion plans and turn to face the new threat with his reputation untarnished. Whether he planned it or not, Genoa finally pushed the Allies over the edge; the great armies of France, Austria and Russia were on a collision course.

The French army, encamped along the Channel coast since summer 1803, was the finest assembled throughout the Revolutionary and Napoleonic Wars. For two years the army lived and trained together in vast sprawling camps on or close to the coast of northern France and extending into Holland and Hanover. These camps, built by the soldiers themselves, formed permanent homes. They consisted of barrack huts, streets, squares, and even gardens. Each day the soldiers assembled to train and manoeuvre in every tactical combination of the army: from company to corps. Battalions drilled daily, brigades on alternate days, and divisions every third day. At other times they honed their skill in musketry and practised fieldwork construction. With officers and men living and working together, each gained confidence in, and respect for, the other.

These were important factors in an army where class barriers had been removed by the Revolution. Each of the great camps formed the nucleus for one of seven separate army corps: miniature armies – containing elements of infantry, cavalry and artillery – able to fight on their own or combine with other corps for larger engagements. The majority of units remained in these same formations from training to combat, boosting their morale or esprit de corps. Two of the corps were in occupation, I Corps (Maréchal Bernadotte) in Hanover and II Corps (Général de division Marmont) in Holland, while the smallest of the formations, VII Corps (Maréchal Augereau), encamped close to the port of Brest in Brittany. The remaining four corps – III Corps (Maréchal Davout), IV Corps (Maréchal Soult), V Corps (Maréchal Lannes) and VI Corps (Maréchal Ney) – were those assembled closest to Boulogne. With the addition of the Garde Impériale and Reserve Cavalry formations the total force amounted to about 190,000 men.

The basic infantry building block was the battalion, which could be either line (*ligne*) or light infantry (*légère*). Both consisted of nine companies. At full strength, a battalion numbered 1,078 officers and men, though these numbers fell rapidly on campaign. Generally, two battalions formed a regiment, one or two regiments a brigade, two or three brigades formed a division, and two or three divisions – augmented by a light cavalry brigade or division and artillery support – created a corps. Clearly, the size of a corps could vary greatly. The light cavalry regiments – hussars and *chasseurs à cheval* – suffered from the desperate shortage of horses in France in 1805, which meant they rarely attained 50 per cent of their full strength, fixed at just under 1,000 sabres. Two or three light cavalry regiments formed a brigade, and, generally, two brigades a division.

The shortage of mounts also had a serious effect on the dragoon regiments, which either formed separate divisions or added their strength to the corps. At the outset of the campaign in 1805 it became necessary to allocate a large number of men to formations of dismounted dragoons, but even so, barely 50 per cent of the reduced mounted target was achieved.

Heavy cavalry regiments – *cuirassier* and *carabinier* – formed separate reserve divisions operating outside the corps organisation. With each established at around 540 sabres, Napoleon put great effort in bringing these regiments – his shock troops – up to strength, and managed, on average, to mount 80 per cent of full regimental strength.

The final reserve formation, the Garde Impériale, formed two regiments of infantry, each close to their full strength of 1,700 men, but again the cavalry regiments were short of their establishment.

Although this army spent two years training, many of the soldiers already had significant military experience. Some 25 per cent of the army had served since the early Revolutionary battles, while another 25 per cent had fought at either Marengo or Hohenlinden in 1800. In all, about 44 per cent of the rank and file had seen previous service and virtually all officers and NCOs could boast similar experience.

This army – no longer the 'Armée d'Angleterre' but now operating as Napoleon's first 'Grande Armée' – waited: well trained and ready for action, keen to exchange the monotonous drudgery of camp life for the adrenaline rush of combat. All but one of their corps commanders had recently entered the newly created ranks of the *Marshalate*, and each was an experienced soldier with years of combat experience behind him. They too were keen to march and test their commands under conditions more exacting than parade ground manoeuvres or mock battles.

The Russian army destined to oppose La Grande Armée had entered a period of necessary reform in 1801. During the earlier reign of Tsar Paul the army had taken a step back, towards the rigid doctrine of the era of Frederick the Great of Prussia, at the same time that France was successfully introducing a more fluid style of warfare. Prior to his accession to the throne, Paul became obsessed with the military, a passion he indulged by creating his own small private army on his estate, which he delighted to drill and parade. When Paul became tsar he extended his outdated views to the rest of the army, and under the auspices of the strict disciplinarian Count Alexsei Arakcheev, began to introduce these retrograde changes, which had an unsettling effect on the army. However, following one of his dramatic mood swings, Paul dismissed Arakcheev from his service in 1799. Four years later, as war clouds gathered once more, Alexander – now enthroned as tsar – looked for assurances from his senior commanders that should diplomacy fail, the army was ready for war. With none forthcoming, he turned to the hated and feared Arakcheev, recalling him to office in May 1803. Appointing him inspector-general of artillery, he tasked him with developing that arm, and ensuring that, when the day for war should come, the army would be ready.

For the average soldier in the Russian army life was tough. Recruited by a levy on the population, the army drew the vast majority of its manpower from the serfs, the lowest social order in the Russian Empire, inured to a life of virtual slavery. Conscripted to the service for twenty-five years, few survived the hardships to return home again and were considered 'dead' by their families when the army escorted them away. But the personal experience of the serf – of blind obedience and stoicism in the face of great hardships – made for a solid, reliable and determined soldier: one well-prepared for a life on campaign.

The main infantry weapon of the Russian army, the 1798 pattern musket, was far inferior to the Charleville musket of the French. At 7.5kg it outweighed the Charleville by 70 per cent, making it difficult and cumbersome to handle in combat, and, much to the frustration of their officers, encouraged the men to fire from the hip, greatly reducing its effectiveness. Perhaps this excessive weight contributed to the Russian soldiers' legendary fondness for the bayonet.

The officer corps of the army attracted much criticism. Generally drawn from the provincial gentry, although considered loyal and hardy, the ordinary line officers lacked education – many were barely literate – and with little chance of advancement, generally avoided excessive military activity. Above them the nobility populated the higher ranks, but although they passed through officer cadet schools, this level rarely showed any aptitude for staff or administrative work. Many with limited military knowledge or training, but with good connections at court, sought postings at general headquarters, which promised a more comfortable and less demanding way of life. To compensate for the lack of good quality senior officers, many foreign nationals were offered staff appointments in the Russian army.

Infantry regiments were of three types: musketeer, grenadier and *jäger*. Originally having two battalions, Alexander increased regiments to three in 1802. Grenadier regiments had one grenadier battalion and two of fusiliers, while musketeer regiments had one grenadier battalion and two of musketeers. At full strength, a battalion of grenadiers or musketeers numbered just over 700 men, and the *jäger* just over 500.

In the cavalry, heavy *cuirassier* regiments and dragoons numbered a little over a 1,000 men, while the larger hussar and *uhlan* (lancers) regiments mustered just under 1,900. However, as in France, dramatic shortages of horseflesh meant these targets were unachievable in 1805.

Arakcheev's modernisation of the artillery had begun to take effect but it remained generally inferior to French guns of similar categories. This fact was compounded by the poorer quality of Russian powder, which affected the striking power of both artillery pieces and muskets alike.

Although Tsar Paul introduced new drill regulations across the whole of the armed forces, many regiments abandoned these following his death and reverted to their own regimental versions, leading to a lack of overall consistency. Only for six weeks of the year, each summer, did officers and soldiers benefit from the experience of drilling and manoeuvring in any formations larger than the regiment. However, these combinations never became permanent and on campaign regiments and brigades regularly moved from one formation to another as needs arose, preventing senior commanders building a working relationship with their subordinates.

When the time came for the leading Russian army to march to war in 1805 it relied heavily on the Austrians to make good their great shortage in transport and supplies. Yet on the eve of war the Austrians faced numerous problems of their own.

Archduke Charles (Erzherzog Karl), a younger brother of the kaiser, and the man charged with the responsibility of reforming the Austrian military system after defeat in 1800, was well aware of the enormity of the task. As such, he felt an extended period of peace was absolutely essential, and he vehemently opposed those who sought an early return to conflict. He began with an extensive overhaul of the archaic administration of the army, but this earned him much criticism from those who felt he should focus his attention on problems within the structure and organisation of the armed forces themselves. Yet despite a massive reduction in the military budget of 60 per cent between 1801 and 1804, Charles managed to introduce improvements. The first steps towards a permanent General Staff were taken with the appointment of FML Duka as Quartermaster General in March 1801, a title normally conferred only in wartime, along with a number of officers solely allocated to staff tasks. At a regimental level, junior officers were poorly paid, with the consequence that the army no longer offered an attractive career for the sons of the upper nobility. The necessity to widen the recruiting base of the officer class meant a further drop in the generally low educational standard they attained, but Charles pressed on with efforts to improve low morale and encourage esprit de corps.

Recruitment to the army was in the main by conscription, but so many individuals were exempt – or avoided selection – that only additional voluntary enlistment kept the numbers up. To help prevent large numbers 'disappearing' rather than taking their place in the ranks, Charles reduced enlistment terms from twenty-five to ten years in the infantry, twelve in the cavalry and fourteen in the artillery and engineers. The very nature of the vast Habsburg Empire meant that the army was multi-national, drawing Germans, Hungarians, Italians, Walloons, Poles, Croats, Serbs and many smaller eastern ethnic groups together to fight for the kaiser.

Economic restrictions made it necessary for the army to house many of its troops in the far-flung corners of the empire, where living was cheaper. Others, after basic training, spent long periods at home on unpaid furlough, limiting the opportunity for regular large-scale manoeuvres. When these manoeuvres did take place they often drew criticism from Charles's opponents. One commented that they highlighted the 'capabilities of the rank and file and the total ineptitude of the officers'.[4]

In 1803 joint foreign ministers, Franz Colloredo and Johann Cobenzl, felt convinced of the necessity of a new alliance with Russia, but faced constant opposition from Archduke Charles. Besides the unprepared state of the army, Charles also voiced his doubts over Russia's reliability and the likelihood of any British intervention in Central Europe. Without these, he argued, Austria would once again risk facing the brunt of any French attack alone. Frustrated by Charles's negative views, Colloredo and Cobenzl began to undermine his position. In doing so, they introduced a retired army officer, FML Karl Leiberich Mack, to present an opposing view on the state of the army. Mack's disastrous period in command of the Neapolitan army in 1798 had tarnished a well-respected earlier career, during which he earned widespread admiration in the campaigns in the Low Countries (1792–1794). But his positive views appealed to the kaiser, who drew increasingly towards this strong faction.

The signing of the treaty between Austria and Russia in 1804, without Charles's involvement, confirmed the weakening of his position. The pressure against him continued to mount until in April 1805, he was forced to dismiss FML Duka and accept the appointment of FML Mack as the new Quartermaster General, with direct access to the kaiser. Duka, like Charles, maintained it would take six months to bring the army to a war-footing. Mack suggested he needed only two to achieve the same result. As such, Austria only began to mobilise in July 1805: just a few weeks after Mack had introduced major structural changes in the army.

Under Mack's belated changes all cavalry regiments, whether light or heavy, increased to eight squadrons: a strength previously only maintained by the hussars. This he achieved by reducing squadron strengths to 131 men in heavy and 151 in the light cavalry regiments. However, as with all other nations in 1805, a shortage of horses made it impossible to attain these numbers in the field.

The reorganisation was more dramatic in the infantry. Until 1805 regiments formed three field battalions, each of six companies of fusiliers and one garrison battalion of four companies. In addition, there were two grenadier companies, but these generally fought in combined grenadier battalions. Under Mack's changes all regiments were authorised to change their establishment to six battalions: four field and one depot battalion of fusiliers and one battalion of grenadiers, each battalion restricted to four companies. However, it seems clear that not all regiments introduced these changes before war commenced in 1805. The frustrations felt by those who did push them through are expressed by an officer who bemoaned the fact that the 'common soldiers no longer knew their officers and the officers did not know their men.'[5] There was no time for Mack to attempt any last minute reorganisation of the artillery and the great shortages of men, equipment and draught animals ensured that it was woefully understrength when war broke out.

Mack added one final late change. The army would now follow the French example of living from the land. By drastically reducing the amount of baggage accompanying the army, he hoped to see a corresponding improvement in its mobility. But an army that for generations had relied upon a regular food supply on campaign now found itself required to adapt to foraging to boost a meagre daily flour allowance.

Britain, the other main signatory to the Third Coalition, possessed only a small army when compared to the might of Austria and Russia. While she planned to send forces to support the flanking actions of the Allied plans, the joint forces of the kaiser and the tsar would undertake the main thrust of the campaign. But Britain's contribution was essential to the plans of the coalition. The treaty between the three nations required Austria to raise 250,000 men and Russia 115,000 for the war – and Britain, under Pitt's leadership, was to subsidise the cost to the tune of £1.25 million per 100,000 men.[6]

And so a revitalised and confident French army, under the inspired leadership of the Emperor Napoleon, held aloft their new eagle standards and carried them eastwards into battle for the first time. Against them, the armies of Austria and Russia hastily completed their final preparations and mustered beneath the shared ancient imperial symbol of the double-headed eagle. As these eagles of Europe sharpened their talons, the armies of emperor, kaiser and tsar unfurled their banners and prepared to march across Europe – to glory or ignominy.

Chapter 4

'Every Delay and Indecision Causes Ruin'*

The grand strategic plan conceived by the signatories of the Third Coalition unleashed five separate Allied attacks against France and the territories she occupied. In July 1805, while the diplomats bound their nations together with treaties and protocols, the military men concocted the complex combinations necessary to bring their plans to fruition.

The Russians entrusted their negotiations to the able General Maior Baron Ferdinand Wintzingerode. German-born and having served in the Hessian and Austrian armies before joining the Russian army in 1797, Wintzingerode quickly established himself and was appointed an aide to the tsar in 1802. His experience and knowledge ideally placed him to undertake this important role. For Austria, Mack sat at the negotiating table, along with FML Schwarzenberg, a brave soldier–diplomat and vice president of the Hofkriegsrat, the Imperial War Council. There was no place for Archduke Charles. The plans they hammered out called for a Russian force of about 16,000 men to join the 12,000-strong Swedish garrison of Stralsund on the Baltic coast and drive into Hanover, where, reinforced by British troops, they would press on into Holland. In the south of Europe, as many as 25,000 Russian troops, based on the island of Corfu and at the Black Sea port of Odessa, supported by up to 9,000 British troops from Malta and Gibraltar, would land in the Kingdom of Naples. Then, in conjunction with the Neapolitan army (some 36,000-strong), they were to defeat the French in that region and drive north to support the offensive in Central Europe, where the main thrust of the Allied campaign would take place.

The main Austrian army, under the command of Archduke Charles, was to assemble in north-eastern Italy, behind Verona on the Adige river, from where it could advance into Lombardy and push on Milan. With the French driven back, Charles could then continue through Switzerland, and in conjunction with a second Austrian army on the Danube, press on into France. While

---

* Kutuzov to Alexander, prior to the commencement of the 1805 campaign.

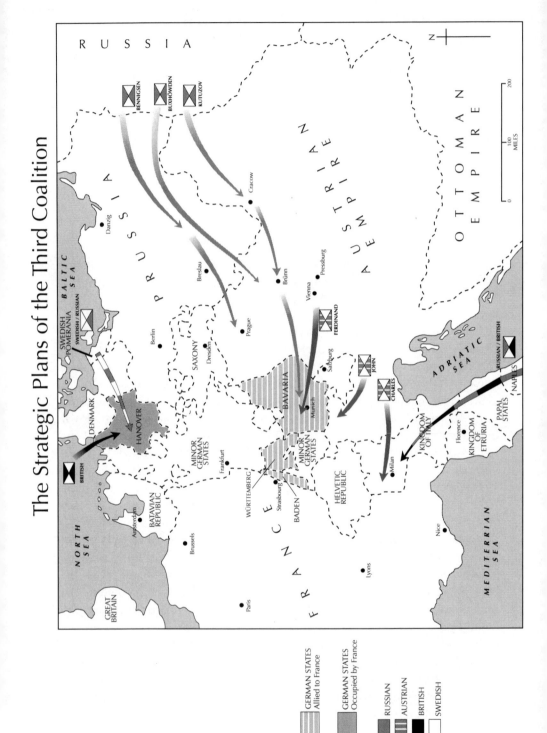

The Strategic Plans of the Third Coalition

Charles launched his attack, this second army would fulfil more of a holding role. Under the command of the 24-year-old Archduke Ferdinand d'Este, a close relative of the kaiser, this army was to cross the border into Bavaria, gain the support of the Bavarian army and await the arrival of a Russian army, led by General Mikhail Kutuzov. Only then would it join the advance into France. Linking these two Austrian armies was a smaller defensive force located in the mountainous Tirol region between Bavaria and the Austrian provinces in northern Italy, under the command of Charles' younger brother, the 23-year-old Archduke John. Kutuzov, with a Russian army of 46,000 men was to march with all speed from the western edge of Russia to Braunau on the River Inn, the border between Austria and Bavaria, where it was to regroup. The date for the commencement of Kutuzov's advance was set for 16 August, but a delay in Wintzingerode's departure from Vienna officially put the start date back to 20 August.[1] Further to the north, General Bennigsen would advance through Prussia and Bohemia before driving into Franconia (northern Bavaria) at the head of a Russian army of about 40,000 men. From here he could support the attack on Hanover and Holland or align with Kutuzov on the Danube. Another Russian army, 50,000 men on paper and commanded by General Leitenant Buxhöwden, would march later, between Kutuzov and Bennigsen, able to switch to the support of either as circumstances dictated.

There is no doubt that the plan looked impressive, and if it could have been made to work then it would certainly have caused Napoleon problems. But even before the campaign got underway the plans were thrown into confusion. Much of the strength of the plan depended on Prussia joining the coalition and granting permission for Russian troops to march through her territory: but with Prussia resolutely clinging on to her neutrality, permission was not forthcoming.

In Austria, command issues threatened the preparations too. The tsar insisted that when Kutuzov linked with the Austrian forces on the Danube the supreme commander should hold a high dynastic rank. With Archduke Charles destined for Italy, the kaiser assumed the responsibility of this position, but in the meantime, Archduke Ferdinand would remain in command and lead the army into Bavaria. However, Francis then appointed FML Mack as Ferdinand's chief of staff and handed him secret orders empowering him to override Ferdinand's military decisions. By this authority Mack became the de facto commander of the army on the Danube. It was a fatal decision, one that would play havoc with the command structure in the coming weeks. Meanwhile, endless diplomatic delays, disputes and negotiations held back the proposed flanking attacks in Hanover and Naples. By the time they got underway it was too late to influence the campaign.

Throughout the spring and early summer of 1805 Napoleon's agents brought him reports of increasing Austrian military activity in Tirol and northern Italy, as well as in Upper Austria. Alerted to this development he began to woo Bavaria, Württemberg and Baden: their military contingents would prove useful additions to his army, but more importantly, should war follow, unrestricted passage for his army through their territories would allow him to strike swiftly on the Danube. The pressure on Prussia to form an alliance increased too, with the prize of Hanover on offer in exchange. In return for this territorial expansion, Napoleon required Prussia to mobilise an army on her border with Bohemia to face any Russian incursion. Prussia made soothing noises but determinedly declared her neutrality, nervously veiling the defensive treaty agreed with Russia the previous spring.

Matters intensified in August when reports reached Napoleon that Austrian contractors were openly filling magazines with supplies in Swabia, a region encompassing much of south-west Bavaria and the Black Forest. By 23 August he had heard enough. On that day he despatched a letter to Prussia declaring his intention to march on the Danube and rejoicing 'at the new bonds which will draw together our states', before offering the prize of Hanover once again. He well understood the threatening effect a belligerent Prussia would have on the war plans of Austria and the release of his troops currently occupying Hanover would boost the forces available for the war. But Prussia would not sign and continued to affirm neutrality.

On the same day that he issued this latest offer to Prussia, without waiting for a reply, Napoleon turned from diplomacy to matters of grand strategy. If the strength of the coalition was to be broken before it could combine against him, he needed to strike fast. He accurately assessed the impact of the flanking threats as minimal to the outcome of the coming campaign, and the option of transferring the majority of his army from the Channel to join those already stationed in northern Italy would risk too great a delay. Instead, he entrusted command of the Army of Italy to the reliable Maréchal Masséna. His command amounted to some 65,000 men, although depots, garrisons and hospitals distributed along the lines of communication reduced his effective strength to around 40,000. With these men Napoleon expected Masséna to check and delay the advance of Archduke Charles and the main Austrian army of about 94,000 men. Général de division Gouvion St Cyr marching north from southern Italy with 18,000 men, released by the extraction of a treaty of neutrality from the king of Naples, offered valuable support. Instead, Napoleon targeted the closest enemy formation to La Grande Armée, the Austrians assembling on the Danube. With a rapid advance he hoped to knock them out of the war before Russian reinforcements arrived from the east.

The following day he issued orders for the *cuirassiers* and dragoons to march for the Rhine, where the dragoons were to observe a 100-mile stretch of the river, extending either side of Strasbourg. On 25 August further instructions authorised them to extend their observations beyond the Rhine towards Bavaria, along with Oudinot's elite Reserve Grenadier Division. Then on 26 August, after two years of intensive training, La Grande Armée received the order to turn their backs on England and march for the Rhine. Maréchal Ney and VI Corps headed for Schlettstadt, 30 miles south of Strasbourg, Soult (IV Corps) and Lannes (V Corps) for Strasbourg itself, and Davout (III Corps) to Hagenau, roughly 20 miles north of Strasbourg. All destinations suggested Napoleon intended following the traditional invasion route into the Danube Valley through the Black Forest. Further to the north, Marmont (II Corps), in Holland, received orders to march for Mainz, situated at the junction of the Rhine and Main rivers, approximately 115 miles north of Strasbourg. Bernadotte (I Corps) was instructed to evacuate Hanover, except for a garrison left at the town of Hameln, and march for Göttingen, 130 miles to the north-east of Mainz. And far off to the west, Augereau began the long march from Brittany, heading for the Upper Rhine around Basel. Behind them Napoleon left some 30,000 troops to remain on the coast and guard against any British landing.

At this point, Napoleon knew little of Austrian intentions on the Danube, but he believed that by rapid movement he could intercept any Austrian advance into Bavaria somewhere between the rivers Lech and Inn. However, it appears that during the evening of 27 August he received information that Allied preparations were more advanced than he anticipated. An Austrian army assembling at Wels on the Traun river, was only 45 miles from the Bavarian border, and other intelligence indicated that the Russians might have begun to move. A quick consultation of the map revealed the possibility that this Austrian army could concentrate on the Rhine before all his formations arrived. Reacting quickly, Napoleon ordered a general shift of the southern formations northwards the following day. Now only Lannes' V Corps and Murat's cavalry would head for Strasbourg, with Ney, Soult and Davout redirecting their line of march between Hagenau and Speyer. These new positions enabled Napoleon to plan an advance targeted on a 30-mile stretch of the Danube lying between the city of Ulm and east towards to Dillingen, one that offered a central position against an Austrian advance into Bavaria or a Russian move from Bohemia.

While the army adjusted to life on the move and set out on the 350-mile journey from the coast to the Rhine, Napoleon sent three trusted men ahead to gather as much intelligence as possible. Murat, disguised as 'Colonel de Beaumont' made an extraordinary reconnaissance, taking him from Mainz to Strasbourg via Würzburg, Bamburg, Nuremberg, Regensberg, Passau, the Inn river, Munich, Ulm and the Black Forest, a distance of 600 miles in about three weeks. Général de brigade Bertrand, an aide to the emperor, engaged on an even longer journey. From Munich he made for Passau and the Inn river, which he then followed upstream to Kufstein. From there he moved to Salzburg before returning to Munich and continuing along the Lech to Ingolstadt and Donauwörth on the Danube, then turning north he headed for Bamburg. A return to the Danube at Ulm followed before he headed back to the Rhine via Stuttgart. The third reconnaissance was entrusted to GD Savary, the man who carried out the execution of the duc d'Enghein. Savary undertook to explore the roads from the Rhine, north of the Black Forest, to the Danube. For this purpose he recruited an old contact, Charles Schulmeister, a trader (and highly successful smuggler) who lived in Strasbourg. Because of his extensive knowledge of the area and numerous contacts, Schulmeister had been of much use to Savary in earlier military campaigns on the Rhine. More recently he had supplied Savary with information on the movements of the duc d'Enghien prior to his abduction. Now, accompanying Savary, and with both men in disguise, they set out to study the roads by which Napoleon's army would advance. Later, Schulmeister would fulfil a far more pivotal role.

While this intelligence gathering was underway, the Allies were preparing to march. The first Russian army to move formed at Radziwilov in Ukraine close to the border with the former Polish land of Austrian Galicia. On 25 August, the 46,000 men began to cross the border at Brody. Then, having divided into six columns of between 7,000 and 8,000 men each, they began their march towards Moravia at 24-hour intervals. But the man appointed to overall command of the Russian army, Mikhail Kutuzov, had taken no part in determining its plans or strategy.

Mikhail Illarionovich Golenshchev-Kutuzov was rapidly approaching his 60th birthday in August 1805. For the last three years he had lived in exile from St Petersburg, residing on his estate at Goroshki in Ukraine, and it was there that he received a message from the tsar ordering him back to the city. Kutuzov had enjoyed a long, distinguished military and diplomatic career. He first saw action against the Poles as a nineteen-year-old infantry company commander and his bravery under fire drew attention during the war against the Turks in 1768. However, Kutuzov was prone to high spirits and an account of his parody of the army commander reached headquarters. His target, Count Rumyantsev, was not amused and immediately dismissed him, but granted permission for him to transfer to the army operating in the Crimea against the Turks. It brought a change over Kutuzov, who it was said became more self-contained, held back his opinions and distrusted the motives of those around him. During the storming of Alushta in 1773 he received a near fatal wound. The bullet destroyed some of the muscles attached to his right eye, causing great pain and dizziness, but which fortunately did not impair his vision. After an extended period of leave, during which he travelled to Berlin and Holland for medical treatment and visited London and Vienna, Kutuzov returned to the army in 1776. Back in the Crimea he served under the revered Russian military leader, Alexander Suvorov, who greatly influenced his thinking. War broke out against the Turks again in 1787 and at Ochakov Kutuzov received another wound behind his right eye, in almost the same spot as that of fifteen years earlier. Although it was again feared fatal, Kutuzov rapidly recovered, however his vision suffered this time as his eye sat awkwardly twisted in its socket. For the next two years Kutuzov, now a major general, continued to perform great heroic deeds in battle and, despite this physical handicap, further enhanced his reputation as a fierce, energetic and intelligent commander.

In 1793, with the war at an end, Kutuzov exchanged battlefield skills for those of diplomacy, following his unlikely appointment as ambassador to Turkey. But Kutuzov adapted well and created a favourable impression in Constantinople. The following year he received a recall and was sent to command the Russian army in Finland, a task he fulfilled until 1797, when the new tsar, Paul, sent him as ambassador to Berlin. A brief period as governor-general of Vilna followed before he returned to St Petersburg in 1800, as acting governor-general of the city. Yet the intrigues building against the tsar made life extremely difficult and required all Kutuzov's diplomatic skills to avoid complicity in the plot against the tsar's life. Following Paul's murder, Alexander appointed Kutuzov full governor-general of St Petersburg, yet he constantly fretted over whether Kutuzov believed him a party to his father's death. To rid himself of this constant painful reminder he began to exert mounting pressure on Kutuzov, until, in August 1802, Alexander was able to announce that Kutuzov had been 'dismissed at his own request'. Now, virtually in exile, Kutuzov retired to his estate in Goroshki to concentrate on farming. His health began to suffer and increasing rheumatism contributed to his aged appearance, then his battered right eye finally failed and he lost his sight. He grew portly but retained his fondness for alcohol and kept his one roving eye for the women. He remained cunning, shrewd, diplomatic and dogged and was still the best commander the army had. When the call came from Alexander to serve his country, Kutuzov responded once more with alacrity. He disapproved of the Allied plans, but as the campaign was already underway, headed off to lead the army into Bavaria to confront the French.

Kutuzov's greatest fear was that Austria would send her army into Bavaria too early. A marathon 650-mile march from Russia to Braunau lay before the army and uncertainty over Prussia's stance, combined with delays in preparation meant his army started five days later than planned.[2]

On 7 August, Alexander wrote to Frederick William, the Prussian king, seeking permission for Russian troops to march through Prussia. While he awaited the king's response, Buxhöwden's army marched towards the border at Brest-Litovsk, in readiness to continue across Prussian territory towards Warsaw. Similarly, Bennigsen's men advanced through Lithuania, awaiting confirming orders to enter Prussia. Russia and Austria agreed (with British consent) that if Prussia refused the request then Russian troops would enter Prussia aggressively. Communications dragged on, and Alexander ordered his two armies to halt at the border, allowing time for Kutuzov to advance far enough to add a further threat from the south to that now presented from the east.

On 4 September, Alexander warned Frederick William that his troops would cross the border into Prussia on 16 September. Then, against the wishes of Czartoryski and the Austrian minister, Cobenzl, Alexander decided he should personally join his armies at the front and share their fortune. Prussia continued to express her neutrality, leading to an extension of the deadline, while Alexander travelled to Brest-Litovsk, where he arrived on 27 September after a seven-day journey. Here he found a letter waiting from Frederick William and in response sent his aide, Prince Peter Dolgorukov to Berlin, in a final attempt at reasoning with the Prussian king. On 3 October, while awaiting the result of this embassy, Alexander retired to the Czartoryski family estate at Pulawy. Meanwhile, Bennigsen, Buxhöwden and their armies remained on the border, already way behind schedule.

With everything static on the Prussian border, Kutuzov pushed his army on as best he could. There were 46,405 men under his command, but only a few days into Galicia, Kutuzov received an order to detach one of his six columns for service on the Turkish frontier. When the kaiser heard of this weakening of the Russian force he immediately appealed to the tsar. In response, General Leitenant Rosen's men were recalled, but because of the inherent delays in communication between Vienna, St Petersburg and the army, he trailed far behind Kutuzov's advance and never reached the Inn, reducing the effective command to around 38,000 men. The leading column reached Teschen, on the border between the Austrian provinces of Galicia and Moravia – the halfway point to Braunau – on 22 September, covering the 320 miles in twenty-nine days. Here Kutuzov received dramatic news: the French had already abandoned their camps on the Channel coast and were heading for the Rhine.

Kutusov's men had suffered badly on the march – poor roads and bad weather taking their toll – but at Teschen the Austrian authorities urged him to push on with greater speed. For this purpose they provided over 2,000 horse drawn carts to hasten the Russians on their way. Exhausted though his men were, Kutuzov ordered them to abandon all excess baggage and make ready to march on, utilising the carts to transport detachments in relays and reassigning his fittest horses to pull the infantry ammunition carts. The artillery teams could not maintain this accelerated rate, so in order to preserve their battlefield effectiveness, they were allowed to continue at their own pace. Although conscious of the need for speed, Kutuzov insisted on maintaining one day's rest for every four spent marching, to prevent exhaustion totally destroying his army. As a result of these changes his progress dramatically increased, but despite his caution, cohesion broke down as more and more men struggled to keep up the relentless pace. This endless tramp along bad roads in chilling rain destroyed the soldiers' shoes, and reduced to marching barefoot, the men suffered greatly. Any unable to keep up were left to come on as best they could.

Kutuzov himself took a detour via Vienna before arriving in Braunau on 9 October. The first column arrived three days later, ahead of schedule, completing the march of 330 miles from Teschen in twenty days. Allowing for three days' rest, these men progressed at the tremendous pace of almost 19 miles a day. However, another two weeks would pass before the last of Kutusov's five columns struggled in. By then, momentous events elsewhere had made their prodigious efforts worthless.

Chapter 5

To the Danube and the Rhine

'Soldiers, we will have forced marches to make,
fatigues and deprivations of all kinds to endure
…we will not rest until we have planted our
eagles in the territories of our enemies!'*

As their Russian allies gradually began to close the great distance between the
two armies destined to serve together in Germany, the Austrian army made its
final arrangements for the campaign. On 29 August, at Hetzendorf, on the
outskirts of Vienna, the senior Austrian commanders met to thrash out the
plan of campaign. It was the first in a series of meetings, but by the time they
reached a conclusion on 5 September, Napoleon's army was already nine days
into its march for the Rhine.

At the first of these meetings Archduke Charles presented his 'General
Principles' of the campaign. He would lead the main army in Italy, for he was
convinced that the greatest threat to Austria lay along her Italian border with
France. In March 1804 he wrote of this threat to the empire, posed by French
forces so close to Austrian lands. He stressed: 'It seems quite indisputable that
the bulk of our forces should be allotted to the Italian theatre of operations'
and added, 'Hence it is on the Adige that we must expect the first and principal
operations, and it is there that the Austrian Armies should assume the
offensive.'[1] Therefore, Charles insisted the army on the Danube hold a position
on the Inn river, until the Russians arrived.

However, this was in direct opposition to Mack's view, which demanded an
Austrian advance into Bavaria in early September, in order to gain time to
absorb the Bavarian army. Mack, who had completely won over the kaiser by
this time, also recommended that Francis should assume his role as
commander-in-chief with himself as quartermaster general (chief of staff).

---

* Napoleon's Proclamation to La Grande Armée, 30 September 1805.

This would give Mack authority to communicate directly with the chiefs of staff allocated to the armies in Italy, Tirol and on the Danube.

Archduke Ferdinand, named as commander of the army on the Danube, expressed concern that according to his calculations, the French could have 150,000 men at Munich before the Russians reached the Inn. He therefore proposed that only an army of observation of 30,000 to 40,000 men should advance into Bavaria, falling back if pressed by the French. This far-sighted appraisal of the young archduke's gained the support of the kaiser, as well as Charles and his chief of staff, Zach. But Mack was having none of it and launched into a convincing destruction of Ferdinand's calculations, suggesting that Napoleon could only bring a maximum of 70,000 to the Rhine, with great numbers tied up on the coast, in Paris, or confined to hospitals by various epidemics. Indeed, the very suggestion that 150,000 men could march from the Channel to Munich in the time span suggested by Ferdinand seemed highly unlikely to a man of Mack's experience. Eloquent, persuasive, and backed by Cobenzl, Mack, won the kaiser over: consequently, the army would move into Bavaria.

But Anton Mayer, chief of staff to Ferdinand's Danube army, argued that while Charles' plan to attack through Italy was the correct one, when Napoleon did eventually move, the Danube was his most likely target. Mayer had already become frustrated in his dealings with Mack, who had failed to provide him with a plan for the campaign in Bavaria. Mayer turned to Charles for help. Later, however, on 5 September, Mayer gained support for the redirection of some 30,000 troops, earmarked for Italy, to march for the Upper Danube instead. Despite his objections, Charles, with his influence much undermined, was forced to concede. No doubt much to Mack's delight, the kaiser approved this transfer of manpower. The army on the Danube now increased to 72,000 men, on a par with Mack's estimate of the strength Napoleon could bring to this theatre.

Until the arrival of the Russians there was no need for the kaiser to join the army, so he remained in Vienna, as did both Charles and Ferdinand, prior to taking over their commands personally. Mack, however, as the kaiser's representative, had already issued orders on 2 September for the army to assemble at Wels, in preparation for the march on the Inn, two days later. Mack's presence with the army made Mayer's position difficult, even before it became known that Mack carried secret orders authorising him to override Ferdinand's decisions. As it was, Ferdinand did not join the army until 19 September, allowing Mack plenty of time to stamp his authority over Mayer.

Karl Mack, Freiherr von Leiberich's path to power had been unusual. Unlike the majority of senior military men in the Austrian army, who owed their rank to the fortune of high birth, Mack enrolled in the army in 1770 as an eighteen-year-old cavalry trooper. Although the son of a minor Protestant official, Mack gained his introduction to the Catholic-dominated army through an uncle on his mother's side of the family, who served as a *hauptmann* in the 2. Karabinierregiment. Mack found army life agreeable and eighteen months later earned his first promotion, to the rank of *korporal*. Further promotions followed until in 1777, after excelling in the role of regimental adjutant – a position held by a senior NCO in the Austrian army – he gained his reward, a commission in the regiment, as *unterleutnant*. Mack's big break came the following year when chosen to act as secretary to Feldmarschall Lacy, the honorary colonel of the regiment, on an inspection tour of the Bohemian border. He continued to serve Lacy through the War of the Bavarian Succession (1778–79) and impressed everyone with his energy and devotion to duty. This taste of command outside the regimental structure appealed to Mack, so in 1783, with the rank of *rittmeister* (cavalry captain), he transferred to the Quartermaster General staff. He continued to earn high praise, gaining further promotion and in 1788 came an appointment as ADC to Kaiser Joseph II.

Mack's star continued in its ascendancy in the following years. In 1789, while serving against the Turks, he gained promotion to *oberstleutnant* but crossed swords with the aged Feldmarschall Laudon, one of the great eighteenth century Austrian generals, while serving under him at the Siege of Belgrade. Mack earned himself a severe reprimand: but after his successful attack on the Turkish-held city, he was promoted to *oberst*, and was awarded the Order of Maria Theresa and the title *freiherr* (baron).

After his exertions Mack became ill and took a period of leave from the army, but in December 1790 he returned, as commander of 3. Chevaulegers. However, he spent much of that winter in Vienna lecturing on military matters to the nineteen-year-old Archduke Charles, marking the start of a friendship that was to end bitterly eight years later.

In 1793, with Austria now at war with Revolutionary France, Feldmarschall Prince Coburg-Saalfield requested Mack's services as his chief of staff in the Austrian Netherlands. Through Mack's encouragement of an offensive strategy the Austrian army won a victory at Aldenhoven and again at Neerwinden, where even though struck down by ill health, he persuaded Coburg to abandon plans for a retreat and to fight on.

Wounded later in the year, Mack went on leave to recuperate, returning to Coburg's staff in 1794. He continued to advocate an offensive strategy, but the campaign went badly and with his ill health returning and intrigues building against him in Vienna, he retired from the army. He returned again in 1796 with the rank of *feldmarschalleutnant*, and although the British were keen for him to command in Portugal, he accepted instead the post of chief of staff to the Army of the Interior. Here, in 1798, he clashed for the first time with Archduke Charles over proposed war plans, leading to animosity that brought their friendship to an end. Later that year, with Kaiser Francis' approval, Mack was offered the command of the Neapolitan army, which he accepted. What started as a promising campaign against the French in Rome descended into chaos as his poorly trained army collapsed and was thrown into disarray. Disgusted by the performance of the army and threatened by an angry populace, Mack surrendered himself to the French in January 1799. Taken to France as a prisoner, Mack eventually broke his parole and returned to Austria in 1800 to settle into retirement, preparing documents expounding his views on offensive warfare and the state of the army. He had served the army for thirty years and had risen from a lowly cavalry trooper to the command of a foreign army. It was a remarkable career and one that now appeared to be over: until intrigues in the Viennese court thrust him into the spotlight once more. Championed by the joint foreign ministers, Cobenzl and Colloredo, Mack became the weapon in their war to undermine the position of the Archduke Charles.

Mack was intelligent, energetic, dogged and brave, while also possessing great skills as a persuasive speaker. He was well respected by those who served with him in 1793–94, particularly the British, but he was also pedantic and became bogged down in creating complex and over ambitious strategies that were often beyond the skills of those serving under him to carry out. His enigmatic character has been described as fluctuating between 'extreme rashness and curious irresolution'.[2]

Having gained support for the advance of the army into Bavaria, Mack, unwilling to delegate, wasted no time in setting the wheels in motion. In-between the meetings at Hetzendorf he journeyed the 100 miles to Wels, the main camp of the assembling army. On 2 September he issued orders for the move to the Bavarian border to commence two days later. On 3 September the Austrian government broke off diplomatic relations with France and despatched Prince Schwarzenberg to Munich to inform the Bavarian elector, Maximilian-Joseph, of the Third Coalition's decision to open war against France, and to seek his adherence to their cause. Austria, of course, knew nothing of a treaty Bavaria signed with France in August and confidently expected that the Bavarian army would soon join her own forces.

Maximilian found himself in a difficult position. He felt well disposed towards France, for Bavaria gained new territory in 1803 in compensation for that lost in the Treaty of Luneville in 1800. In this his powerful chief minister, Maximilian Montgelas, supported him. However, the elector was married to another of the ubiquitous, vehemently anti-French daughters of the margrave of Baden. She demanded that her husband side with Austria. Maximilian, under mounting pressure from both sides, swayed one way and then another before finally agreeing to sign secretly with France. When Schwarzenberg arrived at the Bavarian court he found a very powerful ally in Caroline, the elector's wife. Together they began to work on her husband and gradually swung him back towards Austria.

But public opinion turned against Austria as her army advanced to the Inn and began to cross into Bavaria without awaiting the elector's approval. Austrian plans to break up the Bavarian army, allocating one regiment to serve with each Austrian division, caused widespread anger amongst the army officers too. With this groundswell of opinion, Maximilian finally decided to side with France. On the night of 8–9 September he and his court left Munich for Regensburg, from whence they travelled on to the city of Würzburg, which they reached on 12 September. So as not to alert the Austrians, orders for the mobilisation of the army were not issued until 7 September. Initially the army formed in two groups with orders to avoid contact with the Austrians, one centred between Munich and Regensburg, the other on Ulm. Schwarzenberg discovered the deception on the morning of 9 September and immediately left Munich to find Mack and acquaint him with these unexpected developments.

The leading Austrian units crossed the Inn river into Bavaria on 8 September in two columns: this first wave comprised thirty battalions of infantry and thirty-one squadrons of cavalry. One column passed the river at Schärding, marching westwards to the Isar river at Landshut. The hope that this column would intercept any Bavarian units in the area was not realised: most of those assembling between Munich and Regensberg withdrew northwards across the Danube. The second column crossed further south, at Braunau, heading for Parsdorf on the outskirts of Munich, some 70 miles away. Both columns were scheduled to reach their destinations by 13 September, but in fact the first units of the second column were at Munich two days ahead of schedule and entered the city on 12 September. The rest of the army followed according to a strict timetable drawn up by Mack until the whole army formed on the Lech river. At the same time FML Jellačič, operating in the Tirol but now released from Archduke John's army to join Archduke Ferdinand, established his main body near Feldkirch on the Rhine, above Lake Constance, and sent an advance guard beyond the northern shores of the lake.

When the news of Mack's rapid march into Bavaria reached Archduke Charles he was incensed, forcing him to express his dissatisfaction to the kaiser and pointing out that Mack was exceeding his authority. It was an unusual situation. The army operating in Bavaria, authorised to play a holding role while the army in Italy launched its offensive, was already marching on Munich. More surprisingly, Charles and Ferdinand – the men allocated to command these two armies – were both still in Vienna. Mack's precipitate actions did nothing to improve Charles's pessimistic views of his strategy, and fearing disaster in Bavaria, he began to entertain doubts as to the wisdom of launching his own attack in Italy. Undeterred, Mack pushed on towards the Lech, which he began to cross on 15 September.

Here for the first time he became aware of the movements of the left wing of the French army from Hanover and the general advance on the Rhine. Napoleon had taken every possible precaution to prevent word of the march of the French army from reaching the Austrians. He managed to obscure his movements for twenty days. Napoleon remained at Boulogne until 3 September, aware that his presence attracted attention. However, a financial crisis in Paris imposed a delay in his progress to the front. While in the capital he received his first report from Murat. Despatched from Bavaria on 10 September and received three days later, the report told that the Austrians had entered Bavaria and gave estimates of the strength of Austrian troops at Wels, Braunau and north of Lake Constance. It also told that the Russian army had crossed the border into Galicia.

Back on the Lech, Mack hustled his men over the river as fast as possible. Then, leaving orders for them to cover the 50 miles to the Iller river with all haste, he rode on ahead to study the state of its defences. The river flowed north, descending from the mountains of Tirol to Ulm where it joined the Danube and created a natural defensive line facing the exits from the Black Forest, the traditional invasion route between the Danube valley and France. However, Mayer, chief of staff to the still absent army commander, began to feel uneasy. He knew Ferdinand favoured holding a position on the Lech but, despite his strongly-voiced protests, Mack pressed on, reaching the Iller on 15 September where he began to lay out fieldworks to defend the river between Memmingen and Ulm. It took two days to get the whole force over the Lech, but Mack did not sit idly waiting for their arrival. He sent an advance guard, commanded by FML Klenau, beyond the Iller – the leading squadrons and *jäger* advancing to the far western end of Lake Constance – while he busied himself with a tour of inspection. He went as far as Lindau, at the eastern end of the lake.

The hurried advance from the Inn to the Iller brought about a rapid deterioration in the condition of the Austrian army. While the first units were arriving, exhausted and hungry, others had still not crossed the Inn into Bavaria. The army was widely dispersed over some 150 miles between the two rivers. The rushed assembling of the army meant that not all had full equipment, while most battalions were short of their full allocation of muskets. Further, the additional requirement for it to forage for many of its own supplies on the march, as required by Mack's recent changes, did little to encourage a spirit of optimism amongst the men. Straggling increased and numbers of men and horses died from exposure to the bad weather. What the army needed now was a period of rest and reorganisation on the Iller, but it was not to be.

On 19 September Archduke Ferdinand finally arrived in Bavaria to assume command of the army. The following day Archduke Charles arrived in Italy. Ferdinand immediately called a halt to the advance and ordered the advance guard back behind the Iller. He also recalled Mack to headquarters. Mack was having none of this, and wrote directly to the kaiser, who was now also in Bavaria. In his letter Mack sought imperial sanction for his moves. He described how:

'All except perhaps 10,000 to 12,000 men who remain to guard the coasts and southern frontier of France are moving on the Rhine, and soon two great French Armies will cross that river; one probably between Hüningen and Strasbourg, the other between Mannheim and Mainz: the former against your Majesty's army on the Iller, the later by Würzburg against the Russians coming from Bohemia.'[3]

Francis confirmed his approval of Mack's distribution, as he had already granted Mack authority to overrule Ferdinand. But a meeting was arranged for 22 September in Landsberg on the Lech river, about 35 miles to the west of Munich, to enable the three men to get together and discuss matters in greater detail.

While the Austrian army trudged wearily towards the Iller, the Bavarian army assembling on Ulm under Generalleutnant Wrede was still occupying that city. With the Austrians approaching, Wrede finally marched out northwards towards Würzburg on the afternoon of 18 September. The next day the first Austrian quartermaster arrived in the city to procure supplies for the army, followed by the first units on 20 September. The tireless Mack also entered Ulm that day and having studied the decaying defences authorised the enrolment of civilians to assist in the work necessary for their improvement. With that task underway he departed for Landsberg.

The meeting at Landsberg was frosty, both Ferdinand and Mayer speaking out against Mack's handling of the army and its advance to the Iller. Such were Mayer's protests that Mack, against Ferdinand's wishes, pressed the kaiser to dismiss him. The bewildered, Mayer suddenly found himself ousted from the staff and commanding a brigade of grenadiers. Undeterred by this strong opposition Mack took the opportunity to argue his strategy in the most persuasive manner.

Mack felt sure the French army intended to advance through the Black Forest. The Iller represents the first significant natural line of defence against such a move, secured in the north by Ulm and the fortresses of Memmingen and Kempten in the south. Ulm itself held a hypnotic fascination for Mack. Not only did it offer the practical advantage of providing a bridgehead across the Danube, but he saw it as a solid bulwark, one which had effectively held off the French in the campaign of 1800. The fact that its fortifications and those of the entrenched camps on the Michelsberg and Frauenberg, beyond the city walls, had fallen into a state of disrepair, did not appear to cause him undue concern. While the French attacked on the Iller, Jellačič offered a threat to their right flank and the army could receive local supplies from the magazine set up at Memmingen. Furthermore, a position on the Iller protected the passes into Tirol. In contrast, a position on the Lech would force the abandonment of these to the French, thus threatening the security of the army in Italy – or, according to Mack, would require 30,000 men to defend them. If French pressure forced the army back from the Iller, each of the subsequent rivers, descending from the mountainous Tirol and flowing all the way to the Danube, provided further natural barriers behind which he could stand and delay the French advance until Russian support arrived. Should the French confound his theories and advance north of the Danube, the army could swing to meet them on interior lines, secure behind this dominant river and anchored on Ulm. The position of the Prussian territorial enclave of Ansbach, positioned like a bastion north of the Danube, prevented any threat to his rear, for Prussia assured Kaiser Francis that they would resolutely defend their neutrality.

Satisfied with Mack's confident analysis of the situation, Francis approved all his dispositions, leaving Ferdinand seething with frustration. Orders issued from Landsberg required the full assembly of the army in five corps by 3 October. Schwarzenberg's command was to reunite west of the Iller, maintaining contact with Jellačič's men operating near Lake Constance. Behind these formations, Werneck's corps occupied the Allgäu region east of Memmingen between the Iller and the Lech, with Riesch's corps also between those rivers but occupying the ground northwards to the Danube. The final formation, Kienmayer's corps, was furthest to the rear and designated as a flank guard.

Centred on Neuburg and Ingolstadt on the Danube, Kienmayer was to keep an eye on the Bavarians and watch for the arrival of the Russians. With everything agreed, Francis ended the meeting by appointing Mack to replace the dismissed Mayer, and further infuriated the already angry young army commander by suggesting he should take heed of the advice of his more experienced new chief of staff. However, Francis preferred not to indicate Mack's ultimate sanction – trusting that Ferdinand would acquiesce to his new chief of staff's greater military experience. Convinced that everything was under control, Francis left Landsberg on 26 September and returned to Vienna, intending to return when the Russians arrived and joint operations commenced. He left behind in his wake a confused command structure, riven by rivalry and distrust.

Archduke Charles arrived in Italy to take command of the forces gathering there on 20 September. He found an army in disarray, lacking money, supplies, horses and equipment, some even without uniforms or muskets. Charles' initial gloomy view of the prospects of success sank lower. He began to try and instil some order in the chaos, and erroneously believing himself to be outnumbered by the French, Charles opened negotiations with Masséna, agreeing an armistice pending news from Bavaria. Masséna was happy to agree. On 27 September Charles received a request to transfer more of his men to the Danube theatre of operations. The request from Francis, written as a result of the Landsberg meeting, admitted that 'there can be no doubt any longer that Napoleon intends to strike a major blow before the Russians arrive.' Having already doubted the wisdom of Mack's advance deep into Bavaria, Charles now reluctantly sent the men, but wrote to Francis that he could no longer consider taking the offensive. Charles believed he faced 100,000 French troops in Italy, whereas Masséna's effective force was barely half that. Reduced now to about 70,000 men, Charles determined to preserve his own army, fearing the imminent destruction of that on the Danube.

In France there was but one leader, both civil and military: Napoleon Bonaparte. The problems of rivalry, jealousy and distrust that beset the Austrian high command were irrelevant to him. While some petty jealously existed amongst the members of his newly established *Marshalate*, all owed total allegiance to the emperor.

Having taken the final decision to turn away from Britain, Napoleon's army responded enthusiastically. They were not sailors and the thought of crossing the Channel in cramped unseaworthy vessels must have caused great consternation. But a campaign in Europe, marching on the Danube, was one they understood well.

Three main routes provided the line of march to move the four corps from the Channel coast to the Rhine. Ney's VI Corps marched from Etaples, via Arras, Laon, Reims, Vitray and Nancy to Hagenau. Lannes' V Corps preceded Soult's IV Corps from the Boulogne area via St Omar, Cambrai, Sedan and Metz, where the two corps diverged: Lannes heading for Strasbourg and Soult establishing himself at Speyer. Davout led the northernmost of the Channel corps from Ambleteuse via Lille, Namur, Luxembourg, and Sarrelouis to Mannheim. The leading divisions of each corps began marching on 28 or 29 August, with 48-hour intervals between each of the following divisions. The total marching distance of each corps varied between 350 and 380 miles, with Lannes' corps due to arrive in Strasbourg by 23 September and the others in position two days later. With no danger from enemy attack, Napoleon could break up his corps into their component parts, and by moving them on three separate lines significantly increased their rate of progress. Also, he could call on the resources of France to provide food and shelter for the men as they progressed. To this end, staff officers rode ahead to make arrangements with the towns that would be required to provide succour for the army. But even for Napoleon things did not always go entirely to plan.

Due to the need for Napoleon to delay announcing the redirection of the army to the Rhine, it allowed only limited time to collect together the stockpiles of food and fuel required by the men. Requisitions for supplies often only arrived in towns shortly before the soldiers who needed them and little money was available to pay for them. Securing billets for the men also caused great difficulties. These were supposed to be found close to the road, but often the over-stretched civil authorities forced weary men to march an additional 4 or 5 miles at the beginning and end of the day to secure a roof over their heads. In Lille, the town refused to find quarters for Davout's leading division, a situation he immediately rectified by billeting his men on the inhabitants as though he were in an enemy's country. His following divisions received a warmer welcome in the town. At Vitray, a division of Ney's corps agreed to sleep in the empty barracks there if the town provided straw for the men to sleep on. This they did not do and when the officers complained to the mayor he refused to issue good conduct certificates which were required.[4]

Due to the financial crisis in France it would appear that many French soldiers marched to war lacking certain items of kit: greatcoats in particular were in short supply, as were boots.[5] After the rigours of the march many units arrived barefoot on the Rhine. Horses suffered badly too, as there was little forage available for them, and both Davout and Soult had to cut back on guns or supporting wagons as losses mounted.

The lack of suitable transport forced the requisitioning of farm carts and wagons to convey essential supplies of infantry ammunition, but in these uncovered vehicles it is estimated that between 200,000 and 300,000 rounds were ruined by the weather and had to be abandoned before crossing the Rhine. Needless to say the owners of the carts, pressed into service, did not relish the thought of going to war and took any opportunity to desert, taking their horses with them. Soult reported that of the 1,200 transport horses he needed for his corps, he only secured 700, but he reported four days after crossing the Rhine that 300 of these had already deserted. Nevertheless, despite these handicaps, the four corps from the Channel coast arrived on the Rhine on schedule with 100,000 men. There, another 20,000 men of the Reserve Cavalry and 6,000 Garde Impériale, making their way from Paris, joined them.

Instructions for Marmont's Corps in Holland did not leave Boulogne until 28 August and required him to march on 2 September from Zeist, near Utrecht, towards Mainz on the Rhine. Unable to secure enough transport horses, Marmont wasted no time and arranged instead to move his ammunition and heavy supplies up the Rhine by boat. Thus unencumbered, his corps marched some 230 miles by three roads to their destination via Nijmegen and Cologne. The whole of his corps arrived at Mainz over the 22–23 September. Then, after three days rest, they marched another 80 miles via Frankfurt to Würzburg, where the whole corps assembled on 1 October, having lost only nine men on the march.

Bernadotte, occupying Hanover with I Corps, received his orders on 1 September requiring him to march the following day. To maintain the desired level of secrecy, he was instructed to report that his command was returning to France and that Marmont was marching to relieve him. Proceeding first to the fortified city of Hameln, he stockpiled supplies for three months, placed all the artillery he captured during his occupation and left behind as garrison those of his men lacking fitness for the campaign ahead. Then he marched for Göttingen, where he assembled his corps prior to an advance towards Frankfurt. To speed his progress, Bernadotte opened negotiations with the elector of Hesse-Cassel, whose territory lay across the most direct route. With permission secured, Bernadotte moved off but then received new orders redirecting him towards Würzburg and informing him he could not draw supplies from Frankfurt as they were reserved for Marmont. He arrived with his tired, hungry and exhausted men in Würzburg on 27 September, only to find that supplies supposed to be waiting for him had not yet arrived.

The arrival of Marmont and Bernadotte at Würzburg by the end of September added another 35,000 to the growing French force deployed along the Rhine and Main rivers. This increased further when Bernadotte received instructions to take command of the 23,000 men of the Bavarian army too. In a month Napoleon had gathered a force of about 184,000 men, extended in a great arc stretching for almost 200 miles from Strasbourg to the Bavarians' position at Bamberg, all ready to descend on the Danube. Behind them a further 14,000 of Augereau's VII Corps made steady progress across the breadth of France. Unaware of the strength of the storm gathering against him, Mack attentively watched the exits of the Black Forest for the emergence of the leading elements of the French army. He estimated they could muster no more than 70,000 men and remained confident that his army of 72,000 could hold them until the Russians arrived. But on 26 September, the day that Kaiser Francis left Landsberg to return to Vienna, Napoleon arrived at Strasbourg and his vast army began to cross the Rhine.

Chapter 6

Refuge in Ulm

'Ulm – the Queen of the Danube
and the Iller, the fortress of Tirol,
the key to one half of Germany.'*

As La Grande Armée marched towards the Rivers Rhine and Main, Napoleon
began to plan the second stage of the campaign. This plan, finalised on 10
September, required the army to cross the Rhine on 1 October, then swing
down to the Danube, arriving along a 40-mile stretch of the river between Ulm
and Donauwörth by 9 October. Three days later, on 13 September, Napoleon
learned from the first of Murat's reports that the Austrians had crossed the
Inn. Then, on 18 September, he received a further report from Murat
informing him that the Austrians had crossed the Lech and were pushing
forward towards the Iller. This was a development Napoleon had not expected,
but it presented him with a great opportunity. If he moved quickly and
interposed his army between those of Austria and Russia, he had a chance to
defeat his opponents separately before they could unite.

On 20 September he realigned his line of march further to the east, allowing
more space in which to get behind the Austrians. With Donauwörth now
selected as the central point of the advance, he directed the army against a 65-
mile stretch of the Danube between Günzburg, about 9 miles east of Ulm, and
Ingolstadt. The French army commenced crossing the Rhine on 26 September.
The Austrians' rapid advance to the Iller made it clear to Napoleon that his
opponents expected him to attack through the Black Forest. To maintain this
impression for as long as possible, a feint was prepared through that difficult
terrain. The longer he could hold the Austrians in this advanced position, the
greater his chance of getting behind them.

One other important decision was made at this time too. On 17 September
Napoleon received a communication from his aide in Berlin, Général de division

---

* FML Karl Mack, Freiherr von Leiberach.

Duroc, who had been engaged in persuading Prussia to commit to an alliance with France. Duroc, fearing the failure of his mission, strongly recommended to the emperor that he should avoid sending Bernadotte's command through the Prussian territory of Ansbach. Instead he advised that Bernadotte march via Würzburg and Bamburg, avoiding Ansbach completely. Duroc sensed that any violation of Prussian territory could bring the vacillating King Frederick William firmly down on the side of the coalition, crucially adding at least 150,000 men of the Prussian army to those of Austria and Russia. But Napoleon remained firm in his conviction. He recognised the danger posed by a belligerent Prussia, but also accurately concluded that any physical opposition would be slow to materialise. In the meantime, speed was of the utmost importance if he was to gain the advantage over the isolated Austrians in Bavaria. Accordingly, Bernadotte received orders to proceed through Ansbach. Other aides were despatched to Baden and Württemberg to win over support for the emperor's cause, and gain approval for the advance of the army through these lands.

On 25 September Murat, now back on the Rhine after his exhausting spying mission, crossed the river at Kehl, near Strasbourg, with three dragoon divisions and a division of heavy cavalry, accompanied by Maréchal Lannes at the head of Oudinot's Reserve Grenadier Division. These men were detailed to push through the Black Forest and occupy the attention of the Austrians.

Napoleon arrived in Strasbourg on 26 September. On arrival in the city, he was rapturously greeted by his army as they prepared to march. Cries of 'Vive l'Empereur' filled the air as the soldiers marched past, their hats decorated with sprigs of greenery; veteran and new recruit alike filled with enthusiasm for the task ahead. On the 27 and 28 September Napoleon despatched a number of letters in which he expressed his great wish that the Austrians would remain facing the Black Forest for another three or four days. He confided his view that: 'If they will only allow me to gain a few marches on them, I hope to turn them and find myself with my entire army between the Lech and Isar.'

Murat's cavalry, pushing through the Black Forest, soon encountered Austrian patrols, but the difficult terrain favoured the opposing light troops. Napoleon wanted prisoners from whom he could gain information to help unravel Austrian plans, but in this task his cavalry failed. The Austrians fell back as French columns threatened to overwhelm them, but although clouds of mounted men showed at the exits from the forest, they appeared reluctant to press on. In fact, having made a show of passing through the forest, only one dragoon division remained in front of the position. The rest of Murat's cavalry and Oudinot's grenadiers slipped away, back to the Rhine, to join the main advance.

Napoleon's army pushed on from the Rhine as quickly as possible. By 1 October their right was at Stuttgart and the left at Neckarelz. Marmont and Bernadotte remained for the present at Würzburg and the Bavarians at

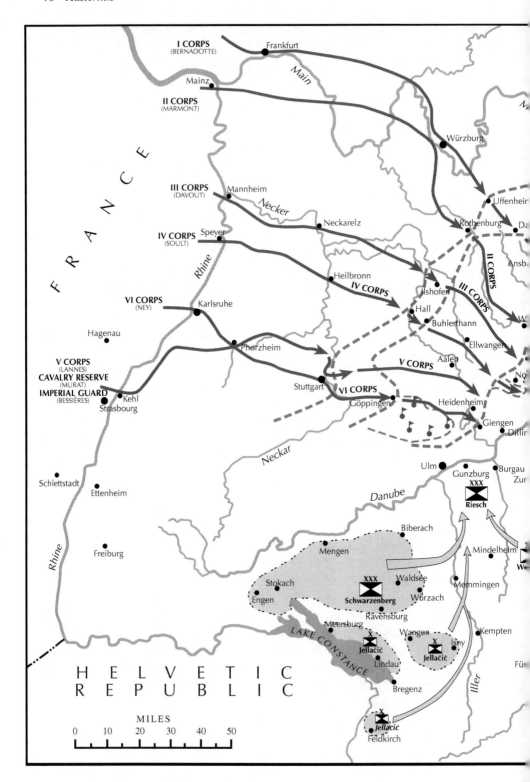

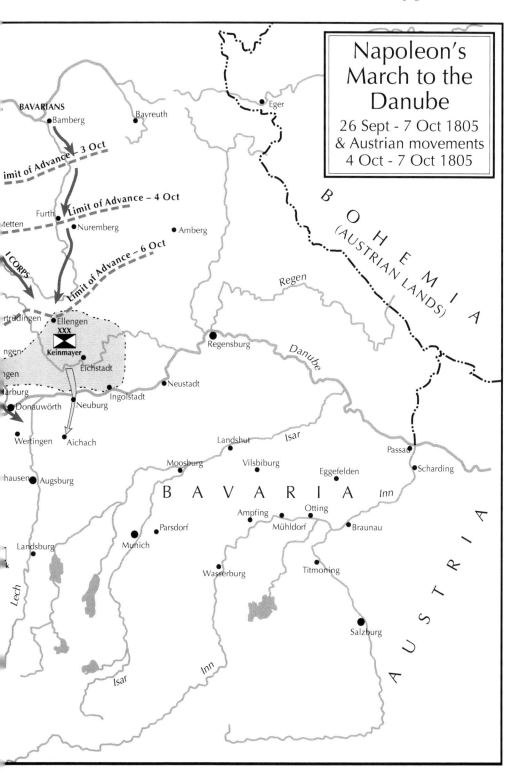

Napoleon's
March to the
Danube
26 Sept - 7 Oct 1805
& Austrian movements
4 Oct - 7 Oct 1805

Bamberg. That same day, before he left Strasbourg with the Garde Impériale, Napoleon had one last meeting. Savary had returned from his spying mission to Bavaria and had grown in admiration for the special talents of his companion, the former smuggler Charles Schulmeister: talents that he felt could be exploited to the benefit of the French army. Schulmeister claimed to have friends in important positions in the Austrian army – in the field and in Vienna – and offered to infiltrate their headquarters as an agent of France. With Savary's recommendation Napoleon agreed: Schulmeister was added to Savary's pay roll and the following day the two men, spy master and master spy, set out for Stuttgart to finalise their plans.

With his army on the move, Napoleon left Strasbourg to conclude the diplomatic missions his aides had begun in Baden and Württemberg. By the time he departed he had secured about 7,000 Württemberg and 3,000 Baden troops for service on his lines of communication. Quite how the three fiery Francophobe daughters of the margrave of Baden – the tsarina of Russia, the queen of Sweden and the electress of Bavaria – reacted to their father's decision is not recorded.

In the absence of any clear information on Austrian movements, Napoleon relinquished command of the left wing of the army – I and II Corps as well as the Bavarians – to Bernadotte, while he retained control of the rest of his forces. On 3 October the front of the army contracted to around 125 miles, its progress closest to the line of the Danube shielded by wide-ranging cavalry screens: but prisoners still eluded them. However, Napoleon still had a network of spies operating in Bavaria and a report of 2 October told of the construction of entrenchments around Ulm, along the Iller and in front of the passes exiting from Tirol. Then, a report on 4 October suggested that the Austrians were withdrawing from their positions west of the Iller and pulling back towards Ulm.

The report was correct. Mack also had spies and scouts out in all directions and finally information from Kienmayer's patrols, probing north-west from Donauwörth, reported the approach of large bodies of the enemy. There could now be no doubt that the French move from the Black Forest was a feint and Kienmayer had located the main body approaching from Stuttgart and beyond. Yet Kienmayer was still unaware that French troops under Bernadotte had, on 3 October, entered Ansbach, the Prussian territory that Francis had assured Mack was inviolable. Seemingly unperturbed by the news of the French approach, Mack issued orders for the army to swing into new positions behind the Danube facing north. Schwarzenberg's corps was to occupy an area just south of Ulm, Riesch's men headed for positions in and around the city, while Werneck's command received orders to line the Danube between Leipheim and Günzburg. All units were required to take up these new positions by 8 October. To strengthen the position, Austrian troops removed planking from the bridge at Elchingen on 3 October, then two days later destroyed the bridge at

Thalfingen. This meant the first intact bridges east of Ulm stood at Leipheim and Günzburg, at least 23 miles away.

As it now appeared likely that the Austrian army was redeploying on the Danube, and he knew of Austrian activity north of the river (Kienmayer's troops), Napoleon demanded that Murat bring in some of these men: 'What I want is information – send out agents, spies, and above all make some prisoners.'[1] But again the Austrians avoided capture.

By 5 October the entire Grande Armée occupied a front narrowed to 65 miles, the only obstruction between them and the Danube formed by the 16,000 men of Kienmayer's corps strung out over 35 miles between Nördlingen and Eichstadt. In fact it was on the extreme far right of this thin Austrian line, where little likelihood of danger was expected, that a weak detachment of three battalions of infantry and a regiment of hussars under Generalmajor Nostitz discovered Bernadotte's army of 37,000 men rapidly approaching from Prussian territory. Clearly Kienmayer could not contain this overwhelming force massing against him and on 6 October he withdrew rapidly across the Danube at Neuburg, sending detachments to protect the bridges at Donauwörth, Rain and Ingolstadt. Later that day, Vandamme's division of IV Corps arrived at Harburg, only 5 miles from Donauwörth. Alerted to their proximity, the Austrians in the town began breaking up the bridge, but around 8.00pm – before the task was even half completed – French troops arrived in overwhelming numbers and drove the defenders away. By the following morning the bridge over the Danube at Donauwörth was secure and repaired. While Vandamme consolidated this important gain, the entire French army hovered within a day's march of the Danube.

The march had been a tremendous achievement for the French army, yet it had not been without problems. The opening of the month of October brought a great change in the weather. The warm sunny days of September gave way to rain, cold winds and even a little snow, and Napoleon's determination that the army should proceed with all speed allowed little time for foraging. One man who experienced the hardships of the march left this revealing description:

'The extremity of fatigue, the want of food, the terrible weather, the trouble of the marauders – nothing was wanting ... The brigades, even the regiments were sometimes dispersed, the order to reunite arrived late, because it had to filter through so many offices. Hence the troops were marching day and night, and I saw for the first time men sleeping as they marched. I could not have believed it possible. Thus we reached our destination without having eaten anything and finding nothing to eat. It was all very well for Berthier to write: 'In the war of invasion as the emperor makes it, there are no magazines; it is the Generals to provide themselves from the country as they traverse it'; but the Generals had neither the time nor means to procure regularly what was required for the needs of such a numerous army. This order was an authorisation of pillage, and the districts we passed through suffered cruelly. We were often hungry, and the terrible weather intensified our sufferings. A steady cold rain or rather half-melted snow fell incessantly, and we stumbled along in the cold mud churned by our passage almost up to our knees – the wind made it impossible to light fires.'[2]

The appalling conditions made life difficult for the Austrian forces too. Mack's widely deployed army trudged slowly through the dreadful weather to their newly allocated positions. The poor road conditions also delayed messengers, and it was only on the morning of 7 October that Mack, in Ulm, heard of the loss of the Donauwörth bridge. In response he ordered Riesch, whose command was forming around Ulm, to proceed towards Günzburg, and for Jellačič to leave a brigade between Lake Constance and the Iller, a detachment in Memmingen, and then march with the rest of his men to Ulm. At 4.00pm Mack arrived at Günzburg, about 30 miles upstream from Donauwörth, to check the position and prepare to threaten any French formations crossing the Danube. Here he heard for the first time that French troops had passed through Ansbach, contrary to everything he had been assured by the kaiser. Surprised by this revelation Mack later wrote: 'The situation of the army was certainly gravely compromised by the sudden appearance of an enemy more than twice its superior in numbers, but I did not consider it desperate.'

Mack's immediate thought was to gather the army together, push through the French units already established south of the Danube, and join forces with Kienmayer for a retirement on the Inn. However, his army was already following redeployment orders and in the atrocious weather it would prove an enormous task to locate all the dispersed units and issue new instructions. Instead, he decided on a concentration on Günzburg and Burgau while awaiting Russian support. He held ample supplies west of the Lech and by maintaining communications with Kienmayer, now at Aichach on the road to Munich, he could offer a double threat to French movements. Additionally, the bridges near Günzburg offered him the opportunity to cross to the north bank of the Danube and present a threat to French communications. Finally, the French violation of Ansbach held the possibility of immediate Prussian armed intervention.

Under the circumstances Mack was not unduly worried. Expressing his confidence on the morning of 8 October, he despatched a letter to Kutuzov, whose arrival on the Inn he anticipated within the next two weeks: 'We have enough to live upon in the district west of the Lech – more than enough in fact to last us until the Russian army reaches the Inn, and will be ready to move. Then we shall easily find the opportunity to prepare for the enemy the fate he deserves.'[3]

Mack now prepared new orders for the army, while the formations closed on their original objectives. One of these, FML Auffenberg's division, nearing the end of a long march from Tirol, was heading towards the Lech, where he expected to form a junction with Kienmayer's corps. After an eleven hour overnight march, Auffenberg arrived with his exhausted and hungry division in the town of Wertingen at 7.00am on 8 October. Awaiting him were instructions from Mack cancelling his march on the Lech. These ordered him to fall back 12 miles to Zumarshausen, situated on the road to Augsburg, where he was to form the advance guard of the force Mack intended to collect near Günzburg to oppose the French. The order must have dismayed Auffenberg. He had under his command some 5,000 infantry and 400 cavalry, but his men were exhausted and he felt they must rest before retracing their steps. At about midday reports arrived in Wertingen of French troops approaching on the road from Donauwörth. To investigate, Auffenberg despatched a force of two cavalry squadrons and four companies of infantry towards Pfaffenhofen. Before they could reach this village they encountered the leading elements of Murat's cavalry and Lannes' V Corps. It was no contest and the Austrians streamed back towards Wertingen to raise the alarm.

On the previous day, 7 October, the French began crossing the Danube in numbers. While repairs to the bridge at Donauwörth were underway, Murat rode a few miles upstream and discovered the bridge at Münster standing undefended. He crossed and returned towards Donauwörth on the southern bank, driving away any of Kienmayer's detachments still lurking in the area. Soult's IV Corps was now crossing at Donauwörth and Lannes' V Corps marched to Münster.

Napoleon arrived at Donauwörth the same day and convinced himself that the only logical move for Mack was to march from Ulm, through Augsburg to Munich. He dismissed the idea of an Austrian move north of the Danube. Accordingly, he issued orders for IV Corps to advance from Donauwörth and march on Augsburg. Davout, still approaching the Danube, was to cross at Neuburg and continue southwards to Aichach. Marmont, following over the river at Neuburg, marched downstream to Ingolstadt to prepare the bridge there for Bernadotte's I Corps and the Bavarians. Ney, with VI Corps, initially received orders to remain on the north bank of the Danube, but to send one division over to the opposite bank to form a link with Lannes. Napoleon, convinced no garrison of any strength remained in Ulm, informed Ney: 'I cannot imagine that the enemy could have another plan, other than to withdraw itself on Augsburg or Landsberg or even Füssen. It is possible, nevertheless, that he hesitates and in this case it is up to us to ensure that none escapes.'[4] The remaining formations of the army – Murat's Cavalry Reserve and Lannes' V Corps – were to move southwards to cut the Ulm–Augsburg road at Zumarshausen. Directly in their path lay the startled Auffenberg and his isolated division.

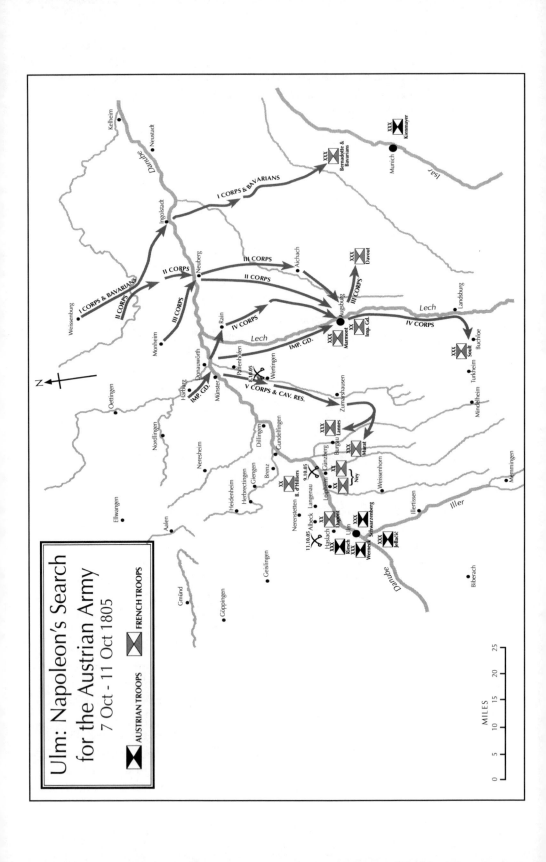

Ulm: Napoleon's Search for the Austrian Army
7 Oct - 11 Oct 1805

AUSTRIAN TROOPS   FRENCH TROOPS

MILES
0   5   10   15   20   25

Although surprised, the Austrian general reacted quickly, placing four grenadier battalions on the high ground to the left of the Günzburg road with $2^1/_2$ squadrons of *cuirassiers* protecting his flank. The rest of the infantry occupied positions in Wertingen or formed detachments in the surrounding hamlets. The most forward of these detachments, close to 200 infantry at Hohenreichen, threw back the first two attacks by dismounted dragoons, but the third attack, involving eight dismounted squadrons from Général de division Beaumont's 3ème Dragon Division – perhaps 900 men – succeeded in capturing the ramshackle collection of buildings. Remounting, the dragoons reformed and, joined by the 1er Dragon Division and supported by artillery fire, they cleared the other outlying Austrian detachments and isolated the defenders of Wertingen from their grenadier battalions drawn up in square on the hill.

When Murat arrived with the rest of the cavalry, the dragoons were unsuccessfully attacking these battalions. Then over to the right of the French position, Lannes arrived at the head of Oudinot's Reserve Grenadiers, having marched to the sound of the guns. Murat and Lannes quickly resolved to break the Austrian defence before nightfall and devised a plan to outflank Auffenberg's hill top position. The Austrian general, realising the danger, ordered his four battalions to begin withdrawing in square, while his remaining cavalry prepared to deter any would-be attackers. But vastly outnumbered, the Austrian horsemen could not hope to stem the tide for long, and eventually they were driven off. With Oudinot's grenadiers rapidly closing on the slow-moving formations and clouds of cavalry hovering all around, the Austrian squares finally broke. Only 1,400 infantry, one cavalry squadron and two artillery pieces made it safely to Zumarshausen and Burgau: although another 1,000 stragglers eventually rejoined their units. The Austrians gave their losses as 101 men killed, 233 wounded, and 1,469 captured. In addition, the French seized three Austrian standards and six artillery pieces. Amongst this haul was the valuable prize of Auffenberg himself. The French gave their losses in killed and wounded as 319 men.

Napoleon was delighted with this overwhelming victory and particularly with the haul of prisoners, the first taken in the campaign. From these he learned that the Austrians were between Memmingen and Ulm with between 60,000 and 70,000 men, and that Mack was at Günzburg where Archduke Ferdinand was about to join him.

Mack and Ferdinand heard of this disastrous encounter at 1.00am on 9 October in Günzburg, the day of the intended concentration of the army. It was obvious that the French were over the Danube in far greater numbers than previously imagined. In response, Mack cancelled the move and recalled those formations already on the road. An intense debate followed as a number of senior officers began to strongly suggest the army should retire on the Tirol. But Mack, having no intention of exposing the Russians to the full might of the

French army, announced a new plan. The army would cross to the north bank of the Danube, clear away any French units remaining there and march east down the river via Donauwörth, Neuburg and Regensburg to link up with Kienmayer and Kutuzov. Mack spent many hours drawing up a detailed plan of operations for the crossing, which included the abandonment of Ulm, and, maintaining some pretence of a chain of command, he submitted it to Archduke Ferdinand at around 4.00pm on 9 October. At the same time the sound of artillery fire north of Günzburg caused renewed alarm.

Following the receipt of Napoleon's orders, Ney led the three divisions of VI Corps towards Ulm on the morning of 9 October, leaving the temporarily attached divisions of Gazan (V Corps) and Baraguay d'Hilliers (Foot Dragoons – Cavalry Reserve) on the Brenz river at Gundelfingen and Herbrechtingen respectively. It was a miserable day as icy winds blew sleet and snow across the whole area. Dupont's division approached Albeck, Loison's men moved towards Langenau and Malher marched his division in the direction of Günzburg, where he hoped to cross the Danube and establish contact with Murat and Lannes. Although the Austrian troops defending the river were instructed to send a detachment across to the north bank to watch for any French movements, this detachment, commanded by Baron d'Aspre, kept too close to the river and were surprised by the sudden appearance of Malher's men.

The bridge over the Danube at Günzburg crossed a short stretch of river, where it divided into a number of separate arms and islands. Approximately 2 miles to the west another bridge crossed at the village of Leipheim, and three-quarters of a mile to the east a third passed over the river between Günzburg and Reisenburg. Malher decided to split his division to launch simultaneous attacks on all three bridges. Entrusting the attack near Reisenburg to two battalions of the 59ème Ligne, supported by the eight guns of his divisional artillery, he then stripped the elite companies from all his battalions, reforming them into an ad hoc battalion for an attack on the bridge at Leipheim. Finally, he collected together his other six battalions (three battalions 25ème Légère, one battalion 27ème Ligne and two battalions 50ème Ligne), in the centre and prepared to attack Günzburg, holding a battalion of 27ème Ligne in reserve.

To gain time for the main body to organise a defence of the river, Baron d'Aspre advanced with about 200 *jäger* to delay the French moving against Günzburg. Almost immediately he discovered a second column approaching Reisenburg. Up until now the bridges remained intact because Mack planned to use them to allow his army to cross the river, but now work commenced in earnest to deny them to the French. Archduke Ferdinand, now in the town, ordered forward three battalions of IR3 Erzherzog Karl and twenty artillery pieces to line the riverbank and defend the Günzburg crossing. Four battalions of IR20 Kaunitz, supported by four squadrons of cavalry, covered the bridge at Reisenburg and three battalions of IR38 Württemberg prepared to deflect any attack on Leipheim. Here the French attack came to nothing. Struggling through the waterlogged marshy ground the attack bogged down and the combined battalion fell back in some disorder. In the centre, however, Malher's men made progress. The *jäger* gained a little time for the Austrian engineers to disrupt the bridges, but when the French charged forward it meant there was no escape for d'Aspre and his intrepid little band, only a few evading capture. Malher's men pressed on to the main island in the Danube but could not proceed across the broken bridge in the face of a fierce fusillade of musketry and artillery fire. A number of volunteers came forward to attempt repairs to the bridge in the face of this storm of fire, but with casualties rapidly mounting, Malher pulled his men back to the tree-lined north bank of the river. The attack on the bridge near Reisenburg also met little success. Now that these attacks appeared to have run their course, the Austrian commander, FML Riesch, prepared to switch over to the offensive as the late afternoon light began to fade. In the gathering gloom he quickly repaired the Reisenburg bridge and formed a column of seven battalions, headed by IR20 Kaunitz, to drive the French back. The French did not attempt to interrupt this work, but as the column crossed they launched a fierce counter-attack against the leading battalion of IR20. In the confusion the Austrians broke and poured back, causing disruption in the battalions to the rear, as the two French battalions of 59ème Ligne rushed forward and captured the bridge. Austrian cavalry charged the French, who quickly formed square, but were unable to dislodge them. Malher rushed reinforcements towards this bridgehead from the force opposite Günzburg and consolidated his foothold on the south bank. French troops pursued the Austrians back to Günzburg but were unable to capture the town and drew back. It was clear to both Mack and Ferdinand that it was now impossible to cross the Danube at Günzburg, or to remain where they were. Ferdinand proposed they should either march rapidly back to Elchingen and cross there to evade the French, or give up the Danube and fall back on Tirol. Mack refused either option and ordered a retreat to Ulm, much to Ferdinand's increasing anger and frustration. The retreat commenced at about 8.00pm. After many days of marching and counter-marching, of appalling weather and lack of food, discipline finally broke down and the army fell back on Ulm in disorder and panic.[5] One citizen of Ulm witnessed the arrival of the dishevelled army in the city:

> 'As 11.00pm struck the Austrians in the greatest disorder began to arrive in Ulm. Infantry and cavalry mixed up together in small groups and individual soldiers. The confusion was general. The weather was terrible. From 9 October it began to rain and rained continuously up to 14 October. In addition an icy wind blew, causing the rain occasionally to turn to snow. The troops suffered terribly. Their shoes and coats tattered, their weapons covered with thick rust.'[6]

Malher's division advanced and occupied Günzburg on the morning of 10 October, the Austrian rearguard having pulled out, leaving some 300 wounded men behind, which the French added to the 1,000 prisoners they had captured in the battle. Maréchal Ney also arrived in Günzburg that day, where he received news that Loison's division had captured the bridge at Elchingen during the night. Here an audacious attack by 3ème Hussards and 6ème Légère, appearing out of the dark at about 11.00pm on a freezing cold night, smashed into the horrified Austrian outposts on the north bank. Alerted to the attack, the main body of the Austrian battalion defending the bridge opened a heavy fire of musketry and canister from the cover of woods close to the river. A local report breathlessly described the encounter: 'What a sight! Like a nightmare! They now moved forwards up to the bridge, a terrible fire of muskets mixed with the blast of roaring cannon illuminated the hell-black night with a constant bright light.'[7] In response, the 6ème Légère brought up two 8pdrs and overpowered the defenders on the north bank, capturing their single artillery piece and taking fifty-seven prisoners, as the rest poured precariously over the partly disrupted bridge. Attempts to set fire to the southern end failed as the French light infantry followed after them, undeterred by the Austrian fusillade. The Austrian defenders, shaken by the whole experience, fell back towards Leibi and Nersingen, where they joined the retreat to Ulm.

From Günzburg Ney wrote to Napoleon to advise him of his discovery: 'The enemy is at Ulm in much more strength than we thought, he received a reinforcement of 15,000 men near Günzburg, coming from Schaffhausen; it seems that the left wing of the hostile battle line (facing the east) will form at Ulm.' Despite Ney's first-hand experience, Napoleon chose to discount this information, and remained convinced that the main Austrian strength was concentrated well to the south of Ulm. The following day, 11 October, a number of pivotal factors fell into place that brought the campaign to a spectacular close nine days later.

Chapter 7
Jealousy and Misunderstanding

'There existed a degree of jealousy and
misunderstanding among the General Officers
in that army which led to fatal consequences.'*

The early hours of 10 October heralded no improvement in the atrocious weather of the previous few days. A large part of the Austrian army falling back from Günzburg passed through Ulm over to the north bank of the Danube and occupied entrenched positions on the Michelsberg. The men were disillusioned, exhausted, cold and hungry. But the French army fared little better.

Since La Grande Armée crossed the Rhine it needed to find its own supplies, a task which proved extremely difficult to fulfil. On 9 October one general wrote that his division 'had neither bread nor meat, and only most scanty supplies of forage ... The villages I have had to occupy have been completely cleared out by preceding columns.' On the same day, GD Suchet, commanding an infantry division attached to V Corps thankfully reported that he still had bread to issue to his men, but the rest of the corps was without. Elsewhere, GD Vandamme, commanding a division of IV Corps, also wrote of the exhaustion of his men and their need for food. Such was the general state of exhaustion in IV Corps that it remained at Augsburg for two days to draw rations and recover.

In the face of these desperate shortages the army showed little compassion for the Bavarian population. Davout, commanding III Corps, considered the situation so out of hand by 11 October that he wrote to Berthier, seeking permission to shoot some men guilty of plundering the locals as an example. In his letter he expressed the need 'to put a stop to marauding and pillaging, which have reached the limits of excess'. He went on to state that the Bavarian villagers were faring worse at the hands of their French allies than they did

---

* Sir Arthur Paget, British special envoy in Vienna, reporting on the Austrian army in Ulm, 1 November 1805.

when France invaded Bavaria as enemies in 1800. He concluded that 'terrible examples are necessary to stop this evil'.[1] Unfortunately, there appears to be no record of a reply.

Napoleon spent the night of 9–10 October at Zumarshausen. In the morning he determined to ride to Munich, where Bernadotte, with I Corps and the Bavarians – the left wing of the army – were marching from Ingolstadt, hoping to discover the latest news of Kienmayer's corps and the movements of the Russians. The centre – II, III and IV Corps and two cavalry divisions – was to continue its concentration on the Lech near Augsburg. The emperor placed the right wing of the army – V and VI Corps plus Murat's cavalry – under the overall command of Murat, while he prepared to head eastwards to the Bavarian capital.

However, this decision clouded the overall picture. Although Murat now commanded this wing, including Ney's corps, with orders to probe southwards towards Mindelheim where Napoleon expected him to find the main Austrian army, separate instructions issued to Ney required VI Corps to take Ulm. Following his own orders, on the morning of 10 October, Murat ordered Ney to bring the whole of VI Corps to the south bank of the Danube so it could operate with him. Coming under Napoleon's influence, he believed that other than a small rearguard in Ulm, the Austrian army was south of the city, preparing either to fight or retreat to Tirol, in order to unite with Archduke John's army. When he received this order Ney objected strongly. Intelligence Ney received from Baron d'Aspre and other prisoners captured the previous day suggested the Austrians intended attacking north of the river. If he moved his whole corps to the south bank, the only French troops remaining to protect their communications and baggage would be a single division of dragoons. The animosity that already existed between the two corps commanders boiled over as the argument dragged on, neither willing to give ground, and as the day drew to a close little had been resolved. Dupont's division doggedly remained north of the river, supported some way to the rear by the dismounted dragoon division of Baraguey d'Hilliers, while both Malher's and Loison's divisions occupied positions on the south bank, close to the river, following their battles the previous day. Loison's men spent the day making themselves unpopular with the inhabitants of Elchingen by slaughtering all their cattle and seizing their horses.[2]

During the day Ney passed on the intelligence he had gathered from his prisoners to Napoleon, who received it in Augsburg. Gradually, Napoleon began to recognise the possibility of a force stronger than a rearguard in Ulm. By evening he began to doubt whether the Austrians were making for Tirol at all and issued new orders. Writing to Murat, he directed the Cavalry Reserve and V Corps to cancel the march on Mindelheim and move towards Ulm via Burgau. Should the Austrians manage to evade Murat's wing, Napoleon felt sure that Marmont at Augsburg and Soult at Landsberg would halt them on the Lech. Elsewhere, Bernadotte and the Bavarians were to continue to march on Munich with Davout in support, while the Garde Impériale was to join Marmont at Augsburg. Napoleon remained at Augsburg, having abandoned his plans to travel to Munich, and ended his orders to Murat by exhorting him to 'march upon the enemy wherever you find him, but with precaution, and keeping your troops in hand. Take no chances, for the first rule of all is to have a numerical superiority.' But Napoleon had again misjudged Allied intentions and the great blow he planned to unleash on the retreating Austrian formations threatened nothing but thin air. No Austrian forces of any strength remained south of the Danube.

As the Austrians struggled back to Ulm on the night of 9–10 October, the dissension amongst the officer corps increased. The animosity that existed between Archduke Ferdinand and Mack since the Landsberg meeting erupted as Mack refused to be shaken from maintaining his presence at Ulm, while Ferdinand demanded that the army break free from the tightening French noose. The situation worsened further when Ferdinand received a letter that evening from the kaiser, which, following up his recommendation to the archduke at Landsberg, put in writing that he should follow the advice of Mack. In response Ferdinand declared that now, deprived of all initiative, he would no longer accept any share of responsibility. A feeling of suspicion and distrust permeated throughout headquarters. Confirmed as holding supreme command, Mack now busied himself reorganising the structure of the corps under his command and instructed Ferdinand to forward all reports to him. In a despatch sent to the British government on 1 November, Sir Arthur Paget, the British special envoy in Vienna, reviewing the situation wrote that:

> 'there existed a degree of jealousy and misunderstanding among the General Officers in that army which led to fatal consequences ... By degrees it arrived to such a pitch that no communication took place between the Commander-in-chief (the Archduke Ferdinand) and General Mack, but in writing: No General Officer would attend General Mack unless accompanied by another General Officer to bear witness of what passed. Councils of War were held, and questions of importance were agitated, but General Mack had the means of reducing every body to silence. He had in his pocket a Carte Blanche signed by the emperor to act as he pleased.'[3]

Mack received a report on the condition of the city's decaying defences. It declared that the city could not withstand a determined French assault, but while Mack recognised the problem, he affirmed that there was little likelihood of Napoleon attacking Ulm in the immediate future: 'It rains, it snows, the enemy stays calmly in his dwellings and we will do the same.'[4]

While Mack remained in Ulm, content to wait for the Russians, his troubles were about to take a turn for the worse with the arrival in the city of Charles Schulmeister. Having left Stuttgart on 10 October, Schulmeister wasted no time in gathering information in inns and eating houses along the way, where his generous budget provided the wine that loosened tongues. Elsewhere in the city two of his trusted colleagues were at similar work. Schulmeister then searched out an old hunting friend, Hauptmann Wendt, head of Mack's intelligence gathering staff. Having renewed their friendship, Schulmeister wasted no time and infiltrated the Austrian command structure with ease by offering his services to Wendt as a spy, which were accepted, probably on 11 October. But before he could begin to influence matters another battle took place, where Napoleon had least expected it.

Following the day of confusion in VI Corps, Ney finally issued orders for the 11 October, in response to instructions received during the evening ordering the capture of Ulm: 'It remains the aim to take possession of Ulm, which is important under all circumstances. His majesty gives you a free hand to arrive at this goal before the end of tomorrow (11 October). The dismounted dragoons will be subordinated to you.'[5]

Accordingly, Ney ordered Dupont to lead his division towards Ulm, where, having taken up a threatening position on the heights behind Haslach, he was to demand the surrender of the city. Ney also informed Dupont that Baraguey d'Hilliers' division of dismounted dragoons would march forward from their positions on the Brenz river and form his reserve at Albeck. South of the river, Ney's other two divisions also received orders to advance on Ulm. Malher's division was to lead with Loison in support. Unfortunately, Ney's orders suffered a serious delay in transmission.

Unusually, the orders for Dupont and Baraguey d'Hilliers were entrusted to one staff officer. He left Günzburg at 3.00am on the morning of 11 October in a storm of rain and snow and soon became disorientated in the dark. It was only after daybreak that he regained his bearings. Although he was required to deliver the orders to Baraguey d'Hilliers first – to allow this reserve some time to close the gap – finding himself closer to Albeck, he decided to deliver Dupont's orders first, arriving there at about 9.00 or 10.00am. He then set off to locate Baraguey d'Hilliers and encountered the leading elements of his division at Stötzingen, roughly 10 miles to the rear. Although the reserve division received its orders at around 11.00am–12.00 noon, with his division spread over a wide area, it was not until around 3.00pm that the commander could begin to march in support of Dupont.

In the meantime, Dupont had rapidly assembled his men and was on the road towards Ulm by 11.00am. Around an hour later he approached Haslach, where his leading men encountered an Austrian cavalry patrol. After an exchange of shots the cavalry retired to the Michelsberg with this new intelligence. The senior Austrian army commanders were all in Ulm when these first shots alerted them. According to Mack's account, as soon as the gunfire was heard, Archduke Ferdinand, with Feldzeugmeister Kolowrat, several other generals and their ADCs, all immediately rode out of Ulm without requesting Mack to join them or leaving instructions as to where they were heading. Mack presumed Ferdinand would make for the Michelsberg, 'the key of our position', as he called it, but when he arrived on the hill, there was no sign of the archduke or his entourage. Then, while Mack surveyed the scene from the left of the position, information reached him that Ferdinand was in an entrenchment far away on the right. During the ensuing battle, with no communication possible between the two most senior officers, the left and right operated completely independently of each other. Despite having established his seniority over Ferdinand it seems Mack still considered his role mainly to formulate and dictate strategy, not to direct the army in battle, for he later wrote: 'Our right remained inert, because it was not my place to send orders to his Imperial Highness.'[6]

From his position at Haslach, Dupont could clearly observe that the Austrians were in force on the Michelsberg – perhaps 20,000-strong. This was not the rearguard garrison he expected to encounter. Malher too, approaching Ulm from south of the river, discovered the strength of the force ahead of him and halted. However, despite orders to avoid combat with superior forces, Dupont decided that if he drew back his force of about 5,000 men the Austrians may recognise his weakness, encouraging them to pursue him aggressively. Alternatively, if he confidently took up a position and prepared for battle, he hoped the Austrians would presume him to be the advance guard of a much larger force and delay their own preparations before committing to battle.

Dupont formed the first line of his division in front of Unter- and Ober-Haslach. The two battalions of the 32ème Ligne to the left of the Ulm road and two battalions of the 9ème Légère to the right of it with artillery across the road and protecting the left flank. The two battalions of the 96ème Ligne formed a second line behind the twin villages. He placed the 1èr Hussards on the extreme left flank and his other two cavalry regiments, 15ème and 17ème Dragons on the right behind the 96ème Ligne. Then, as Malher had done at Günzburg, Dupont formed a composite battalion from the grenadier and *carabinier* companies of his regiments and despatched them to defend the village of Jungingen on the western approaches to Haslach. Finally, with battle fast approaching, Dupont directed an aide to find Baraguey d'Hilliers and urge his arrival on the battlefield. It was rapidly approaching 1.00pm, and unfortunately for Dupont, it would be another two hours before this reserve even began to march.

Having been surprised, it took a while for the Austrians to form themselves for battle. FML Loudon moved forward on the left toward Jungingen in what developed into the main aggressive thrust. He commanded IR8 Erzherzog

Ludwig (three battalions), IR11 Erzherzog Rainer (two battalions), IR20 Kaunitz (three battalions) and IR54 Froon (three battalions). However, all were well below strength and Kaunitz was still recovering from the heavy casualties suffered at Günzburg less than forty-eight hours before – Loudon probably commanded around 6,000 men.[7] On the right, Ferdinand was indeed apprehensive of Dupont's position, believing it must herald a major attack. As such the right appears to have taken much longer to get into a position between the villages of Örlingen and Böflingen. Ferdinand, commanding close to 6,500 men from four regiments, then awaited the French onslaught. Dupont's bold strategy was working.

FML Loudon's column closed with Jungingen where it first encountered skirmishers outside the village. After brushing these aside he pushed ahead with IR8 and IR20 until discovering the main body of the composite battalion, some 400 men, aggressively defending every building, wall and feature, but particularly the barricaded church. More and more Austrian infantry poured into the village, effectively clearing it except for the church, which proved impossible to overcome. And all the time the defenders were exacting a heavy toll on the frustrated attackers.

Dupont, aware of the importance of Jungingen to the stability of his position, decided that with the Austrians now disorganised by the fighting in the village, and encouraged by the lack of movement shown by the Austrian right, he should launch a counter-attack. For this he ordered forward both battalions of the 9ème Légère, supported by both battalions of 96ème Ligne and a few artillery pieces, leaving just the 32ème Ligne, the rest of the artillery and hussars to oppose Ferdinand.

The 9ème Légère stormed forward with the 96ème Ligne in echelon to their left – some 2,300 men in all – with bayonets fixed. This dramatic onslaught swept up those Austrians emerging from the village and threw them back into the confused struggle around the church. Now surrounded in the village, with little chance of escape, the Austrians surrendered in great numbers. Those who did get away were in no condition to take part in renewed Austrian assaults. Determined to clear Jungingen, Loudon ordered forward IR11 and IR54, leaving just the grenadier battalion of IR54 as a reserve, making repeated assaults against the village during which it changed hands five times. With all his infantry on the right now fighting desperately, Dupont continued to gamble on the inaction of Ferdinand. To support the struggle, he ordered one of his only two uncommitted battalions of the 32ème Ligne to plug the open gap on his right flank between two isolated woods. This move prevented the gap being exploited by the 4. Latour Chevaulegers, who were moving up in support of the infantry attack on Jungingen. Instead, the Latours attacked a battalion of the 96ème Ligne, which formed square and repulsed the attack but then suffered badly from the fire of an Austrian cavalry battery.

In an effort to remove the pressure on the battalion of the 96ème Ligne, Dupont ordered forward his last reserve, the 15ème and 17ème Dragons. With the 15ème leading, the dragoons passed between the woods and emerged into the open just as FML Schwarzenberg arrived with two heavy *cuirassier* regiments, 3. Erzherzog Albert and 6. Mack. Although the Austrian squadrons were probably only at half strength, they still outnumbered the dragoons: first the 15ème were overthrown, then the 17ème. However, both regiments fell back, reformed, and bravely charged again. The ensuing mêlée swirled around with neither side appearing to gain the upper hand, French aggression going some way to balancing their shortage of numbers. However, the Latour Chevaulegers now threw themselves into the combat and their numbers swung the matter decisively in favour of the Austrian cavalry as the Chevaulegers captured an eagle standard of the 15ème Dragons, the first lost by La Grande Armée.

During the actions around Jungingen Mack had inexplicably advanced with the cavalry and become involved in the fighting around the village. During this engagement he sustained a bullet wound, forcing him to retire from the field. With the French cavalry retreating in disorder, Schwarzenberg lost control of his victorious horsemen who careered off in pursuit. They did not stop until encountering the baggage of Dupont's division near Albeck, which they preferred to ransack rather than using their strength to threaten the rear of Dupont's command. Meanwhile, some three hours after the first move against Jungingen, Archduke Ferdinand finally began a tentative advance towards Haslach, leading with just one regiment, IR15 Riese. These men quickly became the target of concentrated artillery fire, followed by an attack against its right flank by 1èr Hussards before it marched into musket range of the lone battalion of 32ème Ligne facing them. Assailed on all sides IR15 fell back, pursued by the battalion of 32ème Ligne with artillery support.

The French pursuit almost got as far as Böflingen before the combined efforts of IR17 Reuss-Plauen and IR36 Kolowrat halted it. Yet the Austrians, lacking artillery and cavalry on the right, found it difficult to drive the French battalion back. Eventually, sheer weight of fire forced the French to retire towards Haslach, while the battalions positioned near Jungingen also fell back. The French finally abandoned the village as the last Austrian battalion on the left, the grenadiers of IR54 Froon, moved forward. Ferdinand's infantry similarly began a steady advance in pursuit of the retreating battalion of 32ème. Recognising he could no longer hold his position, Dupont began a general retreat, being driven back towards Albeck before turning off the road and heading across country towards Langenau. The anticipated support from Baraguey d'Hilliers never arrived. At around 5.30pm that officer reached Albeck with an advanced party of about sixty mounted men. Here he encountered the Austrian cavalry ransacking Dupont's baggage. He quickly gathered together as many French cavalry stragglers as he could find, reformed them, and drove off the remaining looters: but not before they had removed twenty-three of the wagons.

The battle at Haslach-Jungingen was unusual in that both sides claimed victory: and with some justification. Dupont set out with limited forces to present an aggressive front, in the hope that it would delay or deter any Austrian moves while he awaited the 5,000 men of Baraguey d'Hilliers' division in support. That they never arrived meant he faced Mack and Ferdinand with between 5,000 and 6,000 men but held his ground until nightfall. Although the Austrian commanders drew together almost 23,000 men for the battle, the acrimony within the command structure meant the full strength could never be brought to bear on the outnumbered French. Attacks made in isolation enabled the French to fight on better terms than they could have hoped for. It appears that perhaps 7,500 Austrian infantry and 500 cavalry held in reserve took no part at all. Despite this, the French had eventually been driven away and the road to Albeck and a path to the north of the Danube cleared. Losses on both sides were heavy. Dupont appears to have lost about 900 men as prisoners to the Austrians, with killed and wounded taking the total up to some 2,000.[8] The Austrian figures are more elusive. In some sources the French claim to have taken 4,000 Austrian prisoners during the struggle for Jungingen. However, the regimental history of the 9ème Légère, the regiment credited with capturing most of them, claims to have taken only 1,500.[9] Austrian casualties probably consisted of approximately 400 killed and 1,100 wounded.

Back in Ulm, Mack, having received treatment for his wound, was delighted with the outcome of the battle, and with the discovery of a copy of Ney's orders to Dupont – found in the captured French baggage wagons – which revealed that the French general was isolated on the north bank (the remainder of the French army being deployed south of the river). This information provided the perfect opportunity for Mack to resurrect his plan – thwarted by the French victory at Günzburg two days earlier – of marching along the north bank and linking up with the Russians; and with the 'victory' at Haslach-Jungingen boosting the sagging morale of his soldiers, he proposed to make the breakout the following morning, 12 October.

Mack presented his plan to the senior officers, but in the tense atmosphere of distrust and animosity that pervaded Austrian headquarters, he received vociferous opposition. In particular, FML Werneck, whose corps would march first, opposed the plan with what Mack described as 'improper violence'. Werneck claimed his men were too exhausted after the battle and were desperately in need of food before they could march. It appears Mack, angered by Werneck's refusal, offered to personally lead the men in his place, but Ferdinand refused to sanction this, and in the face of such vehement opposition, Mack relented and did not claim his authority over Ferdinand on this occasion. Perhaps the best chance of saving the army slipped away at this meeting. As a consequence, the Austrian army spent 12 October resting and reorganising. Changing circumstances during the day caused Mack to rewrite his plans three times.

The 11 October had proved a day of revelation for Napoleon. While Dupont had been fighting the Austrian army single-handed at Haslach-Jungingen, he had lost control of that wing of the army and was unaware of the circumstances in which it found itself. In the meantime, he continued to direct his army to a battlefield unoccupied by his enemies. During the day doubts first entered his mind. A false report that Ferdinand had escaped to Munich fuelled a belief that the Austrians had passed to the south and were escaping to Tirol. But other, stronger reports, now suggested they were still in some strength at Ulm. Bernadotte pressed on towards Munich, reporting some 20,000 Austrians to his front (these were Kienmayer's 16,000 men who continued to fall back towards the Inn) and that Russian troops were expected to be on the Inn in the next day or so. In this he was correct. However, the Inn was still a long way from Ulm. Concerned by these reports, Napoleon ordered Davout to close towards Bernadotte and also sent him d'Hautpoul's *cuirassier* division. Having taken these steps to cover any developments in his rear, Napoleon issued orders for the rest of the army that he believed would bring about a battle on the Iller on 12 October. Writing to Davout he detailed these moves:

> 'Maréchal Soult, with his army corps [IV], is on the march to Memmingen. GD Marmont with two French divisions of his army corps [II] is on the march so as to place himself on the heights of Illertissen, on the Iller. Maréchal Lannes [V] is at Weißenhorn, Maréchal Ney [VI] athwart the Danube near Ulm. Lastly, the Garde Impériale is marching on Weißenhorn.
>
> 'On the [11 October] all the dispositions will have been taken; [12 October], the day of battle, the enemy shall be destroyed, as he is encompassed all around.'[10]

During 11 October Ney and Murat heard distant firing from the direction of Albeck but continued to follow their orders in anticipation of battle next day. However, during the night of 11–12 October Ney received Dupont's somewhat over-enthusiastic and misleading report of his action at Haslach. In it Dupont declared: 'The success was complete; night has come on, and we remained masters of the battlefield. Four thousand prisoners of war, the flags, and the cannon are our prizes for the victory.'[11] Reassured by Dupont that everything was under control north of the Danube, orders requiring him to hold his position were not despatched until morning. Other orders, sent to Baraguey d'Hilliers and Bourcier's roaming dragoon division, required them to cross the river and join the great force building up south of the Danube. But by the time Dupont received his orders a panic had sent his shaken division back to the

Brenz river in some disorder, from where they were not able to move again until 14 October.

Murat sent Dupont's report to Napoleon with another report from Lannes, in which that marshal disputed the assumption that the strength of the Allies was south of the Danube and urgently requested permission to cross to the north bank. Murat had refused to grant Lannes' request, concerned it would upset Napoleon's plan: instead he forwarded it to the emperor, who received both reports at 10.00am on 12 October at Augsburg. This news of an action on the north bank and Lannes' concerns now turned Napoleon's attention away from the Iller. Accordingly, he left Augsburg and headed for Günzburg, then on to Murat's headquarters at Pfaffenhofen. He was appalled to discover the lack of accurate information as to the distribution of Ney's VI Corps. Eventually, he discovered that Dupont no longer held Albeck, where everyone thought he was, and the bridge at Elchingen remained unsecured because of a strong enemy presence. Instead three companies of infantry were merely observing it from the south bank. Napoleon was furious, and severely reprimanded Ney – somewhat unfairly – for leaving Dupont without support, for losing communications between his divisions, for abandoning Albeck and Elchingen, and for not advising the emperor of the movements of his division: all factors where the real blame lay with Murat.

Realising for the first time the danger that existed on the north bank, Napoleon began to reorder the marches of his corps around Ulm and commanded Ney to capture the bridge over the Danube at Elchingen the following morning, 14 October, without fail. Lannes received orders to follow Ney and support him, while Murat was to assemble his cavalry in the Günzburg–Weißenhorn area, just to the south of the Danube, repair the bridge at Leipheim, and be prepared to cross to the north bank if required. Meanwhile, Marmont was to continue his march towards the Iller to prevent the Austrians moving south from Ulm to Memmingen, but also be prepared to change direction and support Ney if called upon. Soult's corps, the furthest to the south, was to cross the Iller at Memmingen and cut off any escape routes from Ulm to the south-west. Only now did Napoleon recognise the true position of the Austrian army and the opportunity on offer – if he moved quickly – to surround it at Ulm: the encirclement of the city was underway.

The open opposition from his generals and lack of support from the petulant Archduke Ferdinand left Mack experiencing the loneliness of command. Three times during 12 October he changed his plans for the following day in the face of opposition from his senior officers, and in reaction to reports detailing confusing French movements.

Mack's final plan, issued at 2.00am on 13 October, reflected the news that a strong body of French troops were marching in the direction of the Iller and that Ney's corps had crossed to the south of the Danube (presumably based on Baraguey-d'Hillier's and Bourcier's movements). These movements seemed odd to Mack, as Ulm sat largely on the north bank of the Danube and any army intending to attack from the south would then first have to force a passage over the river. However, it appeared that the road north of the Danube was now clear and a route to safety lay open. Of the four army corps, Jellačič would leave Ulm and march south up the Iller towards Memmingen, destroying the bridges as he went. Then, picking up the detachments he had left in and around Memmingen earlier in the campaign, he was to retire back into Tirol. FML Werneck, forming the left of the army, furthest from the French, was to march towards Heidenheim on the Brenz river, then on to Nördlingen with the reserve artillery, heavy equipment and baggage wagons. In the centre, FML Riesch, having detached a small force to escort the artillery and baggage with Werneck, was to march close to the north bank of the Danube. FML Laudon was to lead this march with half of Riesch's corps, having responsibility for breaking all bridges between Elchingen and Gündelfingen. On 14 October Laudon was to continue with his task, disrupting the bridges up to Donauwörth. The plan anticipated Riesch reaching Elchingen on the night of 13 October and arriving in Gündelfingen the following evening. Schwarzenberg's corps was to remain south of Ulm on the 13 October, forming the right of the army, sending strong reconnaissance patrols towards Weißenhorn, where the French were reported to be. Then, on 14 October, he was to withdraw through Ulm, and leaving just one brigade as a garrison, follow Werneck on the road to Heidenheim.

The plan was a good one. Werneck faced a clear road, with Riesch protecting his right flank and closing all river crossings to the French, while Schwarzenberg kept the French occupied. Yet the constant changes to their orders merely increased the ill feelings many of the senior officers held towards Mack. Following another freezing, rain-soaked night, the Austrian army finally broke camp on the morning of 13 October. It was the beginning of the end for the army of FML Mack.

Chapter 8

The Emperor of Spies

'all respect to Charles [Schulmeister] ... he was
worth an army corps of 40,000 men to me.'*

The movements and actions of any spy are notoriously difficult to follow with
complete accuracy. Those of Charles Schulmeister, 'Monsieur Charles' to
Napoleon, are no different, but that he was present in Ulm and instrumental to
the outcome of the campaign is indisputable.

Schulmeister left Napoleon's Strasbourg headquarters with GD Savary on 2
October, but their movements are unclear until the two men arrive in Stuttgart
six days later. On that same day Napoleon entered Donauwörth and the
opening battle of the campaign brought France victory at Wertingen.
Schulmeister operated a network of agents and two of these, Jean Rippmann
de Kork and another man, Hammel, had already passed through Austrian lines
and were feeding back information from Ulm. It therefore seems likely that
Savary and Schulmeister were aware that Mack ordered the army to abandon
the line of the Iller on 4 October and to reassemble on the Danube four days
later. When Napoleon left Strasbourg he believed an Austrian retreat on the
Inn or into Tirol as the most likely moves: he did not anticipate Mack holding
a position at Ulm. To Savary and Schulmeister, Mack's new position anchored
on Ulm awakened them to the possibility that if he remained static for a few
more days the French army could completely surround him. Accordingly, on
10 October, Schulmeister departed Stuttgart on a mission to confound Mack:
but before he set out he arranged for couriers to carry two despatches to Ulm.

Schulmeister arrived in Ulm on 12 October and immediately traced an old
friend, Hauptmann Wendt, who hailed from the same town as Schulmeister in
Baden and who just happened to be Mack's chief of intelligence. In Baden,
Schulmeister had claimed to be the grandson of a displaced Hungarian
nobleman and this pedigree allowed him to ingratiate himself into a wide circle

---

* Napoleon to his generals, Ulm, 20 October 1805.

Ulm: Austrian Breakout and French Encirclement
13 Oct - 18 Oct 1805

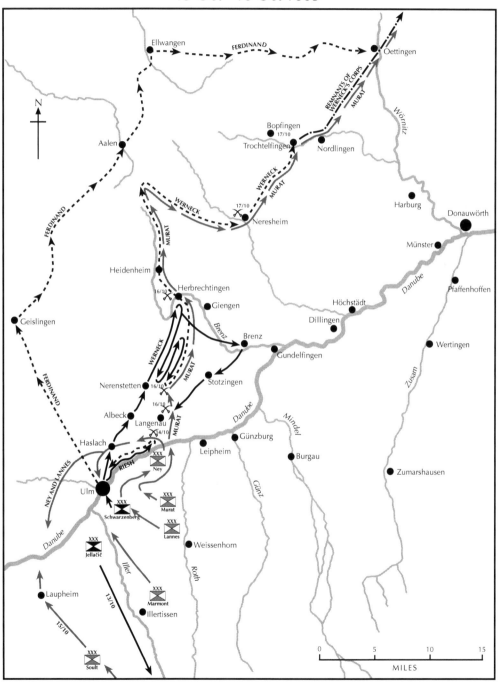

of contacts, Wendt being one of these. Having previously served on the staff of FML Klenau, Archduke Ferdinand appointed Wendt to work under Mack. Once in Ulm, Schulmeister offered his services to his friend as a spy for the Austrian army, revealing that he had gleaned much information detailing growing dissatisfaction in France with Napoleon's rule. Lured in, Wendt introduced Schulmeister to Mack later that day. Schulmeister immediately set about disclosing all he 'knew', backed up by carefully prepared false papers and documents. This information appealed to Mack. Trouble in France would affect Napoleon's plans, but at the moment it was not enough to influence his own thinking. Mack continued with his plans to break out the next morning. But Schulmeister had only just begun to spin his web.[1]

Happy to be on the move again after yet another freezing night, the bedraggled Austrian army set out on the morning of 13 October. Despite the bad weather, Werneck's corps made excellent progress on the road high above the Danube, with his advance guard reaching the Brenz river almost 19 miles away. FML Loudon's leading half of Riesch's corps, some 7,000 men, marched at around 10.00am, heading for Elchingen and encountered a very different situation. From the outset the low-lying roads close to the Danube were in an appalling condition. Riesch described them as some of the worst he had ever encountered:

> 'The narrow sunken roads were impractical, filled with large stones and water up to the chest of the horses, leading between a chain of hills and the Danube bank, lined mostly with thick bushes which were impenetrable for the infantry, forcing them to wade through boggy ground with water up to their thighs.'[2]

As a consequence, it took Loudon's men almost six hours to cover the 7 miles to Elchingen. Exhausted as they were after their efforts, they found themselves now in great danger, as bullets began to fall amongst them. A battalion of the 25ème Légère and two weak regiments of light cavalry had crossed to the north bank of the river earlier that afternoon, and from the village of Ober-Elchingen, opened fire on the leading elements of Loudon's command. For a while, the French held back the startled Austrians, who had not expected to encounter any resistance. But once over the initial surprise Loudon's infantry rolled forward, forcing the overwhelmingly outnumbered French troops to make a break for the Elchingen bridge 1,400 yards away, with their cavalry protecting the retreat. There were, in fact, two bridges: a shorter one of some 35 yards crossing a northern arm of the Danube onto a midstream island, from which a longer bridge of about 65 yards, crossed to the south bank of the river.

The endless delays on the march meant it was impossible now for Loudon to reach Gündelfingen with his main force that night, so instead he sent a few troops ahead to occupy the village. In the meantime, his men began half-heartedly breaking up the northern end of the bridge, but had only removed a short stretch of planking when they came under fire from the French battalion now occupying the woods on the opposite bank. It was already early evening as the Austrians were forced to seek cover.

Riesch set out from Ulm with the second part of his command, roughly 8,000 men, at 2.00pm and found the road even more churned up by Loudon's progress. Alerted by the noise of battle ahead, he moved forward as quickly as possible with a regiment of infantry and a squadron of *cuirassiers* from his advance guard: but the action at Elchingen was over by the time he arrived. With the rest of his column still struggling through the mud, Riesch approved Loudon's decision to remain in strength at Elchingen, but he ordered four battalions and two squadrons to advance towards Leipheim in the early hours of the morning to destroy the bridge there. It was 10.00pm before the last of Riesch's men laboured into Elchingen.

While awaiting their arrival, Riesch discussed the situation with Loudon and his advance guard commander, Mecsery. Mack's orders clearly required the bridge at Elchingen to be destroyed that day, as well as others along the river. At Elchingen the bridge would require a great deal of work to meet the requirements of these orders. The three officers considered their situation, and taking into account the exhaustion of their men, decided to leave the completion of the task until morning. It was a fatal decision, one that jeopardized Mack's entire plan, but such was the lack of respect for the commanding officer amongst his senior subordinates that none felt the urgency of the moment or recognised the importance of their mission. Then a message arrived from Mack, which, although presenting a further change of plans, added to their feeling of security.

New information reached Mack during the morning of 13 October. Two letters arrived in Ulm, one from a Württemberg magistrate, Baron Steinherr, in which he detailed a conversation overheard in a village between Stuttgart and Ulm. Mack considered Steinherr 'a credible witness' and the news his letter contained seemed to solve the great mystery that was puzzling him. Steinherr reported a conversation that told of a British invasion force landed at Boulogne and reported a popular rising against Napoleon in France. The letter also suggested that Prussia, too, was about to stir, following the French violation of her territory. The other report told of a dramatic increase in courier traffic from France, through Stuttgart, towards Napoleon's headquarters. Following on from Schulmeister's news of the previous day, detailing growing anti-Napoleon sentiments in the French press, the veil that hid the 'truth' now lifted from Mack's eyes: or so he thought. With startling clarity the reason for the concentration of the French army south of the Danube was revealed to him. Napoleon must have abandoned his attempt on Ulm, and intent on avoiding battle, was preparing to march back to France with all speed to put down the rising and confront the British forces. But none of this was true. A trap had been set and Mack greedily took the bait: for these were the letters Schulmeister despatched from Stuttgart before he departed for Ulm.

Reinvigorated, Mack sent for Schulmeister, and having discussed the intelligence with his newly recruited spy, instructed him to leave Ulm that evening and return to Stuttgart to verify the stories and discover the latest information. To avoid running into French patrols he was first to ride towards the north-east, advise Werneck of these latest developments, then turn back westwards to Stuttgart. Meanwhile, Mack gave full rein to his 'Dream of the Enemy's Retreat' as he later called it, and issued new orders that he believed would herald the opening moves of the eventual joint advance of his army and Kutuzov's Russians on Paris. Mack now decided to hold Ulm, cancelling the orders for Schwarzenberg's corps to join the exodus to the north-east. However, Werneck and Jellačič were to continue with their original orders, as was Riesch for the time being. Mack intended to redirect Riesch once he knew more details of the French movements and Werneck had secured the retreat of the reserve artillery and baggage.

That night, at Elchingen, FML Riesch received a copy of Mack's 'convictions', which spelt out the commander's new understanding of the military situation. Although many French campfires were visible from the abbey at Elchingen, in a great arc on the south bank of the Danube from Leipheim to Weißenhorn, Riesch and his commanders fully anticipated continuing their march unmolested in the morning. But even as they settled down for the night, Maréchal Ney was preparing an assault on their position.

Having caught up with Werneck's rearguard, Schulmeister spent that night at Neenstetten, about 3 miles to the west of Nerenstetten. The next day he joined Werneck, and while updating him on the developments in Ulm, secretly compiled a detailed breakdown of Werneck's command. Back in Ulm, Archduke Ferdinand looked on helplessly, fuming with frustration, as the army he believed was rightly his to command followed instead the constantly evolving orders of FML Mack. He expressed his helplessness and anger at Mack's handling of the army in a letter written to Archduke Charles that evening:

'In a whole book one could not describe our situation and the madness of Mack. Mack, at least a complete fool, has by his eternal marching to and fro, plan-changes etc. brought us to the point, where without striking a blow, we see the whole army dissolving into nothing. His majesty, the kaiser, gave him complete power and I am in the most unpleasant, I can probably say desperate, situation in the world. I must, so to speak, watch the whole army collapse before my eyes under my signature.'

In the next twenty-four hours Ferdinand's festering contempt for Mack reached breaking point.

Napoleon's verbal attack on Maréchal Ney, for leaving Dupont's division exposed on the north bank of the Danube, left the commander of VI Corps boiling with anger towards Murat, who had ordered him to make the dispositions against his own judgement. Now the emperor ordered Ney to take the bridge at Elchingen and lead his men across the Danube. Nothing was going to stop him carrying out his orders, not the river, nor Riesch's corps on the opposite bank. He returned to his headquarters at Leipheim from where he issued his orders. At 7.00am on 14 October the remains of Dupont's division standing on the Brenz was to advance once more towards Albeck, close to the scene of their battle at Haslach-Jungingen. Loison, whose division had seen little action so far, would lead the assault across the river, while Malher's division, blooded at Günzburg, formed the reserve. In addition to his infantry, Ney had eighteen artillery pieces and two light cavalry regiments from his own corps and Bourcier's attached dragoon division. In all, Ney could call on around 15,000 men to storm across the Danube. By the early hours of the morning all was ready. The troops were in a high state of excitement and houses in the surrounding villages had been broken down and wood removed to provide planking, with which to repair the partly demolished bridge. A civilian observer in Elchingen recalled that the French deployed like a threatening 'black thundercloud' amidst the hail and storm. It was the appearance of this same 'thundercloud' at around 7.30am that advised Riesch of the danger materialising on his flank.

In accordance with orders, FML Riesch had already started his command marching early that morning, and by 7.00am over half of it was already on the road. The rest remained behind to destroy the bridge, while the road ahead cleared. However, the detachment of 2,000 men from Loudon's division, sent to destroy the bridge at Leipheim, reported it already held by a large enemy force of 10,000 men (actually Baraguay d'Hilliers' dismounted dragoon division of around 5,000). Unable to complete their orders, they fell back on Elchingen. The main body of Loudon's men were recalled when the French appeared opposite the bridge.

The other detachment that left camp early was Mecsery's advance guard of Hessen-Homberg's division. His route took him towards Gundelfingen, but near Langenau he encountered Dupont's division marching on Albeck. After a tentative clash of outposts both sides fell back, Mecsery, following orders from Riesch, and Dupont to the Brenz, to protect his communications across the Danube. With all his men back at Elchingen, Riesch aligned his command along the high ground where the abbey and village of Ober-Elchingen stood and which extended towards Unter-Elchingen. In all, he commanded some 15,000 men – about the same as Ney – with fourteen artillery pieces. However, only two battalions and two guns were in position to defend the broken bridge. Others were earmarked for the defence but matters developed too quickly for them to move into position.

During the night Ney formed a battery with eleven of his guns and positioned them by the main bridge on the southern bank of the river. Then, at about 7.30, he appeared at Napoleon's headquarters to receive his final instructions. Before he left, Ney turned to Murat, for whom he now felt nothing but disdain, and in front of the assembled luminaries he took him by the arm. During their heated argument a few days earlier Murat had dismissed Ney's criticism of his strategy by airily stating that he made his plans in the face of the enemy. The two men had almost drawn swords. Stung by this previous insult, Ney now exclaimed loudly, so all could hear: 'Come with me prince, and make some plans in the presence of the enemy!' Murat seethed. A few days later he attempted to gain revenge by accusing Ney of making a false requisition for a large sum of money. Knowing the characters of his marshals, the emperor ignored Murat's letter and concentrated on more pressing matters.

Back at the Danube, Ney gave the order for his artillery to open their bombardment of the Austrian positions. The two Austrian battalions of IR54 Froon defending the river could not hope to stand and face this onslaught of shot and shell and sought what shelter they could. The two Austrian artillery pieces returned fire in what was clearly an uneven contest. Under cover of this heavy concentration of artillery fire, French infantry began to work their way on to the bridge. The Austrian attempts to destroy the bridge meant that, while the beams that ran lengthways across the river connecting the piers were still in place, the cross planking that formed the roadway was missing in places or unsafe. To repair the passage over the river small engineering parties assembled, tasked with laying planks across the beams to form a new roadway. Capitaine Coisel, an aide to Général de division Loison, and a sapper from 6ème Légère carried the first plank. The two men rushed forward but before they could complete their task an Austrian cannon ball smashed the sapper's leg. However, his brave action spurred on others and gradually, plank by plank, the roadway edged across the river.

While this work inexorably proceeded, Loison formed together the elite companies from the 6ème Légère and 39ème Ligne and ordered them on to the partially repaired bridge, while the French guns kept Austrian opposition to a minimum. The *voltigeurs*, *carabiniers* and grenadiers stormed forward across the bridge until the planks ran out. Then, taking to the open beams, they tottered intrepidly the rest of the way before jumping down into the shallows at the river's edge. Once across they fanned out to form a resolute bridgehead while the engineer parties completed their work. From his position on the high ground some 1,400 yards away FML Riesch was unable to halt this flow of men across the river. His decision taken the previous evening, to defer the destruction of the bridge until morning, now returned to haunt him. His men, many of them young and inexperienced, others already bloodied at the hands of the French, watched nervously as the enemy poured across the river.

With the bridge complete, GB Villate led forward his brigade of Loison's division – first the 39ème Ligne, followed by VI Corps cavalry, and then 6ème

Légère. With these 3,300 infantry and 300 light cavalry Ney began to assault the strong Austrian position, while GB Rouget brought his brigade across the river and formed up in support. Although significantly outnumbered, their enthusiasm carried the French troops right up to the foot of the sloping ground on which the Austrians formed their defence before a fierce fire brought them to a halt.

With mounting casualties the 39ème Ligne were forced to fall back, but the 6ème Légère, with Ney at their head, made a ferocious attack on the village and abbey, driving the defenders out. Elsewhere along the line vicious fighting continued. Rouget's brigade (69ème Ligne and 76ème Ligne – about 3,500 men), now advanced to the right of the abbey, where the Austrian infantry of IR15 and IR35 was drawn up in two lines. To the right of Rouget's men VI Corps cavalry (3ème Hussards and 10ème Chasseurs à cheval) and Bourcier's dragoons (18ème, 19ème and 25ème) advanced towards Mecsery's advance guard (three battalions IR42 and two *cuirassier* squadrons). The Austrians put up a stout resistance for a while in the face of the attacking élan of the French. But with their ammunition running low and no chance of replenishment – many of the wagons were still stuck in the mud from the previous day's march – and their confidence already low, they began to give way. Many surrendered. Malher's division of Ney's Corps had now also made the crossing of the Danube and prepared to enter the battle. After around five hours hard fighting Riesch realised the battle was lost and gave the order to retreat.

Although numerically superior to Ney's attacking force, morale-wise the Austrians lacked the same level of conviction for the fight. All order broke down during the retreat and when Riesch finally struggled back into Ulm that evening he retained only about 2,500 of the 15,000 men that had marched out the previous day. Although many of the missing eventually made their way back to Ulm, estimates show that Riesch lost about 4,000 men killed and wounded and perhaps 3,000 as prisoners. French losses are difficult to ascertain but they were probably between 1,600 and 3,000 killed and wounded. It was another disastrous engagement for Mack. Loison's victorious men pursued the fleeing Austrians as far as Haslach before falling back to Albeck, where VI Corps established an advanced position, the main body remaining around Elchingen. Dupont received orders to move his division up towards Albeck. For the moment Ney was unaware of the importance of his victory. Later, in recognition of his remarkable achievement, he received the title 'duke of Elchingen': a reward which drew from him the response: 'Is it not an honour, to be duke of so beautiful a place?'

Ney's attack across the Danube must have made Mack question the veracity of Schulmeister's stories of French retreat, but he did not completely discredit them. In the meantime, the defeat of Riesch's command was not the only bad news. With the French established at Albeck, contact with FML Werneck's column was broken and his situation unknown. In fact for much of the day

Werneck had remained near to Heidenheim, ensuring the safety of the slow-moving reserve artillery and baggage convoy. He heard the distant sound of battle from Elchingen but was unsure whether to march to the sound of the guns or continue to follow his orders. In fact, the distance was such that he could not have arrived in time to alter the outcome. However, it is interesting to speculate whether Schulmeister, now at Werneck's headquarters, had influenced this decision. Elsewhere other developments were further undermining Mack's position.

On the previous morning FML Jellačič commenced his march south out of Ulm, heading up the Iller towards Memmingen, where he intended reuniting with his detachment under GM Spangen. However, the appearance of Maréchal Soult before Memmingen with IV Corps forced an early surrender by the Austrian commander on 14 October with Jellačič only a day's march away. Jellačič veered away towards Vorarlberg, just avoiding Soult's men. In the meantime, advanced detachments of IV Corps crossed the Iller and streamed north to cut off Ulm from the west.[3] Of the five army corps that advanced under Mack into Bavaria, little remained under his direct control. Kienmayer, retiring towards the Inn, had remained out of contact since the French pushed him back beyond Munich. Jellačič was marching for Vorarlberg, Werneck was somewhere north-east of Ulm, Riesch had just struggled back to the city with the remnants of his command, leaving only Schwarzenberg?s corps relatively unaffected. That night tension boiled over in Ulm.

Mack put on a brave face, maintaining his conviction that the position remained strong and advocated its continued defence until the Russians intervened. His senior officers thought otherwise and demanded he attempt to break out towards Tirol. Mack exploded with rage. Archduke Ferdinand had seen enough. Convinced that French forces would soon encircle the city and any chance of escape would evaporate, he represented to Mack that his capture, as a member of the imperial Habsburg family, would be intolerable. Mack attempted to assure him that there was no danger of that happening and he reiterated his belief that the French would commence their retreat to France. Ferdinand was no longer prepared to put Mack's theories to the test, and with FML Schwarzenberg and FZM Kolowrat, prepared to abandon Ulm that night and break out with 2,000 cavalry and two battalions of grenadiers.[4] With his plans complete, Ferdinand offered Mack the chance to ride out with them. He refused and also prevented a number of officers who wished to accompany Ferdinand from leaving on the grounds that they were essential if he was to maintain a defence of the city. At midnight, Ferdinand, Kolowrat, Schwarzenberg and their men departed, with the intention of locating and uniting with Werneck's column. Then Ferdinand hoped to find Kienmayer and link up with the Russians. Mack was appalled.

On the morning of 15 October the French army began closing in on Ulm. Ney's VI Corps marched towards the Michelsberg and supported by detachments from Lannes' V Corps, drove the demoralised defenders out of the incomplete defences and back on the city. Outside the gates they made a stand and succeeded in driving the French back, but they were in a bad position. The French artillery outranged those Austrian guns positioned within the defences (their heavy guns away on the road with Werneck), and threatened a destructive bombardment. By evening, Ney's troops took up the recently vacated positions on the Michelsberg, while the demoralised Austrians crowded into the city.

A citizen of Ulm described the desperate conditions apparent in the congested streets:

> 'Ever more the roads filled with the fleeing and wounded; carts and wagons, emaciated horses, abandoned cannons hindered communications. Hundreds of half-starving soldiers were in every public place. The despondency among the troops took over in such a way that it bordered on resignation and the Austrian soldier represented the starkest picture of human misery.
>
> 'They stood in the rain and snow for two or three days in torn and damaged clothes, many without shoes … While for the most part the officers wandered about the taverns, the soldiers begged for bread with the citizens. In the roads dead horses lay … The condition of the wounded and sick was even more pitiful; more than 4,000 men were in the hospitals, of which about fifteen to twenty died daily.'[5]

With the city surrounded, Maréchal Ney called on Mack to surrender. Despite the suffering all around him, Mack firmly refused. So adamant was he that the city could still defend itself against a French assault that he issued a proclamation forbidding anyone to even discuss the possibility of capitulation. However, he was alone. Nine of his rebellious senior officers objected and prepared a statement urging Mack to make terms with the French, claiming the shortage of food and ammunition made defence impossible. In the face of such constant opposition his determination finally began to dissolve and Mack allowed them to draw up a response to Ney, requesting that the army be allowed to march out of Ulm with all the honours of war back to the Lech. The document, signed by Riesch, Gyulai and Loudon ended with a dramatic flourish. If Ney refused their terms they vowed to defend the city until 'buried in the ruins'. Mack did not add his signature before Generalmajor Moritz Liechtenstein delivered it to Ney in the early hours of 16 October.[6]

Having read the document, Ney forwarded it to Napoleon and awaited a response. It was not long in coming. The emperor categorically refused the request, insisting on the garrison's status as prisoners of war. On receipt of this rejection the three officers immediately sent their courier back to Ney informing him that as he did not accept their conditions they were prepared to entrust their fate to the chances of war. Ney's final response informed that a truce would exist until noon, at which time, if the garrison did not surrender, an attack on the city would commence. With no more word coming from Ulm, Ney's artillery opened a bombardment of the city at midday. A number of small fires broke out but these caused few problems. After a couple of hours the bombardment ceased and renewed discussions took place: but when these broke down it resumed again and continued for a few more hours. That night the garrison made hurried repairs to the city defences, while Napoleon's aide, Général de Ségur, arrived and spent the night negotiating with Mack for an acceptable resolution to the situation.

During the night of 14–15 October, the now isolated FML Werneck received news of Riesch's engagement at Elchingen and also learnt that the French were behind him at Albeck (Dupont's division). As this detachment appeared to be unaware of his presence, he determined to attack them in the morning while the artillery and baggage continued on their journey. He split his corps into two, the first part under his own command marching straight towards Albeck, while a flanking group, commanded by FML Hohenzollern followed a roundabout route via Brenz and Langenau. Werneck reached Nerenstetten, about 5 miles north-east of Albeck at 3.30pm, but as his advance guard drove in the French outposts the sound of gunfire from Ulm reached his ears. With darkness approaching and the French now reinforced by a division of dragoons and no sign of his planned flank attack developing, Werneck decided to pull back and regroup. The orders he sent to recall Hohenzollern did not arrive.

The surprising news that a large body of Austrian troops was operating outside Ulm and presenting a threat to his communications forced Napoleon into action. While the main body of the army tightened its grip on Ulm, Murat received orders to attack any Austrian formations roaming north of the Danube. For this task he created an ad hoc cavalry force, joined en route by Dupont's division and then by Oudinot's Reserve Grenadiers. Setting out on the morning of 16 October, Murat discovered Hohenzollern's command floundering in the mud near Langenau and swept them up before approaching Albeck.

Early that morning the confused Werneck marched back again towards Nerenstetten hoping to find Hohenzollern. Instead he found Murat. The French cavalry smashed into Werneck's advance guard, and while the two sides clashed, Werneck received a message from Mack, written after Riesch's defeat at Elchingen two days earlier, ordering him back to Ulm. Then, another note arrived, this time from Archduke Ferdinand. In it, Ferdinand explained the latest developments in Ulm and ordered Werneck to march towards Aalen, roughly 25 miles north of Nerenstetten, where he would join him. Clearly exposed, Werneck turned again, losing a great many prisoners as his advance guard became the rearguard, and attempted to keep the French at bay while he moved clear with the main body. Ten miles from Nerenstetten, at Herbrechtingen on the Brenz, he hurriedly took up a defensive position on the high ground from where he rejected a summons to surrender. Murat attacked: but after a day of hurricane-like weather that washed away the repaired bridge at Elchingen, his exhausted men fell back in the face of a spirited defence. Undaunted, Murat attacked again after dark, at about 9.00pm, and following a confused struggle Werneck's men abandoned the position, losing perhaps 2,000 men as prisoners to the French.

Whether or not Schulmeister influenced Werneck's marching and counter-marching is unrecorded, but sewing the seeds of doubt and confusion was his forte. That night, however, under cover of darkness, he slipped away from Werneck's headquarters and reported directly to Murat. At around 1.00am on 17 October he handed over a report detailing the direction of the Austrian retreat and their planned rendezvous with Ferdinand at Aalen, as well as the location of the reserve artillery and baggage convoy.[7] Schulmeister, his work done, departed for French headquarters at Elchingen.

Werneck struggled on in the morning, but just a few miles short of Aalen he received a second despatch from Archduke Ferdinand. Not for the first time it contained details of a change of plan. Now he was to march via Neresheim to Oettingen, where the two forces were to unite. Werneck's men now embarked on their fifth day of marching backwards and forwards and they were at the limit of their endurance. The route to Neresheim took them on poor cross-country roads adding further to their misery. The dejected column staggered into Neresheim between 11.00am and 3.00pm and attempted to grab a little rest but within two hours Murat's cavalry appeared, forcing the men on again. Unable to keep up the relentless pace, more and more men fell out, being quickly captured by their relentless pursuers. By the time he reached the flooded village of Trochtelfingen near Nördlingen, Werneck retained only about 2,000 formed men of the 9,000 or so that marched out of Ulm.[8] His men sank down on the waterlogged ground to grab what rest they could.

In the evening, a French emissary approached Werneck and informed him that Hohenzollern's force had surrendered the previous day and offered him surrender terms. Considering the condition of his men Werneck accepted and signed the agreement at about 11.00pm on 17 October. However, while negotiations were underway, most of the mounted officers and cavalry slipped away under cover of darkness and finally did rendezvous with Archduke Ferdinand at Oettingen.[9] A brigade of dragoons completed the bag by rounding up the Austrian artillery and baggage at Bopfingen on the road between Aalen and Nördlingen. By then Schulmeister had already reported to Napoleon's headquarters at Elchingen. Here, to the emperor's delight, he was able to give a thorough briefing on the condition of the army in Ulm, the animosity existing amongst the senior generals, the false information disseminated to Mack, and details of the composition of his command. The Austrian army lay naked and exposed before the emperor.

Napoleon's aide, Général de Ségur, left Ulm early on the morning of 17 October and reported back to Napoleon on his progress. The terms were:

1: The garrison to be prisoners of war and removed to France; or if the Russian army appears on the Lech river near Rain during the course of the day (16 October), the garrison will be granted free passage back to Austria.

2: In either circumstance the officers will return to Austria on parole not to serve against France for the duration of the campaign.

3: Following the surrender, if preferred, three or four French divisions will remain static for five or six days around the city.

Mack would not accept the terms and communications flowed back and forth. Then, at 2.00pm, Napoleon's chief of staff, Maréchal Berthier, arrived to finally settle matters. Mack negotiated an extension of eight days: if the Russians were not in force on the Lech by 25 October he would surrender. Berthier agreed, well aware that the Russians were still assembling east of the Inn. But in return, Mack astonishingly conceded to a request that, in the meantime, the French would be given access to one gate (the Neutor) of the city, granted permission to quarter a brigade within the city, and allowed free passage through it across the Danube. With this extraordinary decision to allow the French access to Ulm, what the outcome of a sudden Russian appearance would be does not appear to be clear.

At 9.00am on 18 October a brigade from Malher's division of VI Corps arrived before Ulm and demanded access. The gates opened, allowing the Frenchmen to enter, and they immediately requisitioned a wide area of the city. The Austrian soldiers were nonplussed. Mack had issued an order forbidding any aggression against the French, yet here were their enemies, swaggering amongst them and forcibly ejecting them from their billets. An Austrian staff officer describing the feelings of the garrison wrote:

'You had to be in Ulm to have an idea of the dreadful situation that surrounded us; it would be much too insulting, too painful, to give a detailed description of all the insults and abuse which we must now endure. Everywhere our soldiers mixed with the Frenchmen, and those who knew only too well their expected fate, looked with contempt on their officers ... The French generals gallop through the streets without slackening and cover us in mud, they dispute our dwellings with us, steal our effects and during the night break into our stables by force, steal our horses and laugh at our objections ...'[10]

Information from inside Ulm, and Schulmeister's report, clearly indicated to Napoleon the poor situation of the Austrian army. Frustrated now by the delays he would incur in line with the agreement Berthier had signed the previous day, he decided to accelerate the process and called Mack to Elchingen that afternoon.

Mack arrived at Napoleon's headquarters with a large number of attendants but without his senior officers and suffered the indignity of being kept waiting for two hours by the emperor. Finally, when he at last appeared, Napoleon pressed Mack on the question of why he had decided to defend such a poorly situated and fortified place as Ulm. Mack vehemently defended his decision, continuing to promote his belief in the strength of the position, but answering that circumstances dictated he must surrender.[11] At that point Napoleon decided to acquaint Mack with the facts. He informed him of the surrender of Memmingen five days earlier; that the Russians had not yet crossed the Inn; and that 60,000 troops were ready to oppose them (Bernadotte, Davout and the Bavarians). Further, he added that Werneck's corps surrendered on 17 October and on the 18 October Archduke Ferdinand was fleeing towards Bohemia with Murat in pursuit. The news hit Mack like a bombshell. It was clear now that there was no chance of relief before the deadline of 25 October. Mack was no longer the energetic, dominant figure that had marched confidently across Bavaria up to the banks of the Iller and beyond only six weeks earlier. He now showed the signs of a defeated man, worn down and driven to exhaustion by the constant battles with his own officers as well as the French. A few days earlier, an Austrian staff officer, Count Neipperg, described Mack as looking 'pale, having a night-cap under his hat, wearing a blue frock coat, his arm tied in a scarf [the result of his wound at Jungingen], and supported by a servant'.

Pressed by Napoleon and presented by Berthier with a written guarantee that all the information given was true, Mack agreed to bring the surrender forward and give up the city the next day, 20 October, to save his men further suffering. Yet in his confused state Mack did not think to oblige Napoleon to maintain the French army around Ulm until 25 October, as he would have been forced to do if he had not agreed to bring the surrender forward. Instead, only Ney's VI Corps was required to hold their positions around the city until ten hours after midnight on 25 October, freeing up the rest of the army to march immediately against the Russians. Mack returned to Ulm and called his senior officers together. He announced his decision, informing them that he no longer held any hope for relief; that the French were in overwhelming numbers; and it was therefore pointless to remain in the city for another six days, where food had all but run out. Instead they would march out the next day. The assembled officers voiced their astonishment, followed by protests, threats, uproar and then finally resignation. The French were all around them and amongst them; there was no longer any other option. The army made preparations to march out, the rank and file into captivity and the officers on parole back to Austria.

Elsewhere, the last couple of days proved difficult for Archduke Ferdinand too. Arriving at Oettingen on 18 October, he was shocked to find only the remnants of FML Werneck's column to meet him. Clearly, with the limited resources now at his disposal it was no longer possible for him to influence matters: instead he turned towards Bohemia, hoping to make good his escape. Granted permission to enter Ansbach, he departed Oettingen early on the morning of 19 October, yet even before the rearguard marched out they came under attack from GD Klein's dragoon division. Schwarzenberg, commanding the Austrian rearguard, informed Klein that as they were now in neutral territory the attack should cease. Klein refused, considering it merely a delaying tactic, and stuck to his orders: to pursue relentlessly and attack wherever he found the necessity.

The main body of Ferdinand's command arrived in Gunzenhausen about noon and prepared to make camp behind the village, leaving a battalion of grenadiers to defend the bridge over the river in front of the village. However, as Klein approached, with the French keen on battle, Ferdinand ordered his men to march on towards Schwabach on the Nürnberg road, detailing the rearguard to hold the French back as long as possible. Schwarzenberg continued to negotiate unsuccessfully with Klein, but with Murat now approaching too, Klein ended the discussions by taking captive the grenadier battalion at the bridge, despite protests that it was an unlawful act. Ferdinand pushed on rapidly, losing his baggage and few remaining guns to Klein, and arrived at Schwabach during the night before continuing on again towards Bayreuth after a few hours rest. Attacked vigorously on the afternoon of 20 October near Nürnberg, the rearguard lost many men, but by evening they rejoined the rest closing on Bayreuth.

Murat remained at Nürnberg. He had done enough. Following the receipt of Schulmeister's information he had taken all the Austrian reserve artillery, maybe 500 wagons and captured virtually all Werneck's column – covering some 100 miles in five days.

Archduke Ferdinand finally arrived at Eger (now Cheb) on the Bohemian border, and safety, on 21 October, accompanied by 1,500 cavalry: all that remained of his command.[12]

The campaign in Bavaria was over. Ever with an eye for the theatrical, Napoleon prepared the surrender ceremony with meticulous detail. In the morning, Marmont's corps passed through the city and joined the rest of the troops on the north side of the Danube. Here they formed up on the high ground of the Michelsberg and Frauenberg in a great open square, with Napoleon surrounded by his Garde Impériale. At around 1.00pm the Austrian army emerged from the city through the Frauentor, and with their officers at their head, marched between the lines of French soldiers. Over 20,000 men paraded with drums beating, while the French musicians struck up too. Although most Austrian soldiers were glad their torment was over, others cried 'Es lebe der Kaiser!' in a final gesture of defiance. The staff officer, Count

Neipperg, wrote expressing the despair felt by the army, marching out 'with rage in our hearts, despair in our souls ... the shame which crushes us, the mud which covers us, are inextinguishable.'

Napoleon called the senior Austrian officers to him as the endless column paraded to the Neutor, where the infantry laid down their muskets and the cavalry handed over their mounts to eager, footsore French riders. Napoleon consoled his opponents on their misfortune and entered into discussions on the reasons for the war – which he laid firmly at Britain's door.

And so ended the campaign of Ulm, the first stage of the war of the Third Coalition, brought to an astonishing end. Mack's army – that was in his own words, 'to form the anvil' on which the Russian hammer would smash the French army – had ceased to exist. Yet the Russians were unaware of Mack's dangerous predicament. None of the infrequent messages Kutuzov received from Mack or Ferdinand told of their defeats. At Ulm, Napoleon took the surrender of Mack and fifteen other generals, fifteen staff officers, between 23,000 and 25,000 men, and a vast arsenal of military equipment. Adding the losses suffered at Wertingen, Günzburg, Haslach and Elchingen – as well as those suffered by Werneck and Archduke Ferdinand during Murat's pursuit – plus the garrison that surrendered at Memmingen, the total losses were around 50,000 men out of the 72,000 that entered Bavaria. Only Kienmayer, who was back on the Inn, escaped the French net, along with Jellačič – for now – falling back on Vorarlberg.

Rapid manoeuvre and a unified central command contributed enormously to this remarkable achievement of the French army. Virtually all the significant engagements fell to Maréchal Ney's VI Corps, with support from Murat's Cavalry Reserve and Oudinot's grenadiers, part of V Corps. The enthusiasm of Napoleon's highly trained soldiers proved too much for the Austrian army, many of whom were raw and unprepared for active campaigning. But the influence on the campaign of Charles Schulmeister, Napoleon's 'Emperor of Spies', was crucial. By his ingenious efforts he caused Mack to change his plans and keep part of his army in Ulm on 13 October after he had already determined to depart with his whole force. This gained time for Napoleon and allowed him to correct the mistake made by leaving Dupont's weakened division isolated on the north bank of the Danube, when the rest of the army manoeuvred ineffectively south of the river. Then, taking payment from the Austrians too, Schulmeister attached himself to Werneck's escaping column, passing to Murat details of his route and that of Archduke Ferdinand, leading to the capture of most of their men. Napoleon was not slow to recognise Schulmeister's particular talents. As the Austrian army marched out of Ulm and into captivity, the emperor turned to his entourage and said, 'Gentlemen, all respect to Charles, who I estimate highly, because he was worth an army corps of 40,000 men to me'.[13] For Mack the end of the campaign left him more isolated than ever. A French officer, keen to catch a glimpse of the defeated commander, approached an Austrian officer standing alone and asked him to point out Mack. The officer replied: 'the man standing before you is the unfortunate Mack in person.'

On the morning of 21 October Mack left Ulm and began his long journey back to Vienna. At the same time, far away, off the south-west coast of Spain, Vice Admiral Lord Nelson led the British fleet against Admiral Villeneuve's Franco-Spanish fleet that finally sailed from Cadiz after two months' inactivity. The ensuing British victory at Trafalgar ended forever the dream of a French invasion of Britain. William Pitt had achieved all his initial aims – to prevent any possible French invasion and remove her army from its threatening position on the Channel coastline. But in Vienna the news of Mack's defeat had a devastating effect. With the Austrian army in Bavaria removed from the campaign, Napoleon turned to face the Russians, now forming the only obstacle between La Grande Armée and the Habsburg's imperial capital.

Chapter 9

'From The Ends of the Earth'

'This Russian army, that the gold of
England has transported from the ends of
the earth, shall experience the same fate
as those who we have just defeated.'*

Pressing on with all speed, Kutuzov arrived at the border town of Braunau on
9 October and began to make preparations for the arrival of his exhausted army
at the end of their gruelling 650-mile march. Having set out with just over
46,000 men on 25 August, this reduced within a few days to about 38,000 when
one of his six columns was redirected towards the Turkish frontier. Although
later recalled, they were not reunited until early November. Ordered to hurry
to Braunau as swiftly as possible, the punishing march continued to take its toll
on Kutuzov's army, which began to arrive on 12 October. By the time the final
column struggled in on 20 October he was down to 32,000 men, having been
forced to abandon the stragglers and sick on the road to come on as best they
could.

Information from the Austrians, who Kutuzov knew to be at Ulm, was
limited. He received a letter from Mack written on the morning of 8 October.
Although Mack had learned the previous day of the French march through
Ansbach, he confidently informed Kutuzov that his position at Ulm was secure
and he would hold it until the Russians advanced to join him. But later that day
the Austrians suffered their first defeat at Wertingen and the campaign entered
a new phase. That was the last Kutuzov heard from Ulm. The Russian
commander pushed patrols across the Inn to seek information but generally
remained in the dark.

Then, on 13 October, Kutusov received an unexpected – though welcome –
Austrian reinforcement. Pushed back by the advance of Bernadotte, FML
Kienmayer fell back to a position at Mühldorf, 25 miles west of Braunau.

---

* Napoleon's address to La Grande Armée, 21 October 1805.

Kienmayer formed the right wing of Mack's army, but the sudden appearance of the French on the Danube forced him back, initially towards Munich, and then the Inn. The detached brigade under Nostitz fell back too and rejoined him. But neither officer could offer Kutuzov anything in the way of news from Ulm.

Having just arrived at Braunau, FML Merveldt, an Austrian officer with much military and diplomatic experience, took command of these formations and other Austrian detachments in the locality. This officer was keen to encourage Kutuzov to advance into Bavaria and offer some support to Mack, but the Russian commander wisely would have none of it while his troops were still assembling.

Gradually, snippets of information trickled into Braunau from Ulm, hinting at a setback for the Austrian army. But only on 23 October did the startling truth become clear. On that day, an 'elderly gentleman' – or so he was described by a Russian officer who saw him – arrived in Braunau, requesting an audience with Kutuzov. To the Russian commander's surprise it was Mack in person. Released by Napoleon, Mack, a mere shadow of the man who had marched through the town so full of confidence and enthusiasm forty-six days earlier, was starting out on his melancholy journey back to Vienna. He described to Kutuzov the disasters that led to the surrender of his army and urged him not to venture forward against Napoleon's overwhelming numbers. Kutuzov suddenly felt very exposed. No news whatsoever had filtered through from the other Russian columns last heard of on the eastern border of Prussia, and now he found himself isolated, on what was the frontline, with perhaps a maximum 50,000 Russian and Austrian troops under his command. He did not require any further encouragement to abandon plans for a forward movement into Bavaria.

The news was rapidly relayed to Vienna, from where the kaiser, overcoming the shock and horror of the moment, wrote back immediately. He urged Kutuzov to 'avoid defeat, keep the troops intact and unharmed'. Furthermore, he should 'not enter battle with Napoleon, but hold him back every step of the way, allowing the Archdukes Charles and John and the corps from Russia to reach the theatre of war'.[1] Unimpressed, Kutuzov responded to the kaiser that if he was required to oppose every step of the enemy, then inevitably he would be drawn into a battle, which if it escalated, may result in defeat.

Kutuzov then began to make plans for the withdrawal of his army. Initially, he set his slow-moving wagons and artillery back down the Danube valley, giving them a chance to get ahead. He reformed his Russian troops in and around Braunau and prepared orders with Merveldt for Kienmayer to destroy the bridge over the Inn at Mühldorf on 24 October, and withdraw the following day through Braunau to occupy Salzburg with his 16,000 men, in order to protect the left flank of the army. Nostitz with his *grenz* infantry and 4. Hessen-Homburg-Husaren took a position at Passau, at the junction of the Inn and the Danube, to protect the right.

Back at Ulm, with the great drama of the surrender of the Austrian army complete, Napoleon quickly turned to more pressing matters: the defeat of the Russians. Right from the start, speed had been of the essence to defeat the leading Austrian force before support arrived from the Russians. Having disposed of those Austrians he now needed to bring the Russians to the battlefield before they, in turn, received reinforcements. But also the threat existed of intervention on his flanks from the Austrian army under Archduke Charles in Italy and that of Archduke John in Tirol, as well as the greatly enhanced possibility of Prussian involvement, since Bernadotte's march through Ansbach. Perhaps a more cautious commander would have hesitated from advancing against an enemy force of uncertain strength to his front, while the menace of vast forces massing against his flanks and rear threatened. But Napoleon was prepared to gamble on the reluctance of the Prussians to commit to war, while he dealt with the Russian threat that was both real and immediate.

With the ceremonies at Ulm concluded, Napoleon issued orders from his headquarters at Elchingen Abbey for the army to congregate on the line of the Iser by 25 October. As stipulated in Mack's capitulation, Maréchal Ney's corps was unable to take part in this realignment and remained at Ulm, relegated to the tedium of guarding the prisoners. On 22 October, Napoleon made his way to Augsburg, having selected this town as the major depot for the army. But before he departed an extraordinary opportunity arose to discover the strength and dispositions of the Allied forces opposing him on the Inn.

On 21 October GD Savary received a letter from Schulmeister. Keen to contribute more to the campaign, Schulmeister offered to infiltrate Russian army headquarters at Braunau, before heading for Vienna, in order to report back on affairs in the Austrian capital, where he claimed a police inspector and a secretary to the War Council amongst his contacts.[2] Napoleon, recognising the value of Schulmeister's offer, ordered Savary to make the necessary arrangements. Having received a large sum of money to aid his information gathering, Schulmeister left Augsburg at 1.00pm on 23 October on this new and challenging mission, still clutching the invaluable pass issued to him by Mack some days earlier.

The following day, at 6.00pm, Schulmeister arrived before the Austrian outposts at Mühldorf. He needed all his cunning and guile to pass, but on arriving in the town he searched out an old contact, Leutnant Rulzki, a hussar officer serving as an aide-de-camp to FML Kienmayer. With his generous expense budget, Schulmeister entertained Rulzki extravagantly that evening, and having stated that he had come from Ulm with important information, Rulzki freely advised Schulmeister on the state of Kienmayer's corps, as well as that of Kutuzov's Russians.

Early on the morning of 25 October, Rulzki escorted Schulmeister to Braunau, where he took him to Merveldt. Taken in by Schulmeister's convincing act, Merveldt considered him to be 'an advisor of complete

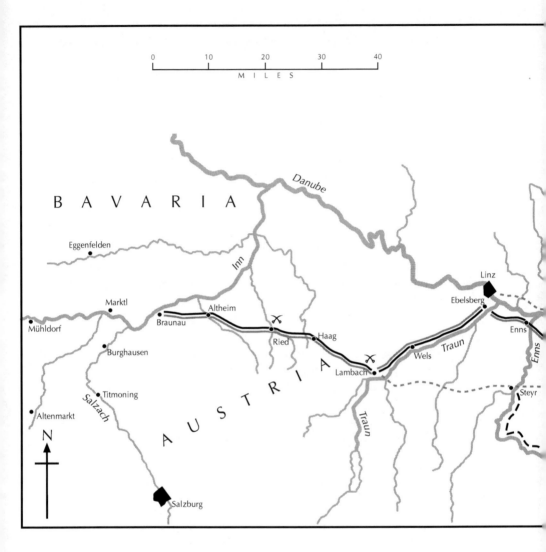

confidence' and listened attentively to the limited information he offered on French movements. He told of Napoleon entering Munich the previous day, and that the divisions of Suchet, Dumonceau and Soult, as well as the Garde Impériale, were about to join him there that day. The information was true, but hardly crucial to the outcome of the campaign. Merveldt forwarded the details to Vienna. In the meantime, the Austrian commander, totally convinced of Schulmeister's veracity, rewarded him with 100 ducats and issued him a new pass, expecting him to return shortly with more information. He never saw him again.

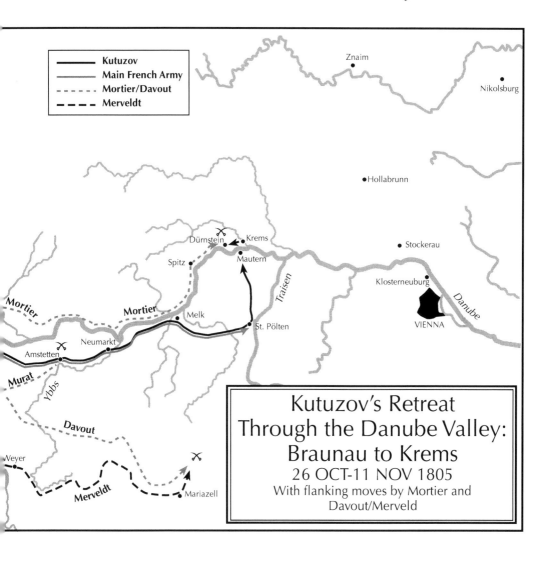

Kutuzov
Main French Army
Mortier/Davout
Merveldt

Znaim

Nikolsburg

Hollabrunn

Dürnstein · Krems

Spitz · Mautern

Stockerau

Traisen

Klosterneuburg

Danube

Mortier

Mortier · Melk

St. Pölten

VIENNA

Neumarkt

Amstetten

Murat

Ybbs

Davout

Weyer

Merveldt · Mariazell

Kutuzov's Retreat Through the Danube Valley: Braunau to Krems
26 OCT-11 NOV 1805
With flanking moves by Mortier and Davout/Merveld

Meanwhile, Schulmeister, donning the uniform of an Austrian officer, mingled amongst the Russian staff officers and learned that Kutuzov would fall back from Braunau and not fight until he received reinforcements. By 3.00pm on 25 October, Schulmeister began his return journey through the Russian and Austrian lines, armed with his new pass. He observed the outlying Russian soldiers pulling back towards Braunau and saw Kienmayer's entire command retiring on the town from their advanced positions at Mühldorf. With the bridge over the Inn at Mühldorf now destroyed, he took a detour back through Landshut, where he stayed that evening before arriving in Munich on 26 October. There, after his round trip of approximately 230 miles, Schulmeister immediately presented a written report to Savary. Besides the movements and strength of the Allied formations, he added much detail describing the appearance and bearing of the troops he encountered, as well as impressions of their uniforms, arms and equipment, the condition of their horses, and their knowledge of the current situation on other fronts. All in all, it was a most complete report.[3]

While Schulmeister gathered his information, Napoleon finally entered Munich on 24 October, as his army assembled along the Iser, preparing for the next phase of the campaign. The city welcomed Napoleon as the liberator of Bavaria and his appearance ushered in celebrations that continued for three days. Then, on 26 October, he launched La Grande Armée over the Iser in three great columns, determined to catch and defeat Kutuzov's army before it received reinforcements.

The news of the capitulation of Ulm changed the nature of the campaign in Italy too. Archduke Charles had already expressed his doubts as to Mack's strategy – doubts he voiced loudly to the kaiser – and as a result, received approval from Vienna on 5 October to delay his own offensive in northern Italy until the outcome in Bavaria became clear. Shortly after his arrival at the front, Charles concluded an armistice with the French commander, the bold and tenacious Maréchal Masséna, while both sides awaited news. The armistice stipulated that six days' notice be given by either side before a resumption of hostilities. On 11 October, Masséna gave that notice, having received notification of the arrival of the main French army on the Rhine. In the early hours of 17 October he launched an attack across the Adige river that separated the two armies. His attack met with success, allowing him to establish a bridgehead across the river, but he then waited for further news from Bavaria before making his next move. Charles used this lull to gradually withdraw his men to a strong fortified position at Caldiero, a few miles east of the Adige.

On 24 October, news of Mack's surrender reached Charles and he informed Vienna that it was his intention to fight a battle at Caldiero. He hoped that by inflicting significant casualties on Masséna, it would deter the French commander from a rapid pursuit, enabling him to fall back to the Danube valley to aid in the defence of Vienna. Masséna only received the news of Ulm on the evening of 28 October and the following morning he launched his attack against Charles's army. Three days of ferocious fighting followed, as Masséna attempted unsuccessfully to break through the Austrian position, and on 31 October, with casualties mounting, he broke off and pulled back.

Charles considered this the appropriate moment to commence his retreat, and so in the early hours of 1 November, he abandoned the Caldiero position, leaving only a small rearguard to disguise his move. It did not take Masséna long to discover the ruse and by 2 November his leading troops were harassing Charles's rearguard as they, too, fell back.

For the next few days Charles and Masséna both handled their respective commands with great skill, but having crossed the Piave river on 5 November, Charles finally broke free. The French commander continued to pursue Charles at a distance until reaching the Isonzo river on 16 November. Having been without any news from the main army for many days, Masséna decided to halt until he was able to establish communications once more. Mindful of the need to concentrate his forces, Archduke Charles issued an order for his brother, Archduke John, to abandon Tirol and to join him in the defence of Vienna. It took over three weeks before the imperial brothers were reunited, and by then the campaign had taken another dramatic turn.

Away to the north, Archduke Ferdinand, having broken out of Ulm, reached safety on the Bohemian border at Eger on 21 October. He continued eastwards towards Pilsen and began to draw together detachments into a new reserve formation. With this concentration underway, he departed for Vienna to inform the kaiser personally of the disaster at Ulm. He arrived in the city on 28 October, a day after Mack, who was forbidden to enter Vienna. Mack remained at a village on the outskirts, where he gave his full account of the entire campaign to officers sent by the kaiser. From there he was escorted to 'some place, which he was at liberty to choose of in the vicinity of Brünn, there to await the [kaiser's] further orders'.[4]

Well received by the kaiser, Ferdinand lost no time in heaping all the blame for the loss of the army at Ulm on Mack's shoulders. Sir Arthur Paget reported that he accused Mack of 'ignorance, of madness, of cowardice, and of treachery', claiming amongst other things that Mack gave information to the enemy of the route he had taken in his retreat.[5] Paget concluded that: 'It is in short impossible that a greater degree of rancour and animosity can exist than that between General Mack and his antagonists.' Reviewing Mack's defence, Paget summarised that the Austrian commander firmly laid the blame at the feet of Ferdinand 'and the rest of the general officers, to whose ill will and opposition he openly attributes his calamities which have happened … he contends that his determination was never to surrender, and that he was driven to that extreme by the protestations of the army against any further resistance.'

The kaiser, perhaps overwhelmed by the vehemence of the accusations, reproached Ferdinand for not having placed Mack under arrest, causing the archduke to remind him 'of the full powers he had invested in the general, and the [kaiser] acknowledged the fault he had committed'. But a scapegoat was required and it would not be coming from the imperial family. Mack was committed to appear before a court martial. Ferdinand remained in Vienna for just two days before returning to Bohemia to complete the formation of his new reserve corps.[6]

As the Archdukes Charles, John and Ferdinand, fell back to positions from where they hoped to play an important part in the second phase of the campaign. Kutuzov, at Braunau, still waited with growing concern for news of Russian support. When he left Russian territory on 25 August the other two main columns were advancing towards the Russian–Prussian border with the intention of intimidating the Prussians to allow their passage through Prussia. Britain and Austria agreed that if Prussia opposed such a move then Russia should enter aggressively. When Tsar Alexander joined his men on the Prussian border on 27 September the Russian columns still waited on a final decision, as King Frederick William vehemently maintained his neutrality in the face of Russian threats.

In fact, the Prussian monarch was becoming concerned – with justification – by Russia's glances toward the former Polish lands now encompassed as Southern Prussia. He knew that the tsar's deputy minister for foreign affairs, the Polish prince, Adam Czartoryski, held much influence over Alexander, and indeed, Czartoryski had encouraged Alexander to believe that if he marched on Warsaw, the Polish nobles would rise under the Russian banner against Prussia. At one point, the tsar confirmed to Czartoryski that he intended following this plan, but later wavered and finally abandoned it, much to the disappointment of the deputy minister.

Alexander sent his aide, Prince Peter Dolgorukov – a staunch opponent of Czartoryski's Polish plan – to Berlin, to make one final attempt at convincing Frederick William to side with the Allies, or at least open his frontier to the passage of Russian troops. Dolgorukov's efforts failed to sway the Prussian monarch and he had set out on his journey back to Alexander at Pulawy, when a messenger from the king overtook him and recalled him to Berlin. Suddenly everything changed. The news – just received – that French forces had boldly marched through the Prussian territory of Ansbach without any diplomatic communication incensed Frederick William. On the very day that Czartoryski informed the Russian ambassador to Vienna, 'His Majesty is firmly decided to start war against Prussia',[7] Dolgorukov sped off with the momentous news that Prussia now granted Russian troops permission to march through her lands to pursue the war against Napoleon.

By the time Dolgorukov reached the tsar, he had already moved to military headquarters, but delighted by the news, he immediately shelved his aggressive plans against Prussia. Frederick William requested a secret meeting with the tsar, but Alexander, determined to show all Europe that Prussia had fallen in with the Allies, insisted on travelling the 400 miles to Potsdam. He set off on 21 October, arriving four days later. Only then did discussions for Prussian involvement in the plans of the Third Coalition take place. But by then Ulm had fallen and Kutuzov looked on in vain for reinforcements that were many, many miles away. He was alone, isolated, and clearly Napoleon's next target.

On 26 October, the day he received Schulmeister's extensive report of the Allied position at Braunau, Napoleon set La Grande Armée in motion once more. He planned a three-pronged attack on the Inn river, with supporting flanking movements. The left of the main attack saw Lannes' V Corps advancing from Landshut, via Eggenfeld, on Braunau; while in the centre, with Murat acting as an advance guard, Soult, Davout and the Garde Impériale marched on Mühldorf. Bernadotte, the Bavarians and Marmont, forming a broad front on the right, moved towards Salzburg. Elsewhere, Ney's VI Corps, which had experienced so much of the fighting around Ulm, was broken up. While Ney headed south towards Tirol with a division and a half of infantry, the other half division and Ney's cavalry remained behind to guard the Ulm prisoner haul. At the same time, Dupont's division joined that of Dumonceau, detached from Marmont's II Corps, marching along the Danube towards Passau, protecting the left of La Grande Armée. Further to the rear, Augereau with VII Corps, having reached the Rhine after his long march from Brest, received orders to occupy Kempten and observe Vorarlberg in conjunction with Ney's wider operations in Tirol. By these moves Napoleon hoped to prevent any threat to the flank or rear of the army by Archduke John.

Presuming that Kutuzov would defend the lower reaches of the Inn, Napoleon intended that the right, led by Bernadotte, would cut across the headwaters of the Salzach river, a tributary of the Inn, and turn the Allied left flank. Advancing towards the Inn, Bernadotte, with I Corps and the Bavarians, repaired the bridges at Wasserburg and Rosenheim, crossed the river on 28 October and entered Salzburg two days later. Marmont headed for the bridge at Tittmoning, between Salzburg and Burghausen. On the evening of 26 October, Davout began to repair the bridge at Mühldorf while Murat waited at Ampfing. The following day Murat sent a brigade over the restored bridge, scattered the few remaining defenders and enabled repairs to be carried out on the bridges at Neuötting and Marktl. Davout's light cavalry then crossed the Inn on 28 October and prepared the way for Davout, Murat and Soult to lead their commands across the Salzach river at Burghausen, about 13 miles upstream of Braunau. On the left, Lannes' corps experienced least difficulties. He reached the Inn opposite Braunau unopposed on the same day that the centre column reached Burghausen, but found the Russians had broken the bridge over the river. With the walls of the town appearing undefended, he sent two detachments of infantry across in boats, whereupon the citizens of Braunau opened the gates to him. Inside, he discovered large quantities of military equipment, food and clothing: but no Russians.

Unable and unwilling to defend the position, and aware that the French were approaching the upper reaches of the Inn, Kutuzov ordered the withdrawal of his army on 26 October.

Having taken his leave from Munich, Napoleon arrived in Braunau with the Garde Impériale on the evening of 29 October, by which time Davout, Soult and Murat were reforming some 10 miles beyond Braunau, centred on Altheim, with Lannes moving north to Schärding.

The route back down the Danube valley offered Kutuzov a number of defensive positions. South of the river the valley extended for about 65 miles on the Braunau line before reaching the mountainous northern spurs of Tirol, but it gradually narrowed and at Enns was reduced to a width of around 35 miles. A number of rivers flowed across the valley from the mountains to the Danube: the Traun, Enns, Ypps and Traisen. Each could be defended and utilised to delay the French pursuit. Kutuzov's initial plan was to fall back 40 miles to Lambach on the Traun. Nostitz's Austrian detachment at Passau received orders to fall back on Linz, while Kienmayer's command at Salzburg was to draw back also, keeping aligned with Kutuzov. Then, protected by a rearguard commanded by General Maior Prince Peter Bagration and supported by a reserve, under General Leitenant Mikhail Miloradovich, Kutuzov set out for Lambach, which he reached on 29 October, assembling his headquarters at Wels. Here Kaiser Francis and a group of high-ranking Austrian officers joined him.

The rapid turn of events had taken their toll on Francis: one officer thought 'he was pale, emaciated, and his eyes were vacant.'[8] Kutuzov now proposed Vienna be abandoned to the French. Once freed of this responsibility, he proposed a stout defence of the line of the Enns until such time that he retreated over the Danube at Krems. Here he could reform the Allied army in safety, await reinforcements and prepare for a new campaign. Concerned by this desire to abandon Vienna, Francis offered a compromise, announcing that he was prepared to forsake his city to the French if necessary. However, if Kutuzov held the line of the Enns for as long as possible, before falling back to fortified positions under construction at Mautern, protecting the Krems bridge, the kaiser hoped Kutuzov could remain south of the Danube. From here, Francis felt he could engage Napoleon until reinforced by the arrival of Buxhöwden's Russian army as well as those of the Archdukes Charles and John. With the meeting over and the matter left in Kutuzov's hands, a despondent Francis prepared to return to Vienna to contemplate the fate of the imperial capital, his ears ringing from the bitter complaints of the local population against Russian excesses.

Those civilians living in the Danube valley were suffering greatly from the passage of these great armies through their locality. The town of Ried, some 25 miles east of Braunau, nervously awaited the return of the Russians. On 25 October one of the inhabitants wrote:

'The enemy is arriving in our neighbourhood. It is thought that the Russians will stop them, but I no longer rely upon them; I am packing up my goods; I wish to God I had done so before these savage men arrived…They have plundered everything…They have, however, been driven from Braunau, and they are now coming, to the number of 30,000 … They can do no more harm to this unhappy country, except to burn the houses, for no inhabitants remain."[9]

It was at Mehrnbach (a village just outside Ried) that the first of the rearguard actions took place. Although the responsibility for leading the advance fell to Murat and his cavalry, he was not the first agent of France into Austrian lands. That honour lay with Charles Schulmeister.

Having handed over his report of the situation to Savary at Allied headquarters in Munich on 26 October, Schulmeister set out again the following morning. In the guise of a German jeweller, with his colleague, Jean Rippmann de Kork, who had been with him in Ulm, he took the road to Vienna on the second part of his mission. He travelled first to Linz, avoiding the main concentration of the French army near Braunau. Here he met a man by the name of Joseph von Rueff, head of the tobacco bureau at Braunau – a customs officer – who Schulmeister may have known previously from his former smuggling escapades. Schulmeister, mistaking von Rueff's loyalties, offered him a sum of money to join them on their mission, which he saw fit to accept.

The three men travelled to Amstetten, where they spent the night. On the morning of 29 October Schulmeister handed a report to Rippmann instructing him to remain until the French arrived and then to hand the report to Murat. While these arrangements were being finalised, von Rueff slipped away and reported his colleagues as spies to the Russian commander in the town. This officer instructed von Rueff to continue his journey with Schulmeister, keeping him under close observation, and had Rippmann arrested as soon as the two men left town. The following day, in Kemmelbach, a village close to Melk, word reached Schulmeister of Rippmann's arrest, but before he could depart von Rueff alerted the authorities, who seized him and placed him under arrest. Despite presenting his pass and claiming he worked for FML Merveldt, Schulmeister found himself behind bars, where Rippmann joined him on 31 October.

Transported to Vienna the following day, the two spies suffered three days of intense questioning before they were transferred to the secure fortress of Königsgrätz for further interrogation. Notwithstanding the importance of these prisoners, the guard escort consisted only of a senior NCO and three men, who appeared less than pleased with their task. Only a day into their journey the escort grew tired of their charges and after giving them a thorough beating, left them for dead by the side of the road on a freezing night. Incredibly, both men survived and decided to separate. Schulmeister, with his clothes in tatters and his body wracked with pain, disappeared into the night. Rippmann, however, was made of less sturdy material and although quickly recaptured, died shortly after in hospital. But for Schulmeister the campaign was not yet over.[10]

Murat began his advance on 30 October with a note of caution from Napoleon. The Austrians were old enemies, but he had never crossed swords with the Russians. The emperor advised: 'The Russians are not yet broken; they know how to attack.' At Mehrnbach, the French cavalry encountered an Austrian hussar regiment, part of a detachment commanded by Generalmajor Schustekh, attached to Bagration's rearguard. The 1er Chasseurs à cheval attacked these hussars, who fell back before them for about 10 miles to Haag, where they turned and checked the pursuit. It was only when Murat sent forward Beaumont's dragoon division in support that the Austrians fell back again. However, by then the hussars were receiving supporting musketry fire from wooded hills close to the road, which allowed the Austrians to pull clear.

The French cavalry resumed their advance in the morning and encountered four Austrian battalions, another part of Schustekh's detachment, as they approached Lambach. Pinned by 1er Chasseurs à cheval and 7ème Hussards, the three battalions of 9. Peterwardein Grenzer and a battalion of IR60 Gyulai defended themselves while FML Merveldt, alerted to the problem, sent to Bagration for help. At the same time, the French cavalry called for support, which saw GD Bisson's division of Davout's corps rushing forward. Bagration was at Lambach with the rest of the Allied rearguard, supervising the destruction of the bridge over the Traun and responded rapidly to the call for help, sending forward a squadron of the Pavlograd Hussars, six infantry battalions (the 6. and 8. Jäger Regiments) and an artillery company. The battle flowed backwards and forwards for about five hours between the two evenly matched sides, until eventually, a French cavalry charge broke Allied resistance and the rearguard, under pressure, fell back across the Traun, completing the destruction of the bridge behind them.[11]

On 1 November, while Kutuzov's army fell back towards the line of the Enns, where he intended making a stand, the French established themselves on the Traun. Napoleon ordered Davout to form his corps at Lambach and sent a small advance guard to scout the road towards Steyr, on the upper reaches of the Enns. Soult marched north to Wels while Murat extended down the Traun towards the Danube to repair the bridges. Lannes was to march on Linz and occupy the city while Marmont marched on Lambach. Bernadotte received orders to leave Salzburg and march with his corps and Generalleutnant Wrede's Bavarian division for the Traun, while the other Bavarian division, commanded by Generalleutnant Deroy, was to cooperate with Ney in Tirol.

As the Allies fell back on the Enns, Kutuzov authorised a slight restructuring of his command. He retained direct command over Nostitz' small brigade that had just disrupted the bridge over the Danube at Linz and retired on Enns, but the rest of the Austrian troops now marched towards Steyr under Merveldt's overall command to hold the southern extreme of the line. Bagration continued to lead the Russian rearguard. He was a fine rearguard commander and carried out his task with determination. Pursued all the way by Murat, the two forces arrived at the bridge at Enns almost simultaneously. A detachment of the Pavlograd Hussars, commanded by Podpolkovnik Joseph O'Rourke, an officer of Irish descent, was the last to cross. Then, under a hail of canister and directed by O'Rourke, these men set alight the incendiary material placed on the bridge and completed its destruction. The two sides continued to exchange fire across the river for the remaining daylight hours of 3 November. During the day, while Bagration delayed the French advance, Kutuzov ordered fieldworks constructed along the river for the defence of the line of the Enns.

While Kutuzov prepared his defensive line, 300 miles away to the north, Tsar Alexander embraced King Frederick William of Prussia over the tomb of Frederick The Great, each swearing an oath of eternal friendship and thus sealing the Treaty of Potsdam. But at a time when urgent action was required the treaty failed to deliver. Prussia virtually demanded the breaking up of the new Kingdom of Italy by seeking territorial indemnities for the king of Sardinia, who had lost lands to Napoleon, and a drawing of the Austrian boundary in Italy on the Mincio. In addition, Prussia called for the independence of Naples, Holland, the German states and Switzerland. Napoleon would never agree to the terms, but Prussia offered mediation between the warring nations and threatened, if refused, to join the Allies. Without consultation with Britain, the tsar offered Prussia and her Saxon allies the same British financial subsidies as granted to Russia and Austria and also – extraordinarily – pledged to use his influence to gain Hanover for Prussia.

Having decided upon a period of one month for France's response to these terms, the responsibility for delivering them to Napoleon fell to the Prussian foreign minister, Count Haugwitz. But having argued that the army would not be ready to move until mid-December, he delayed his departure for another ten days, with the king's approval, leaving Napoleon untroubled by Prussian threats. On 5 November Alexander left Potsdam to rejoin the army, but decided first on a detour to visit his sister, who had married the crown prince of Saxe-Weimar. He finally ended his leisurely family visit on 13 November. The following day Haugwitz finally set out to complete his mission. By then Napoleon was already settling into the imperial capital of Vienna.

In Vienna anxiety began to manifest itself in a population starved of official information: since the war took a turn for the worse, official sanctions suppressed the newspapers. Sir Arthur Paget wrote to London expressing this unease:

> 'The consternation which prevails here is at the highest pitch, and although I am far from supposing that it would have been an easy task to calm the public mind at a moment like the present, I cannot help thinking from the facts which have come within my observation that the conduct of the Government is of a nature to augment rather than diminish the dismay which has become so general.
>
> 'There is in truth too much reason for this dismay. The culpable pains which are taken to keep the public in the dark with respect to the situation of affairs, naturally increases the alarm...The emperor instead of shewing himself at Vienna is living at a miserable country house, in order as the people say that he may be enabled to effectuate his escape with greater facility.'[12]

Despite the lack of information, it was clear to the ordinary citizens of Vienna that the war was not going well. This became even more obvious when many found themselves pressed into service for the defence of their city. At the end of October one man wrote:

> 'The aspect of affairs is very melancholy ... for all the citizens are obliged to mount guard. All foreigners are ordered to quit Vienna in eight days, and the Hereditary States in ten days. No carriage can quit Vienna without a passport from the Police. All inhabitants are called out for the defence of the country. In a word it seems as if the enemy were close to us. No young men were seen in the streets for fear of being taken by soldiers. Every one is taken who is capable of carrying arms.'[13]

Paget, commenting on the raising of this levy, reported that the city required 7,000 men and strove to achieve this number 'with a degree of severity perfectly unexampled'. Yet these citizens were not just afraid of the arrival of a victorious French army in their midst. As Paget related: 'The greatest apprehension begins to prevail on account of the Russians of whose excesses loud complaints are beginning to be made. Their arrival here is as much dreaded as that of the French.' A typical story that aroused these fears came from Enns:

> 'We are constantly shut up – we dare not appear at our doors or windows. By adapting this precaution, we have hitherto escaped bad treatment; but alas! we see what our neighbours suffer. The order of

the Regency is, to give each Russian 1 pound and a half a day of meat, 4 pounds of bread, twelve potatoes, and a jug of beer. They have no sooner dined than they want supper; as soon as they have that they call for their next day's breakfast; and as soon as they are satisfied, they beat their unfortunate hosts. Some poor families have twenty, and some as many as eighty to lodge.'[14]

While fear and confusion spread, urgent efforts to pack up and evacuate the state archives continued unabated, yet the vast military resources of the Vienna arsenal remained untouched and were left for the French. Paget, dryly questioning the Austrian government's priorities, informed London that amongst the papers removed were 'those even of the Chancery of Bohemia, which no Frenchmen or foreigner that ever existed would give himself the trouble to read a line'.

On 4 November the kaiser called a council of war: the city's defences were in a poor condition and there were questions over the mood of the population. As recently as July, social unrest broke out in what became known as the 'Baker Riots', when dissatisfied civilians protested against increases in the price of bread, an insurrection only brought to a halt by the intervention of the military, resulting in 10 dead and 100 wounded.

Therefore, to preserve the city intact, the imperial family, government and garrison evacuated, making no attempt at defence. While the kaiser arranged his departure for 7 November and planned to move to Olmütz, where he hoped to meet with Tsar Alexander, his family set off almost immediately for Buda in Hungary. The government gave no public notice of the departure of the kaiser, adding to the 'considerable degree of discontent' apparent in the city.[15] Before he left, Francis despatched FML Gyulai (taken captive at Ulm but subsequently released as part of an exchange for French prisoners) to Napoleon with a proposal for an armistice. This meeting took place in Linz on 8 November and resulted in Napoleon presenting Gyulai with an ultimatum: break the alliance with Russia and hand over Venice and Tirol to France – only then could talks commence. Overwhelmed by these demands and in no position to accept them, Gyulai returned swiftly, adding further to the kaiser's gloom and uncertainty, and heralding in a period of shuffle diplomacy, as Gyulai constantly moved backwards and forwards between the two camps.

In this unsettled state of affairs Paget bemoaned what appeared to be a total breakdown in the Austrian intelligence network. Until his capture, Schulmeister offered the French command a flow of detailed information during the operations around Ulm and then again during the advance on Braunau, but the situation was very different in Vienna. On 1 November Paget informed London that in his opinion: 'It is not possible to be more ignorant of the movements of the enemy than this Government is ... as to any detail whatever, I am persuaded that nothing is known here or at headquarters.' Seven days later he lamented further: 'I still observe that the ignorance here and as I am informed at headquarters respecting the movement of the enemy is beyond all credibility. They have not such a thing as a spy belonging to them.'[16]

Against this background of confusion in Vienna, 90 miles to his rear, Kutuzov prepared to honour his pledge to Francis and hold the line of the Enns river for as long as possible, gaining time for the intervention of General Buxhöwden and Archdukes Charles and John. But as the wet and windy weather of October turned into the icy blasts and snow of November, rapidly changing circumstances saw this resolve quickly melt away.

Chapter 10
'A Day of Slaughter'*

The confusion prevailing in Vienna during the first days of November soon affected those elements of the Austrian army still engaged at the front. Since the capitulation at Ulm, Vienna had confirmed Kutuzov's position as overall military commander, but FML Merveldt, now the senior Austrian commander in the field, still received direct orders from Vienna, as well as those from the Russian commander-in-chief.

The Allies began falling back from their positions on the Traun river on 1 November to the new line on the Enns, where a determined defence was to take place. On 4 November Kutuzov concentrated his Russian troops on the Enns, centred on the town of the same name, near to its junction with the Danube. FML Merveldt was occupying Steyr, 15 miles upstream, having detached Kienmayer with thirty-six cavalry squadrons about midway between the two towns. Work immediately began on the construction of fieldworks as the Allies awaited the French onslaught. On 4 November, and again on the following day, Francis wrote to Kutuzov, urging him to make a resolute defence. He concluded: 'I put too much confidence in your intelligence to enter into details on the importance I place, initially, to the defence of the right bank of the Enns, then, that of a slow retreat to Krems and finally to the conservation of the bridgehead in front of that place.'[1]

While Kutuzov deployed his army on the Enns, Napoleon established his headquarters at Linz, from where he ordered his army forward. Murat, with the cavalry, followed by Davout with III Corps, kept up the pursuit of the Allies towards Steyr, where Merveldt, defending the crossing, was in receipt of a stream of confusing and contradictory instructions from Vienna. Then, as the French began closing on the river, Merveldt received an order to take his force of 6,000 men and march away from Steyr. These orders sent him into the Styrian Mountains via Weyer, Mariazell and Bruck an der Mur to Graz, where he was to make contact with Archduke Charles, marching from Italy.[2] Having

---

Report of the Battle of Dürnstein, 22nd Bulletin of La Grande Armée, St Pölten, 13 November 1805.

received a direct order, Merveldt abandoned the town and began to move away, leaving Kienmayer to support the Russians. By the time countermanding orders arrived, compelling him to remain with Kutuzov, it was too late. As soon as the Russian general learnt that his left flank was completely open he ordered the army back from the line of the Enns. Kutuzov later wrote: 'All the weak points of the river were defended, and I hoped to be able to hold this position for a long time; but soon, the corps placed at Steyr being forced to give up this station, I found it necessary to abandon the Enns and march on Amstetten.'[3] The resolute defence of the river lasted barely a day.

Murat, now unopposed at Steyr, swiftly repaired the bridge over the river and the following day, at the head of two brigades of light cavalry, followed by Oudinot's Reserve Grenadiers from Lannes' corps, he once more set off in pursuit. Their route led them towards Amstetten, where the roads from Steyr and Enns merged to form the main road through the narrowing Danube valley towards Vienna. Elsewhere, Soult and Lannes continued their march as soon as they had crossed the Enns, while Bernadotte marched to rejoin the army. Marmont received orders redirecting him south towards Styria to watch for Archduke Charles, and Davout, at the head of III Corps, set out for Vienna on a more mountainous southerly route than Murat's, to ease pressure on the overburdened road capacity in the valley. Unfortunately for the Austrians this route directed him on a collision course with Merveldt's detachment.

The road between the Enns and Amstetten extends for about 18 miles, presenting few opportunities for strong rearguard positions, with part of the route running through extensive pine forest. However, between Strenberg and Amstetten, the road emerged from the forest into a large clearing, now carpeted with a layer of fresh snow. While the main Russian army continued its retreat, Prince Bagration formed his rearguard here for battle, strengthened by an Austrian force of four battalions of *grenz* infantry and three regiments of cavalry. These men formed the front line with a Russian horse artillery battery and the Pavlograd Hussars, while behind them Bagration arranged his Russian infantry: three battalions each of the Kiev Grenadiers, Azov Musketeers and 6. Jäger.

Murat, riding at the head of the pursuing force, harried a small fleeing cavalry rearguard through the winter landscape. Emerging from the confines of the forest into the clearing and observing the Allies drawn up before him, Murat did not hesitate from recklessly launching an immediate attack with only his escort squadron. Seeing such a tempting target, the Allied cavalry counter-charged and within moments Murat and his men were tumbling back in retreat. An aide-de-camp of Maréchal Berthier, Capitaine Lejeune, who was riding with Murat, described the dramatic events that followed:

'The enemy overtook us, their ranks mingled with our rearguard, our men were swept down, many were taken prisoners, and we ourselves were in danger of being captured. Murat's horse was killed under him, mine fell in the confused rush down the steep path, and I was flung off.'[4]

Lejeune only saved himself by diving behind two artillery pieces, which the officer in command was double-loading with canister. As the cavalry mêlée swirled around in front of the guns, a gunner shouted a word of warning seconds before the gun spewed forth its massive charge. The shock waves brought the snow crashing down from the trees all around and the shot caused a great number of casualties amongst the Allied cavalry. As they turned and rode away in confusion, 'great death-dealing icicles, falling from a height of more than a hundred feet, crashed upon the helmets of the fugitives with a resounding noise.'[5]

More French troops rushed forward and the encounter quickly developed into a fierce battle, but in the face of repeated attacks the Allies held their ground. Kutuzov personally witnessed the clash, and fearing the outcome, ordered Miloradovich forward with the reserve, exhorting them to 'Act as befits Russians.'[6] In fact, they arrived just as Bagration began to retire. Miloradovich fed his four infantry regiments into the battle, supported by the Mariupol Hussars. The bitter struggle continued, swinging one way and then the other. Murat tried an attack on the Russian right but was driven back: he launched another against the left but was similarly repulsed. The Russians then threw forward the grenadier battalions of the Apsheron and Smolensk Musketeers against Oudinot's grenadiers. Miloradovich ordered them not to fire: instead he urged them to remember how Suvorov taught them to use their bayonets in Italy.[7] The Russian attack forced Oudinot's men back, but fighting continued with no quarter given until both sides were exhausted. For many French troops this level of ferocity was a new experience. An officer wrote:

'In this moment where the French infantry and Russian infantry approached corps to corps, Oudinot's grenadiers showed the greatest intrepidity, the Russians a wild courage: wounded, mutilated, they fought with fury, even when we had disarmed them; these same prisoners attacked their escort.'[8]

After some five hours of relentless fighting, which carried on into the night, the exhausted French gave ground and fell back, taking their prisoners with them. Miloradovich, having achieved his aim of delaying Murat's pursuit, did not linger on the battlefield any longer than necessary. He began to retreat once more, through Amstetten and across the Ypps river on the trail of the main army, heading towards Melk. Both sides claimed victory as silence once more descended on the forest clearing: its carpet of snow now stained red with the blood of the fallen.

The determination of the Russian rearguard made a deep impression on Napoleon and convinced him that they would soon stand against him in a major battle. Studying the map it appeared the most likely spot for such a confrontation would be at St Pölten on the Traisen river, the last defensive position of any strength on the road to Vienna. To add to Kutuzov's difficulties, Napoleon created a new provisional corps. With this formation he hoped to threaten Allied communications with Moravia by blocking the strategically important bridge over the Danube near Krems, and to delay any reinforcements heading towards Kutuzov from north of the river. This ad hoc corps, commanded by Maréchal Mortier, was created by drawing in the divisions of Dupont (VI Corps) and Dumonceau (II Corps), which, separated from their own corps after Ulm, had marched down the Danube via Passau to Linz. To these Napoleon added Gazan's division from V Corps and the 4ème Dragons, and on 6 November they crossed the Danube at Linz.

Mortier's orders were to march along the north bank of the river, in conjunction with Lannes' advance on the south bank, but keeping to his rear. He was to keep a watchful eye on Bohemia to the north, where Archduke Ferdinand had escaped after Ulm and where any possible Prussian intervention may appear, and push cavalry patrols far ahead to search for signs of the enemy. A large flotilla of boats of all sizes was authorised to maintain communications between Mortier and Lannes across the Danube. Yet there were flaws in this plan. At Linz, Napoleon was already some distance behind Murat and the leading elements of Lannes' corps – on 6 November the distance was close to 40 miles – and communication was suffering.

As Mortier led his men across the Danube on 6 November, Murat and Lannes, having recovered overnight from their fierce encounter at Amstetten, tentatively pushed forward again. Expecting at any moment to run into another determined rearguard, they were puzzled to find an empty landscape. They increased their pace for the rest of the day, and the following day too, through the eerily deserted countryside without finding any trace of the Allies. It was as though the Russians and Austrians had vanished. North of the Danube, in an effort to keep up with these two rapidly moving corps, Mortier pushed Gazan's division ahead, leaving the others to come on as best they could along the single narrow road which hugged the north bank of the river.

Elsewhere, the French pursuers were more successful. Davout's corps soon encountered FML Merveldt's Austrian detachment. While Merveldt's route towards Styria took him on higher tracks forcing his men to struggle through deep snow, Davout's corps advanced on a lower roadway where he was able to make up ground before turning towards Mariazell. On 6 November he caught up with a part of the Austrian baggage train trailing behind the infantry. His men joyously raided the wagons, discovering in them, amongst other items, a very welcome supply of sky blue Hungarian infantry trousers, ankle boots, linen drawers and greatcoats: a great boon in the icy weather.

Desperate to escape from their relentless pursuers, grenadiers from IR4 Deutschmeister attached themselves to the artillery harnesses to help pull the cannon through. But on 8 November Davout closed to striking distance and at Mariazell the luckless Merveldt was soundly beaten, escaping with only about 2,000 men through the mountains towards Graz and reaching Geisdorf on 11 November. From there he retired with his dispirited men into Hungary, arriving at Raab, some 70 miles south-east of Vienna, eight days later.

The fruitless search by Murat and Lannes for the retreating Allied army finally came to an end on the same day that Davout won his victory at Mariazell. After two days' exhausting pursuit they came upon the army drawn up in battle order at St Pölten, just as Napoleon had anticipated. Unwilling to tackle such a large formation, Murat despatched the news back to Napoleon, who was still at Linz, now some 70 miles to the rear, urging him to come forward.

Napoleon left Linz on 9 November, already conceiving a plan to surround Kutuzov. However, the Russian commander, alerted to the approach of a French formation along the north bank of the river, had no intention of allowing Napoleon to corner him in such an unfavourable position and prepared to move away from St Pölten at once. He sent officers back to inspect the fortifications protecting the bridge over the Danube near Krems, but, despite the assurances of Kaiser Francis, the work had made little progress. In light of this Kutuzov considered his only choice of action was to abandon St Pölten, and by definition Vienna too, cross to the north bank of the Danube and destroy the bridge behind him. This important bridge was the last crossing point before Vienna, and once safely across he knew he would gain the time he desperately needed to reorganise his exhausted troops and await reinforcements from Russia.

The kaiser still clung to the hope that Kutuzov could be persuaded to protect Vienna, and to this end sent FML Heinrich von Schmitt to headquarters, where he arrived on 6 November. Schmitt bore a letter of introduction from the kaiser, personally recommending his appointment as chief of staff, a function Kutuzov had fulfilled himself since becoming commander of the army shortly after Ulm. Part of Schmitt's mission was to induce Kutuzov to fight a battle before Vienna, but in this he failed. Kutuzov wrote to the kaiser to justify his decision. He informed Francis that the French were approaching his rear and intending to trap him against the Danube and then cleverly went on to explain that in fact he was following the kaiser's original orders to the letter:

> 'I dare to assure you, Your Majesty, that in the full sense of the word I was disputing every single step of the enemy. Bloody battles of the rear guard serve as proof of this. However, I could not have held Napoleon any longer without entering a fully-fledged battle, which would be against the orders given to me by Your Majesty.'[9]

And so, during the night of 8–9 November, Kutuzov fell back towards the Danube. Kienmayer remained before St Pölten with his cavalry, screening the position from the French, with orders to retire on Vienna when pressed. It was not until the evening of the 9 November that Murat recognised the true role of Kienmayer's cavalry. Then, with the last of Kutuzov's men safely over the river and the bridge already burning, the Austrians melted away and fell back to Vienna, 35 miles to the east. Here they joined a force hastily assembling outside the city preparing to defend the massive Tabor bridge over the Danube.

Blinded by the illusionary prize of the Austrian capital, Murat spurred his cavalry forward on the morning of 10 November, urging Lannes and Soult to follow him with all speed. But it is possible that Murat failed to realise Kutuzov had crossed the Danube, and thought him still retiring on Vienna: certainly Napoleon did not expect this move, which would leave Vienna undefended.

Because of the great distances involved, it was not until the night of 10–11 November that the emperor learnt of this turn of events, while at his new headquarters at Melk Abbey. It was a setback to his plans. He realised now that there was no quick end in sight and the Allies would gain time to draw in reinforcements. And this news came on the same day that he was digesting details of the defeat of Franco-Spanish navy at Trafalgar. Seething with anger, he lashed out at Murat. At 3.30am he despatched a peremptory message, calling on him to halt his advance on Vienna and criticising him for not seeking new orders when the Russians passed over the Danube and for rushing on Vienna without knowing the emperor's wishes. He ended with the rebuke: 'You were ordered to pursue the Russians with your sword in their ribs. It is a curious way of pursuing them to move away from them by forced marches.'[10] The order reached Murat just 6 miles from the city. Of the rest of the army, Lannes was marching from St Pölten towards Murat, Soult stood on the Traisen with detachments towards the Krems, Bernadotte had reached Amstetten and orders sent to Davout ordered him to halt his march on Vienna at Mödling. But the real problem lay on the north side of the Danube as Napoleon was now very much aware. The corps of Maréchal Mortier was alone and unsupported and rapidly approaching Kutuzov's army.

In an attempt to keep pace with the rapid advance of Lannes' corps, Maréchal Mortier pushed Gazan's division ahead of the rest of the newly-formed corps, although Napoleon's plan for an extensive flotilla to link the two formations had failed due to a lack of suitable vessels. On the afternoon of 10 November, Gazan's men arrived at the village of Dürnstein, about $3^1/_2$ miles west of Krems. Despite orders requiring him to scout far ahead, the majority of Mortier's cavalry were operating on his left flank, in the passes leading towards Bohemia. It was not until his infantry advance guard approached the tiny twin villages of Ober and Unter-Loiben, just beyond Dürnstein, that he encountered any Allied activity. Here, a small Austro-Russian patrol fell back before him, while in the background, the bridge over the Danube still smouldered. It all contrived to convince Mortier that the Allied army was in retreat. He followed up until he encountered resistance just outside Krems, his advance guard falling back to a position at Rotenhof. Gazan's division prepared to settle down for the night, intending to continue their advance in the morning.

Kutuzov, however, had learnt from some French prisoners that the force advancing towards him formed only a single division of some 5,500 men, its nearest support, Dupont's division, standing at Marbach some 26 miles to the rear, with another division (Dumonceau's) beyond that. With encouragement from FML Schmitt, Kutuzov decided to attack, leaving his new Austrian chief of staff to draw up the plans. A little after midnight, in the early hours of 11 November, two Russian columns, a total of approximately 10,000 men, marched off into the freezing night. They planned to climb the rugged snow-covered hills and swing around behind Gazan's division, descending through narrow passes back down to the Danube by about 8.00am. In the meantime, volunteer 'deserters' entered the French camp to help persuade Mortier that only a rearguard stood before Krems, in an attempt to hold Gazan in the trap. This image Kutuzov reinforced by leaving only 2,500 men under Miloradovich in front of Gazan. The generally poor condition of the Allied army meant the rest of his command adopted supporting or reserve positions and were not involved in the attack. But Kutuzov did receive the welcome addition of General Leitenant Rosen's column. These were the men redirected towards the Turkish frontier in August, then recalled: now they had finally caught up with the army.

At 7.00am on the morning of 11 November Miloradovich moved forward to engage Gazan's advance guard, now reinforced by a few cavalry squadrons. Driving these men back, Miloradovich attacked aggressively and gained the village of Unter-Loiben, but the intensity of French fire from Ober-Loiben drove him back. For the next five hours the two sides attacked each other ferociously until, at noon, it appeared Miloradovich's men were finished. Sensing the moment Mortier ordered Gazan's men forward, driving the Russians all the way back to Rotenhof, where the first exchanges took place earlier that morning, and then further back towards Stein on the very outskirts of Krems. Finally, at about 1.00pm, with the situation looking bad for Miloradovich, the first of the flanking formations, five battalions commanded by General Maior Strik, appeared on the French left. The conditions the troops experienced in the hills were atrocious and only by dogged determination did they fight their way through the snow-covered hills to the Danube.

Now Mortier began to fall back, pursued by Miloradovich, reinforced by four battalions from Rosen's newly arrived column. Reinvigorated, the Russians forced Mortier back in a fighting retreat all the way to Ober-Loiben. Then at around 3.30pm, much to Mortier's dismay, more Russian troops emerged from the hills in his rear and advanced against Dürnstein. After a fierce assault on the town the Russians, under General Leitenant Dokhturov, drove the French defenders out, cutting off Mortier's retreat and forcing him back towards the impassable rising ground which hemmed in the battlefield to the north.

But help was at hand. As the leading elements of Dupont's breathless division finally appeared, they immediately engaged the last of Dokhturov's battalions approaching Dürnstein. Dupont's men gained the upper hand but then the long-overdue appearance of the final Russian column, led by FML Schmitt, emerged from the hills about 2 miles west of Dürnstein, throwing the battle into confusion in the gathering darkness. Dupont pulled back but Schmitt advanced too far and found himself caught between Russian and French crossfire. In the chaos, Schmitt was shot dead, his death a huge loss to the Allied cause. Dupont abandoned his attempt to break through to Dürnstein and fell back to Weißenkirchen: the exhausted Russians were in no position to exploit the situation.

For Mortier the position was now critical: he stood isolated without support, surrounded by Russians on three sides and with his back to a soaring range of steep hills. But after a long day of tortuous marching and intense fighting, numbers of cold, hungry, and thirsty Russian troops began to slip away from their positions after dark to seek food and drink. This weakening of the cordon coincided with a last desperate breakout attempt by Mortier. Striking suddenly towards Dürnstein, the French broke through the undermanned Russian lines and rapidly dispersed into the night. Although taken by surprise, the Russians rallied in time to intercept the tail end of the column, taking many of the 4ème Légère captive.

In the early hours of the following morning Mortier transferred his badly shaken corps to the south bank of the Danube, and it was with great relief that Napoleon received news that, despite heavy losses, he had managed to extricate Gazan's severely wounded division.

Kutuzov spent the day regrouping his army and granted it desperately needed rest. He had not destroyed Gazan's division but he had forced the new corps to retire across the river: a reverse for La Grande Armée. When the news reached Vienna, Kaiser Francis expressed his delight by awarding Kutuzov with the Knights Cross of the Maria Theresa Order. Now, separated from Napoleon's army by the great obstacle of the Danube, Kutuzov at last began to feel secure, and once the Austrians completed the destruction of the bridge at Vienna, he could await reinforcements in safety.

Two days earlier, General Leitenant Buxhöwden arrived at Troppeau, about 180 miles to the north-east, with the second army. Yet this security came at a price: at the Battle of Dürnstein each side probably lost between 3,000 and 4,000 men killed, wounded, missing, or taken prisoner. The 22nd Bulletin of La Grande Armée succinctly summed up the ferocity of the battle: 'This day was a day of slaughter'.

As soon as he knew Mortier was safe, Napoleon began to create a new plan. He believed that if he moved fast he might still be able to gain the bridge at Vienna. Then his army could file across the Danube and attempt once more to cut off Kutuzov from his reinforcements.

On 12 November Napoleon instructed Murat to recommence his advance on Vienna and capture – by any means possible – the Tabor bridge. The Austrian authorities were well aware of the importance of the bridge and plans for its destruction were already in place. With the departure of the kaiser, Count Wrbna remained behind as the imperial representative in Vienna and on 10 November the security of the city became the responsibility of the civilian militia. Three days earlier, FML Fürst Auersperg, drawn reluctantly out of retirement, took command of a reserve corps formed from garrison troops of Vienna. For the previous twelve years he had held only ceremonial commands: now he had 13,000 men under his orders.[11] On the approach of the French, Auersperg was to abandon Vienna, retire over the Danube, and prepare the bridge for destruction. He left the city at 2.00pm on 11 November.

The Tabor bridge was in fact three separate wooden structures, two short ones closest to the city crossing narrower branches of the Danube, then one long stretch, extending for 550 paces over the main arm of the river to Jedlersdorf. Oberst Geringer of the 11. Szeckel-Husaren commanded the rearguard, and he placed twenty men of his regiment under Oberleutnant Herbay to guard the southern gateway of the first bridge. At the northern end of the main bridge, sixteen artillery pieces stood defiantly ready to defend this vital link. The bridge was prepared for burning but Auersperg received a request from Count Wrbna to delay its destruction: there were strong rumours circulating of an armistice and Wrbna insisted he needed the bridge to allow rapid communication with the kaiser. The rest of Auersperg's command stood 3 miles to the north of the river, between Stammersdorf and Gerasdorf on the edge of the Marchfeld, the scene of great battles four years later.

The task of capturing the bridge fell to Murat and Lannes. On the morning of 12 November, as he approached the city, Murat received a deputation from the citizens of Vienna leading a wagon convoy of bread, wine and meat for the French army. They declared Vienna an open city and urged Murat to respect this decision and spare it the horrors of war. He assured them he would – if the Tabor bridge remained intact. Advanced troops entered the city later that day. One man who welcomed their arrival was none other than Charles Schulmeister. Having survived his beating on the road to Königsgrätz he had made his way back to Vienna under cover of darkness, finally arriving in the city two days before the arrival of the French. Savary gave him money and clothes. Schulmeister offered the spymaster his services once more.

That evening, French troops prepared for a ceremonial entry into Vienna to take place the following morning, while a crowd of curious onlookers gathered to watch the invading army. Throughout the night, Count Wrbna kept up the pressure on Auersperg not to authorise the destruction of the bridge, claiming the need to keep open a supply route for the city as well as championing the possibility of an imminent armistice. On the morning of 13 November French forces entered the city as the Viennese lined the streets to watch the army pass. There were no protests, only curiosity. The civilian population had never supported this war and the leading citizens were determined that no harm should come to their city. To this end the city even provided a guide to lead a detachment of French hussars around the city walls to a position from where they could observe the southern end of the Tabor bridge undetected. With great relief, they discovered it was still intact and guarded by a mere handful of hussars.

Oberleutnant Herbay, was under strict instructions. On the first sign of the French army, he was to fire a carbine and retire. At this signal, all troops deployed south of the main arm of the Danube would fall back to the north bank and fire the bridge. What his orders did not cover was the arrival at the bridge of first one, and then another carriage, containing passengers demanding to see Prince Auersperg.

Herbay was confused. The two passengers in the first carriage, Viennese officials, informed Herbay that Maréchal Murat was on his way and wished to speak to Auersperg. While he was considering this development, a civilian arrived in the second coach demanding permission to cross the bridge, as he bore important despatches for Auersperg. Herbay refused permission, whereby the gentleman descended from his coach and vehemently argued his right to cross the bridge, becoming most agitated in the process and causing great confusion. In the light of these requests Herbay despatched details back down the line. Then, in the midst of this turmoil a party of high-ranking French officers appeared with Count Wrbna following behind. They asked when Auersperg would appear and demanded to see Herbay's commanding officer. The group of officers, including such luminaries as Murat and Lannes, as well as Napoleon's aide, GB Bertrand, increased the pressure on the humble lieutenant, as demands mounted on all sides. Herbay sent for Oberst Geringer, but just before he arrived a couple of French soldiers smashed the locks shutting the gate of the bridge. In response the nervous Austrian guards fired the agreed warning shot just as Geringer arrived. The French officers increased the chaos by immediately berating Geringer for opening fire. Bertrand insisted that the bridge remain intact, falsely claiming an armistice now existed and hostilities were over between Austria and France.

Harassed on all sides, Geringer despatched Herbay to ride to Auersperg and advise him of this development, but on demanding written confirmation of the armistice, Bertrand instead offered him the guarantee of his word of honour and requested permission to deliver the news to Prince Auersperg in person. In an effort to extricate himself from this bewildering position, Geringer agreed to escort Bertrand and three other French officers to Prince Auersperg, on the agreement that no French troops would advance on to the bridge in their absence. Herbay, riding ahead, found Auersperg and Kienmayer at Stammersdorf at around 1.00pm. Kienmayer wanted to order the immediate destruction of the bridge, but Auersperg decided they should first see the situation for themselves. As they approached they encountered Geringer and Bertrand, whereupon the French officer repeated his story of the conclusion of an armistice.

Meanwhile, back on the southern bank of the Danube, Oudinot's grenadiers, who had remained hidden in the trees and thick bush growing close to the river, advanced onto the first bridge and pushed on over the second. The road then wound for a mile or so towards the main bridge, but the attackers remained hidden from its defenders by the bends in the road and thick vegetation that grew everywhere. Murat and Lannes now began the final part of their plan. With the grenadiers concealed, they openly advanced towards the southern end of the main bridge, accompanied by their staff, gesticulating and loudly announcing the signing of an armistice. The sentries held their fire as these officers approached, then, brushing aside their protests with talk of the armistice, continued on to final stretch of the bridge. The Austrian gunners at the northern end of the bridge, aware of the general opinion circulating that an armistice seemed likely, hesitated to fire into the confused jumble of Austrian and French soldiery rolling towards them. Only when Oudinot's grenadiers appeared at the far end of the bridge did the artillery suspect something was wrong, but as they prepared to fire, Murat, Lannes and the other senior officers were close enough to the guns to plausibly convince them otherwise.

While this confusion abounded, the French grenadiers moved amongst the gunners and disarmed them without fuss. By the time the shocked Auersperg arrived on the scene, his batteries were turned, mutely facing inland with the French firmly in possession of the bridge. His demand that the French should hand back the bridge fell on deaf ears: Murat, continuing the pretence of an armistice, merely advised him to march away with his men, but that he must leave his artillery behind. Seeing no other choice, Auersperg sent off messengers to carry the desperate news to Kutuzov and the kaiser and then retired. Murat's action – taking the bridge 'by any means possible' – delighted Napoleon and redeemed him in the emperor's eyes. But even amongst the French there were some who did not agree that gaining the bridge by such methods – which Murat called his 'little ruse' – was acceptable, pointing out that GB Bertrand, a senior French officer, had given confirmation of an armistice on his word of honour, when no armistice existed.

As soon as Kaiser Francis heard the news he relieved the unfortunate Auersperg of his command and sent him to the fortress of Königsgrätz to await court martial. FML Johann Fürst Liechtenstein took command of his men as they headed north. After a lengthy trial, Auersperg was found guilty of failing to destroy the Tabor bridge. Three years imprisonment followed, but in 1812 he received an official pardon. Oberst Geringer also found himself incarcerated, for three months. Yet there was no investigation of Count Wrbna's role in the failure to destroy the bridges. And what of the mysterious civilian who distracted Oberleutnant Herbay as the French approached the first bridge? Although never proven, there are strong suggestions that this was yet another example of Charles Schulmeister's contribution to the campaign.

What is certain is that two days later Schulmeister received an appointment as Commissioner General of the Viennese Police – only a week after his beating and narrow escape from death on the road to Königsgrätz! He retained this role throughout the occupation of Vienna and ran an extensive spy network that helped to calmly control and run the city. But for a man of his abilities this was not enough. From Vienna it is reported that his network penetrated the headquarters of the army of Archduke Charles in Hungary, as well as that of Grand Duke Constantine of the Russian Imperial Guard, keeping Napoleon aware of their movements and allowing him to assess their threat.[12]

While Napoleon pressed his advance on Vienna with all speed, Archduke Charles had continued his slow retirement out of northern Italy, fending off Masséna as he went. On the same day that Murat and Lannes captured the Tabor bridge, Charles passed the Isonzo river and finally distanced himself from his pursuers. But he was too far away to be of assistance – about 275 miles across mountainous terrain from Vienna. So in the meantime he continued to march north-east, through Laibach (Ljubljana), Cilli (Celje), towards Marburg (Maribor) on the Drave river, where he hoped to unite his forces with those of his brother, Archduke John.

For John the retreat from Tirol was a tough one. The geographical nature of the area convinced him of the need to distribute his army widely to protect every possible point of ingress into the region. Therefore, when he received the order from Charles to abandon Tirol, he first had to instruct his numerous detachments to regroup on the Brenner Pass above Innsbruck before marching to the valley of the Drave.

Ney, ordered into Tirol by Napoleon, broke through the Austrian defences at Scharnitz and Leutasch on the road to Innsbruck where he arrived on 5 November. Some 50 miles to the north-east, Deroy's division of Bavarians released from Bernadotte's command at Salzburg, attacked the fortress of Kufstein, defended by a single battalion. The Bavarians were reluctant to press their attack against a very strong position and the two sides continued to scowl at each other until, on 10 November, they struck a deal and the garrison marched off to join John.

Ney remained at Innsbruck while Deroy secured Kufstein, then on 11 November he ran into an Austrian rearguard, which delayed him further. Unable to wait any longer, Archduke John commenced his retreat towards the Drave, arriving at Klagenfurt on 20 November without the detachments under Jellačič and Prince Rohan. Jellačič, in Vorarlberg since his march from Ulm, and unaware just how much things had changed since he left the city, had been unwilling to join John, as he felt he could still rejoin the army on the Danube. However, on 14 November Augereau surrounded him and forced his surrender, although much of his cavalry did escape and made it back to Bohemia. Prince Rohan was unable to reach the rendezvous but instead marched southwards and broke through into Italy with just under 4,000 men. He caused much concern until finally being cornered on 24 November at Castelfranco, 25 miles from Venice, by GD Gouvion St Cyr, at the head of a French force marching through Italy from Naples.

In the meantime, Maréchal Ney had failed to catch up with Archduke John. After reaching Klagenfurt, John rested for a couple of days before pushing on and was finally united with his brother, Archduke Charles, on 26 November at Marburg, still 150 miles south of Vienna. Charles now commanded a force of about 80,000 men, but learning that the French already occupied the capital he determined to retire into Hungary before striking north towards the main army congregating in Moravia.

Meanwhile, in Bohemia, Archduke Ferdinand continued to create a new formation at Pilsen. Then, having heard on 4 November of French troops at Linz, he advanced to a position roughly 60 miles to the north of them at Budweis, with just under 10,000 men. However, the rapid progress of the French army soon left him behind. On 14 November he received information that Kutuzov was retiring into Moravia after the battle at Dürnstein. He therefore began to march back towards Prague, about 130 miles to the north, before turning on the road towards Moravia, marching another 80 miles to Czaslau, where he arrived on 25 November. Here he established himself, 60 miles from the Moravian border.

Tsar Alexander was furious when he heard of the bloodless capture of the Tabor bridge. The Russian opinion of the Austrian army, already seriously damaged after Mack's capitulation at Ulm, now took a further turn for the worse. Kaiser Francis, at Brünn, wrote: 'I am full of consternation, this imprudent and inexcusable trick destroys the whole confidence of my Allies at a single stroke and interrupts our good harmony.'[13]

But while tsar and kaiser raged, Kutuzov had no time to consider the moral rights and wrongs of the issue. Unless he moved fast his exhausted army was in very real danger of being surrounded and destroyed by the jubilant Grande Armée.

Chapter 11
'March! Destroy the Russian Army'*

Napoleon entered Vienna with the Garde Impériale on 14 November, setting up his headquarters outside the city in the magnificent surroundings of the Schönbrunn Palace, the Habsburg's summer residence. But he remained there only two days while awaiting news of Kutuzov's army.

Having benefited from the unlikely capture of the Tabor bridge, Napoleon had no intention of failing to take advantage of this coup. Quickly formulating the next stage, he ordered Murat to lead a rapid advance from Vienna towards Znaim. Napoleon rightly believed this road must be Kutuzov's new goal, for beyond Znaim the road led to Brünn and beyond that city marched Buxhöwden's advancing army. After crossing the Danube on 13 November, Murat immediately pushed troops along the road to the north-west, two cavalry divisions advancing to Stockerau and Oudinot's grenadiers reaching Korneuburg. The next day the rest of the Cavalry Reserve, V Corps and IV Corps also advanced on Stockerau, where they discovered a vast depot of supplies and military equipment of the Austrian army. Elsewhere, Napoleon ordered Davout to extend III Corps around Vienna to cover all the approach roads. Gudin's division took up a position towards Neustadt, about 30 miles south of the city, from where he could offer support to Marmont, now in the Styrian Alps, watching for activity on the road to Italy. Friant's division was east of the city, towards Pressburg, and Davout's remaining infantry division (now commanded by Général de division Caffarelli, since the previous commander, Général de division Bisson, fell wounded at Lambach two weeks earlier), moved across the Danube to a position on the vast plain to the north of the city. Convinced that Kutuzov had no choice but to abandon his position at Krems, Napoleon ordered Bernadotte to march for the Danube and prepare a crossing close to the destroyed Krems bridge. Once across, Napoleon anticipated that Bernadotte's rapid pursuit (I Corps and Wrede's Bavarians) of the wily Russian from the west, would crush him against the other great pincer led by Murat from the south.

---

* Napoleon to Murat, 16 November 1805.

Francis I came to the Habsburg throne in 1792 and for the next twenty-three years led Austria through the turbulent period of the Revolutionary and Napoleonic Wars. In 1804 he gave up the title 'Kaiser Francis II of the Holy Roman Empire' and took in its place that of 'Kaiser Francis I of Austria'.

Tsar Alexander I succeeded his murdered father, Paul I, in 1801 at the age of twenty-three. A grandson of Catherine the Great, he saw himself as the arbiter of Europe, once his initial admiration for Napoleon waned.

Karl Mack, de facto commander of the Austrian army that marched into Bavaria. Mack was appointed chief of staff to Archduke Ferdinands's army, but carried secret authority from the kaiser allowing him to overrule the young archduke.

Mikhail Kutuzov, the commander of the Russian forces. Although exiled from St Petersburg prior to the commencement of the campaign, and not consulted on the Russian strategy, he agreed to lead the army into Bavaria. (Sammlung Alfred und Roland Umhey)

Maréchal Michel Ney, French commander of
VI Corps. Ney's corps undertook much of the
fighting around Ulm and was successful in
the battles at Günzburg and Elchingen before
demanding the surrender of Mack's Austrian
army in Ulm.

Maréchal Nicholas Soult, French commander
of IV Corps. Born in 1769 Soult considered a
career as a baker before joining the army in
1785. His corps played a crucial role in the
Battle of Austerlitz.

Prince Peter Bagration, descended from a
dynasty of Georgian kings, was an excellent
rearguard commander and through his resolute defence at the Battle of Schöngrabern
earned promotion to General Leitenant.

FML Michael Kienmayer, an experienced
fifty-year-old cavalryman, led an active and
prominent part throughout the 1805 campaign. He was one of the first Allied commanders to encounter the French army in 1805,
and also one of the last, as Austrian rearguard
commander on the retreat from Austerlitz.

Napoleon harangues Marmont's II Corps at Augsburg on the Lech river. The Emperor arrived in the town on 10 October and left two days later.

At the battle of Elchingen on 14 October Maréchal Ney threw his corps over the damaged Danube bridge and attacked Riesch's Austrian corps. The Austrians formed on the high ground close to the Abbey but were overwhelmed and retreated back to Ulm.

After Mack's disastrous campaign, he agreed to surrender his army on 20 October. Over 20,000 Austrian soldiers marched out of the city to lay down their arms.

(All Sammlung Alfred und Roland Umhey)

A view of the Dürnstein battlefield looking south to the Danube, which runs along the foot of the hills in the background. Between the villages of Unterloiben on the left and Oberloiben to the right Miloradovich locked in combat with the isolated French general, Honoré Gazan.

A distant view of the Pratzen Plateau from the
outskirts of Kobelnitz. The high ground on the
right horizon shows the Pratzeberg, the scene of
the fierce fighting between St. Hilaire's division of
IV Corps, Kamenski's Russian brigade and
Jurczik's Austrians   *(Martin Worel)*

The Santon, the important isolated hill lying
close to the Brünn-Olmütz road on which
Napoleon anchored the left of the army.

Napoleon and his staff on the morning of Austerlitz observing the progress of Soult's attack on the Pratzen Plateau from Zuran Hill. *(Sammlung Alfred und Roland Umhey)*

One of the solid stone buildings in the village of Sokolnitz. The fighting here was both fierce and prolonged, buildings such as this creating stout strongpoints for defence.

GB Rapp returning to Napoleon with news of the successful attack by the French Imperial Guard cavalry against the Russian Imperial Guard. Amongst the trophies and prisoners is Prince Repnin-Volkonsky, a squadron commander in the Russian Chevalier Garde.

Napoleon diligently toured the battlefield once the fighting drew to a close. He organised what help he could for the wounded and here is seen receiving captured Allied officers against a backdrop of Allied standards. *(Sammlung Alfred und Roland Umhey)*

In the early afternoon of 4 December Napoleon met Kaiser Francis at Spáleny mill, about 11 miles south of Austerlitz, with FML Johann Liechtenstein in attendance. The meeting resulted in an armistice between France and Austria.

A French satirical cartoon, 'The Death of William Pitt'. The devil is shown carrying the British Prime Minister down to hell, while the reins supporting George III snap, sending the king towards a dark chasm over a sack bearing the words, 'Depot of crimes of the English government.'

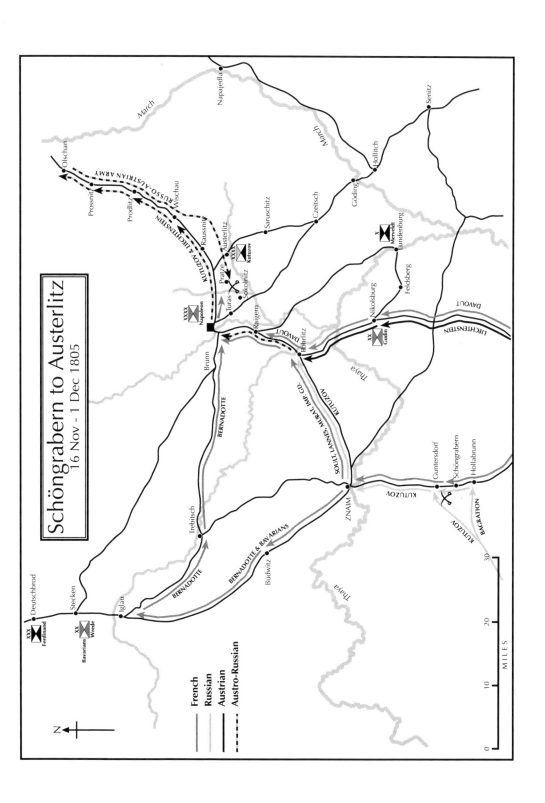

Schöngrabern to Austerlitz
16 Nov – 1 Dec 1805

Deutschbrod
Stecken
Iglau
Trebitsch
Budwitz
Znaim
Guntersdorf
Schöngrabern
Hollabrunn

Brunn
Raigern
Turas
Pratze
Sokolnitz
Austerlitz
Raussnitz

Olschan
Prossnit
Prodlitz
Wischau

Napajedla
March
Senitz
Hollitch
Göding
Czeitsch
Saruschitz

Nikolsburg
Feldsberg
Pohrlitz
Lundenburg

Napoleon
Kutuzov
Merveldt
Gudin
Wrede
Ferdinand

RUSSO-AUSTRIAN ARMY

KUTUZOV & LIECHTENSTEIN

BERNADOTTE

SOULT, LANNES, MURAT, IMP. GD.

KUTUZOV

BERNADOTTE & BAVARIANS

KUTUZOV

BAGRATION

DAVOUT

LIECHTENSTEIN

Thaya
March

Bavarians
Bernadotte

French
Russian
Austrian
Austro-Russian

MILES
0   10   20   30

N

The Austrians, now commanded by Liechtenstein, fell back towards Brünn by a separate road, Murat detaching a dragoon division to follow their movements. While his command assembled at Stockerau during the day, Murat pushed patrols up the road towards Hollabrunn from where, in the early hours of 15 November, he received news of the presence of Russian troops approaching that town.

News of the capture of the Tabor bridge reached Kutuzov at Krems a few hours after the event. Instantly he abandoned his plans:

> 'The forcing of the Vienna bridge by the enemy (an event which was not to be expected) and his march on Hollabrunn forced me to change my plans, and instead of defending the passage of the Danube and waiting patiently for support, I found myself obliged to march with all speed past Hollabrunn to avoid an unequal combat against infinitely superior forces and to follow my first plan of a junction with the army of the General Buxhöwden.'[1]

In fact, Kutuzov now faced a race for survival. On the evening of 13 November Murat's leading cavalry formations at Stockerau were only 15 miles from Hollabrunn on a good road. A quick glance at the map showed Kutuzov that if he was to escape he must push his tired men on a rapid march of some 25 miles, over poor tracks and paths, to reach that same town and access to the main road leading north. Fully aware of the difficulty of the situation, Kutuzov immediately gave the order for his army to prepare to march. Speed was now of the utmost importance. Reluctantly, therefore, he abandoned all the sick and wounded lying in the makeshift hospitals in Krems to the mercy of the French.

Pushing ahead, Kutuzov reached Ebersbrunn later that evening, 15 miles away to the north-east, where he established his headquarters. The rest of the army struggled in during the early hours of the following day. Fortunately for Kutuzov, while Murat needed the 14 November to assemble his full force at Stockerau, back on the Danube, Bernadotte was experiencing great difficulty collecting together boats and bridging materials for his river crossing. There was a glimmer of hope. As Kutuzov waited anxiously for his army, an Austrian officer advised him of a route which by-passed Hollabrunn and reached the Znaim road at Guntersdorf, nearly 9 miles north of the town. Denying his men any rest, Kutuzov drove them on right through the night of 14–15 November, constantly riding backward and forward, encouraging his 'children', as he liked to call his troops, and forever exhorting them to 'Behave like Russians!' But he also realised that this march alone was not enough to protect him from the French pursuit. Before leaving Ebersbrunn he called Bagration to him and explained the position. The only way to save the army was for a rearguard to make a strong defence at Hollabrunn and deny the road to the French while the army made good its escape. General Maior Prince Peter Bagration, a descendant from an ancient dynasty of Georgian kings, had already proved his abilities in battle on many occasions during his twenty-three years' military service. He was considered calm in a crisis and a brave, ferocious fighter. There could be no one better suited for the task.

Bagration received additional Russian troops to bolster his depleted command up to about 7,000 men, as well as Nostitz' battered brigade: the only Austrian formation still fighting alongside the Russians. Then, diverging from the main army, Bagration headed across country to Hollabrunn on his daunting mission. Kutuzov momentarily let his feelings show and wept as they departed, convinced of the inevitable destruction of this meagre force, but he later wrote: 'I would have nevertheless considered it satisfactory to sacrifice one corps for the sake of the army.'[2]

Bagration assembled his forlorn hope at Hollabrunn at midday on 15 November, but was unable to discover a suitable defensive position. Leaving Nostitz covering the approaches to the town with the 4. Hessen-Homburg-Husaren and a number of Cossack detachments, he fell back 4 miles and established his force near the village of Schöngrabern. Within a very short time Murat's advanced cavalry detachments arrived in sight of Nostitz, who drew back to this new position. Bagration feared an immediate attack, but it did not materialise.

In fact Murat, believing he faced the whole of Kutuzov's army, was reluctant to attack until reinforced by IV and V Corps. However, encouraged by the success of his ruse at the Tabor bridge, he sent forward a messenger with a request to speak with the commander of the rearguard. Nostitz approached and was informed of the conclusion of an armistice between Austria and France. Count Nostitz, schooled in the old gentlemanly ways of war, accepted Murat's word, turned his advance guard about and rode off to inform Bagration.

Unlike his Austrian comrade, Bagration was unimpressed with tales of an armistice and stood his ground. Alerted to this development, Kutuzov, more attuned to the changing nature of war than some of his Austrian colleagues, immediately saw an opportunity to gain time for the escape of his beleaguered force. By agreeing to a truce while discussions took place, Kutuzov reasoned that he could withdraw his army unnoticed, shielded from French eyes by Bagration's force. In accordance with this plan, Kutuzov sent two aides-de-camp to Murat to open negotiations for the safe passage of the army back to Russia. This suited Murat perfectly, as he saw it as an opportunity to complete the concentration of his command before commencing the attack. Later that evening, Kutuzov's ADC, Baron Wintzingerode, and Murat's chief of staff, Général de division Belliard, signed the agreement, subject to the approval of Napoleon and Kutuzov. In the meantime, both sides were to maintain their current positions, with either side required to give four hours notice of a resumption of hostilities.

This agreement may have suited Murat, but Maréchal Lannes remained less than impressed. In a brief discourse with Bagration, he responded to the Russian general's flattery with the retort that, if he had his way they would be fighting at that moment, not exchanging empty compliments. By the time Murat's aide galloped off to Napoleon at the Schönbrunn Palace, to advise him of his second great masterstroke, Kutuzov was gaining ground. Only Bagration, with his 7,000 cold, hungry and exhausted men remained to face a gathering army of 37,000 Frenchmen.

Napoleon received Murat's despatch in the early hours of 16 November. He could not believe what he read and for the second time in a few days dashed off a crushing reprimand to his errant brother-in-law:

'It is impossible for me to find words to express my displeasure ... you have no right to conclude an armistice without my orders ... Break the armistice immediately and march upon the enemy ... it is only a ruse. March! Destroy the Russian army. The Austrians let themselves be duped over the passage of the Vienna bridge – you have let yourself be duped by an aide-de-camp of the tsar.'

It was already after midday when Murat received the emperor's rebuke, and in response, immediately prepared to lash out at the Russians, but Lannes insisted on honouring the agreed four-hour notice. Alerted by an increase in French activity, Wintzingerode and Nostitz rode forward to discover its purpose. Angered by the Russians' adept use of his own strategy, Murat held the two officers at his headquarters in Hollabrunn, refusing to allow them return to their own lines for the coming battle. The darkness of an autumnal evening began to descend on the scene by the time the French advanced at 5.00pm. Napoleon set out for Hollabrunn, hoping a great battle was in the offing, but of Bernadotte, hopelessly delayed at the Danube, there was no sign.

Bagration pulled his men back from the village of Schöngrabern, drawing them up in front of the next village, Grund. Having made an effort to strengthen the ramshackle collection of buildings, he placed his artillery in the centre of his line, across the road leading from Schöngrabern. On either side of the guns he placed six weak battalions of infantry, with another two held in reserve. On each flank he posted a Russian cavalry regiment supported by a regiment of Cossacks, holding the Austrian 4. Hessen-Homburg-Husaren in reserve. Murat commanded two divisions of Lannes' V Corps (those of Oudinot and Suchet), two divisions of Soult's IV Corps (Legrand and Vandamme) and most of the cavalry. He placed Oudinot's Grenadier Reserve in the centre, behind Schöngrabern; on their left flank he formed Legrand's division and on the right flank Suchet. Vandamme's division remained in reserve. The cavalry supported the attacks but the ground, much broken with vineyards and boggy areas, restricted their employment.

As soon as the French began to advance, the Russian artillery bombarded Schöngrabern, which quickly caught fire and delayed the movement of Oudinot's division and the artillery. On the French left, Legrand pushed forward against the Russian right, commanded by General Maior Ulanius, but found progress difficult through the vineyards. In fact, the French cavalry were first to test this flank. Ulanius' men held their nerve and by steady musketry repulsed two mounted attacks as the burning village of Schöngrabern cast an eerie glow across the battlefield.

Legrand's division now closed to combat but Ulanius' men still held firm. After some delay Oudinot's division bypassed Schöngrabern and marched against the centre and left of the Russian line, while Suchet moved forward on their right. Here the six battalions commanded by General Maior Selekhov faced fearful odds, but they too stood their ground against overwhelming numbers. Bagration fed in some of his reserve as the two sides hacked and stabbed at each other ferociously. Twice the Russians were surrounded but fought their way out with the bayonet. Bagration now gave the order for a withdrawal, resulting in some extremely desperate fighting within the houses and along the narrow streets and alleys of Grund. However, Bagration kept his men together and battled his way back to the village of Guntersdorf, where he had ordered two battalions and some Cossacks to form a new rearguard to protect his retreat. All the time the French pressed forward. Whenever a chance presented itself the cavalry darted forward and slashed their way into the Russian ranks. But they did not have it all their own way as Jean-Pierre Sibelet, a lieutenant in the 11ème Chasseurs à cheval, later recalled:

'Having passed on the other side of the road to pursue the enemy who were in no position to resist, we found while advancing, some Russian soldiers in groups of ten to twelve, rummaging around and groping forward. On our approach, they threw themselves on the ground with their muskets beside them and, as we passed, they appeared to us to be dead, but hardly had we passed, when they stood up and fired on us from behind. Educated of this manoeuvre we turned our bridles: the soldiers who had fired slept again, but now they all bore the mark of the point of the sabre in the back.'[3]

By now total confusion reigned on the battlefield, yet still the outnumbered Russians did not break. The village of Grund burned too and the cries of the wounded, unable to escape the flames, fused with the smell of roasting human flesh, all adding to the vision of hell in which the desperate men now found themselves. Lieutenant Sibelet, fighting on a battlefield illuminated only by burning buildings, described his bewildering and unnerving experience:

'Our infantry, taking us for enemy troops fired on us; but as it was extremely high, the balls passed over our heads. One moment later we took two Russian artillery pieces that we were obliged to release. The Russians took four of ours which we took back from them ... the soldiers fired one on another. French battalions and squadrons were in the middle of the Russians, and the Russians in the middle of the French; our guns shot at us and Russian guns shot at the Russians. It really was complete confusion.'[4]

The fighting around Guntersdorf continued in this way until midnight, when Napoleon, who had now arrived at Hollabrunn, advised Murat to bring the fighting to an end. After seven hours' stubborn resistance Bagration disappeared into the night with his shattered command. Only in the morning was the true cost revealed. Across the rolling, snow-covered ground between Schöngrabern and Guntersdorf lay the frozen corpses of maybe 1,200 Russian soldiers, and when these were added to the losses in wounded, prisoners and missing, Bagration's rearguard defence perhaps cost around 3,000 men: almost half of his command. Yet the sacrifice allowed Kutuzov to escape and gain two marches on the French.

Bagration forced his army on throughout the night, and by the morning of 17 November he reached Neu Schallersdorf, just outside Znaim. Detaching some cavalry to act as a rearguard, he set out on the road towards Pohrlitz, 25 miles away, a town which Kutuzov reached safely later that day. Here the Russian commander received the welcome support of Prince Liechtenstein, at the head of his Austrian troops. Amongst these was the sixth battalion of IR49 Kerpen. Major Mahler, an officer called out of retirement to command the battalion, only joined his newly recruited men at Korneuburg, north of Vienna. At Pohrlitz, Mahler revealed that, 'During this strenuous march, I lost many men, some of whom had been left behind because of fatigue; others, out of fear, as most were still recent recruits, had headed off home.' The following day, amid scenes of great emotion, Bagration's heroic but savagely depleted force reunited with Kutuzov's in the town. But with no time to waste, the whole force moved off to Brünn, reaching it later that day.

Here Kutuzov received most welcome news: Buxhöwden and his army were now just over a day's march away. He had won the race.

As soon as the diverse elements of the two armies drew together so their relationship began to suffer. Major Mahler viewed the Russians with despair: 'Although they received their provisions separately and despite all our efforts to oppose them, the Russians seized the bread and forage rations from the men of our force, and even carried off officers' baggage and wagons into their camp.'

After his diplomatic mission to Potsdam and pleasant interlude with his sister, the tsar also now reached the army. He joined the kaiser at Olmütz, an ancient fortified town some 45 miles north-east of Brünn, which now assumed the role of Allied army headquarters.

Despite the abundant supplies present in Brünn's magazines and depots, Kutuzov marched again on the morning of 19 November and later that day encountered the leading column of Buxhöwden's army. Both armies then retired to Olschan, about 5 miles south-west of Olmütz, where they set up camp on 22 November in an excellent defensive position. It was the end of a monumental march of over 900 miles, carried out in bad weather, on poor roads, with inadequate clothing and failing supplies, and for the last 250 miles, under the constant threat of French attack. At Olschan, free at last from pursuit, they could rest and begin to recover from their ordeal. But with so many men crowded together and with supplies short, disease quickly struck. Major Mahler recorded that: 'a large number of men had to be conveyed daily to the Olmütz hospital; during our time in the camp at Olmütz I was myself forced to transport away five or six soldiers as they had died suddenly, as well as sending 200 men to the hospital.'

On the morning after the battle at Schöngrabern, Napoleon assumed front line direction of the army for the first time since it advanced across the Isar river on 26 October. On the morning of 17 November he directed it towards Znaim, but other than encountering a little Allied rearguard opposition, the march was unopposed and of the main body there was no sign. By the time his leading troops entered Znaim it was clear to Napoleon that Kutuzov had escaped, and as his army was suffering in much the same way as the Russians, he called a halt, allowing a day's rest at the well-stocked town.

On 19 November Murat continued on the road to Brünn, the principal town in Moravia, where Napoleon decided to set up his headquarters, marking an end to the second phase of the campaign. The emperor entered the city the following day and extended his army in and around it. Again the Allies had abandoned vast quantities of supplies and equipment, which the French eagerly took advantage of. The two armies now stood some 45 miles apart and began to plan their next moves.

An eyewitness observing Napoleon's arrival in Brünn described him riding into the city accompanied by 1,000 Guard cavalry and forty Mameluks:

> 'His outer appearance seized the general attention. He wore a grey coat; a low hat covered his head. Napoleon was small and corpulent, wore a dark green uniform with red facings, golden epaulets and two stars on his breasts. His face was pale, his look bright and wistful. He set up his quarters in the Governors Palace. Often one could see him by the window where he – after he walked through the room – remained standing and observing the square.'[5]

That evening, each household was obliged to illuminate the city by setting two candles in their windows, to welcome the arrival of Napoleon. The French army then seized all the meat in the city and rounded up all the cattle from the surrounding villages and farms, many of which they slaughtered in the Kohlmarkt, one of the city's principal squares, 'where the blood flowed in streams'. By the time the army left the area a few days later, the local population had been relieved of 3,000 horses, 4,000 cattle and 6,000 sheep.

While Napoleon pondered his maps and charts and the tsar and kaiser held strategic conferences, the ordinary soldiers of each army focused their attention on the basic necessities of life: keeping warm and finding food. Such was their condition that they cared little how they acquired it. In the French bivouacs on the outskirts of the city, anything combustible was forcibly removed from the simple peasant houses and when that supply became exhausted the houses themselves were torn down to stoke the fires through the freezing nights. One officer recorded that after the men moved on to a new bivouac the peasants tentatively approached and 'picked their way among the wreckage [of the camp] in search of whatever might belong to them'.[6] Many stragglers trailed miles behind their units and roamed freely through the countryside forcibly taking whatever they could. To combat this Napoleon found it necessary to form columns to round up these men and drive them back to their regiments. However, in excessive cases of pillage, the emperor authorised execution.

In the Russian camp conditions were as hard. General Leitenant Alexandre-Louis Langeron, a French *émigré* officer who had served in the Russian army since 1790, arrived at Olmütz with Buxhöwden's army. He felt that march discipline had been well-observed, but when the newcomers encountered Kutuzov's army all that quickly changed. Kutuzov's men were greatly disillusioned after their ceaseless marching and lack of bread. Langeron observed that the Russian soldier 'is a big eater of bread; he needs 3 pounds a day, and he is unhappy if he does not get this amount. It counts for nothing that you replace his favourite food with meat or vegetables.'[7] The Austrian supply officers had not observed this important part of the Russian diet and as such the soldiers grew resentful. This led to much plundering in the villages the troops passed through and now extended to those surrounding the camp at Olschan. Langeron observed that:

'under the pretext of seeking bread, they took money, property; the inhabitants fled their hearths and the disorder became universal. Soon it was communicated to the army of Buxhöwden ... In the bivouacs of Olschan, hardly thirty men per battalion remained during the day, all the others were widespread in the villages, even to a distance of [10 miles] from the camp, and returned in the evening with bags filled with property, turnips and potatoes which formed their principal food.'[8]

The arrival of Alexander did little to improve the situation. The Russian soldier in general is devoted to the tsar and many senior figures assumed his arrival would, as Langeron put it, 'inspire great enthusiasm in his soldiers'. But the reality was different. The army received Alexander with 'coldness and dull silence'. His entourage included many young and inexperienced officers who held great influence over him and were keen to impress with their enthusiasm and drive. The tsar put great faith in their words of advice, often above those offered by experienced military men. To his comments on the muted reception given to Alexander by the army, Langeron added that the Russian soldier 'often judges men and events extremely well'.[9]

Napoleon now needed to consider his next move. It was two months since La Grande Armée crossed the Rhine. In that time he had crushed an Austrian army at Ulm and cleared Bavaria. His progress forced the Austrians to abandon northern Italy and Tirol, and he occupied the imperial capital of Vienna as well as great tracts of Habsburg territory. His only setback had been his failure to intercept and defeat Kutuzov's army. But now he sat precariously at the end of a long and exposed line of communications, facing an Allied army in a strong position. While the enemy increased in strength as reinforcements began to arrive, the French army required ever more detachments and garrisons to keep communications open. The longer Napoleon took to make his move, the greater the chance the Allies' strength would increase still further. The armies of Archduke Charles and John were still at large, as was that under Archduke Ferdinand in Bohemia. After his defeat at Mariazell, Merveldt had also hastily gathered together a small force. In addition, the Russian Imperial Guard was approaching Olmütz, and another Russian column under General Leitenant Essen I could reach the area by the first week of December.

Napoleon had with him in and around Brünn the Garde Impériale, Soult's IV Corps, Lannes' V Corps and Murat's Cavalry Reserve: about 52,000 men. Following his late crossing of the Danube, Bernadotte, with I Corps and Wrede's Bavarian division, received an order from Napoleon ordering him up through Znaim to take up a position opposing Archduke Ferdinand. Marching through Budwitz and Iglau to Deutsch Brod, around 60 miles north-west of Brünn, Bernadotte took up a position just over 20 miles to the south of Czaslau, at which place Ferdinand arrived on 25 November. Davout's III Corps was widely spread. Caffarelli's division was now close behind the main army at Pohrlitz, 60 miles north of Vienna, while Friant's division had moved to Vienna and Gudin's was 40 miles to the east at Pressburg. Mortier, who remained at Krems with his corps after the mauling at Dürnstein, received the order to march to Vienna with two of his three divisions and relieve Davout. The rest of the army, the corps of Ney, Marmont and Augereau was now too far away to take an active part in any future battles in Moravia.

On the same day that Napoleon arrived at Brünn, he pushed Murat and the cavalry forward on the Olmütz road, where the leading division encountered a large force of Russian cavalry at Rausnitz, some 3 miles north of a town called Austerlitz. From an initial clash of advance and rearguards a full scale cavalry battle quickly developed, with the mass of Allied horsemen pushing back a couple of brigades of Général de division Walther's dragoons. But reinforced by d'Hautpoul's division of *cuirassiers* with Murat at their head, followed by six squadrons of Garde Impériale cavalry, the French gained the upper hand and drove the Russians off. The French cavalry clearly won the day, but those young Russian officers of the tsar's entourage who keenly sought battle took great encouragement from the taking of French prisoners and the captured eagle standard that their men brought back.

The following day Murat pushed outposts as far as Wischau and Soult's Corps moved forward to occupy Austerlitz and a long plateau of high ground between that town and Brünn. Having now secured the area up to Wischau, a distance of about 20 miles, Napoleon rode out as far as the outposts to thoroughly inspect the lie of the land.

Showing a keen interest throughout, on the return journey he stopped on the Brünn-Olmütz road, close to an isolated steep-sided hillock adorned with a tiny chapel on the top, the Bosenitzerberg, rising up just on the north side of the road. He then turned off the road and rode southwards. He followed a stream, feeding the Goldbach, which ran southwards from the hillock, across the front of the Zuran Hill and down through a low valley, passing the villages of Jirzikowitz, Puntowitz, Kobelnitz and Sokolnitz to Telnitz: a distance of just over 7 miles. From here a vast shallow lake extended eastwards to the village of Augezd. Then, dominating the Goldbach valley and running from Augezd back to the Brünn–Olmütz road, rose the Pratzen Plateau. Napoleon led his entourage over this gently rolling feature, carefully calculating distances between highpoints before returning to the hillock by the main road. Of all the country he had traversed that day this area appealed most to him. Before he returned to Brünn, Napoleon ordered that the eastern side of the hillock be dug away to make it more difficult to assault and had eighteen captured Austrian cannon brought up and installed on the top. His aide, GD Savary, recalled that the emperor told his followers: 'Gentlemen, examine the ground well; you will have a part to act on it.'

Chapter 12
'The Russians Are Coming!'

'Soldiers, in much disarray, packed their kits
hurriedly, and with pale faces informed
the inhabitants, "The Russians are coming".'*

While the French army purposefully followed a single direction, at Allied headquarters dissension was rife. There were many differing opinions as to what the next step should be and bickering amongst the rival factions within the Russian command increased, as did the contempt many expressed towards the Austrians. With food supplies around Olmütz all but exhausted, matters came to a head at a council of war on 24 November.

Kutuzov advocated a retreat towards the Carpathian Mountains, opening up new sources of supply and leaving a devastated and barren land in their wake to hamper any pursuit. In addition, by deferring contact with the French, it allowed time for Bennigsen's Russian army to draw closer, and possibly for Prussian intervention too. Other options were presented. General Sukhtelen, a senior officer of Dutch origin, advocated withdrawing into Hungary and forming a junction with Archduke Charles, while General Leitenant Langeron was in favour of a move towards Bohemia to operate with Bennigsen's army and Archduke Ferdinand.[1] Most experienced generals upheld the proposals to delay battle, which was indeed Napoleon's greatest concern. In this they were supported by Adam Czartoryski, who, recognising that the presence of the tsar diluted the authority of his generals, attempted to persuade him to return to St Petersburg. He failed.

Alexander, with no military experience, was encouraged to believe he now had the perfect opportunity to cross swords with the most proven military commander in Europe and to defeat him on the field of battle. His sycophantic circle of friends, advisors and so-called experts airily dismissed Napoleon's earlier successes in the campaign as merely a reflection of the

---

* Satschan parish records, later recorded in the local school chronicle.

weakness of the Austrians. They confidently predicted that fighting the Russian army would be a much tougher experience for the French, as already shown at Dürnstein and Schöngrabern. The French pursuit, an unremitting torment since Kutuzov crossed the Inn a month earlier, had now ceased, a fact these young lions saw as confirmation that the French were overstretched. They saw no need to await the intervention of Archduke Charles or the Prussians or even the 10,000-strong corps of General Leitenant Essen I, which, although originally destined for Bennigsen's army, now marched on Moravia and was only a week away.

The impressionable tsar, military glory beckoning, inclined towards the advice offered by these belligerent young men. The kaiser also approved – although the Russians rarely sought his opinion now – for a successful battle would bring an early end to the French occupation of Vienna. Such was the tsar's position in Russian society that once the decision was made at the council of war on 24 November, his senior generals felt unable to oppose him.

And so Alexander enthusiastically embraced the option that offered the Allies fewest advantages and instead presented Napoleon with his best chance of victory. With the decision taken, the army began preparations for an advance to commence the following day, but almost immediately the plan encountered problems. An Austrian cavalry commander, Generalmajor Stutterheim, reported that: 'it was necessary to take two days' provisions; and these provisions could not arrive till the day after. When that day came, some of the generals had not sufficiently studied their dispositions; and thus, another day was lost.'[2]

The Austro-Russian army finally began to edge forward from the Olschan camps at 8.00am on the morning of 27 November. Confusion and dissension marked their progress.

Langeron estimated the strength of the Allied army near Olmütz at about 69,000 men, of which some 16,000 were Austrian. He noted that while the battalions of Buxhöwden's army numbered between 600 or 700 men each, some of those that had survived Kutuzov's odyssey mustered only 200 or 300. He also estimated that Kutuzov and Kienmayer had lost approximately 11,000 men on their retreat from Braunau to Olmütz, in killed, wounded, sick, and captured. To this he added that Buxhöwden's command left about 5,000 in the hospitals of Troppau and Olmütz.[3] The Austrian infantry brought from the Tabor bridge or swept up by Prince Liechtenstein as he marched north was also weak. Of the sixteen regular battalions present, half were formed by depot battalions, which, according to Stutterheim, had been 'recruited, armed and organised about a month before'.[4] However, on 25 November the army received a timely boost when the Russian Imperial Guard, commanded by the tsar's younger brother, Grand Duke Constantine, arrived at Olmütz. Despite a tortuous march of over 1,000 miles from St Petersburg, the Guards looked ready for action, increasing the fighting strength of the army to between 76,000 and 78,000 men.

Having taken the decision to attack, the task of drawing up the plan of campaign fell to an Austrian officer, Generalmajor Weyrother. Despite the low opinion of the Austrian army held by the majority of the Russian staff, Weyrother had ingratiated himself with Buxhöwden as he escorted his army through Galicia to Olmütz. On his arrival, Kutuzov appointed him as his chief of staff, filling the vacancy left by the untimely death of FML Schmitt at Dürnstein earlier in the month. Yet as the presence of the tsar dominated military matters more and more, the long-standing distrust he felt for Kutuzov came to the fore and the general, so revered by his men, saw his control over the army diminish.

Franz, Freiherr von Weyrother, was fifty-one years old and had served in the army for thirty years. His first appointment as chief of staff came in 1796 and he took on this role again in 1799 under FML Kray before transferring, in a similar capacity, to the army of the Russian Field Marshal Alexander Suvorov operating in Switzerland. A year later he served as chief of staff to Archduke John during the Hohenlinden campaign. Stutterheim considered him 'an officer of reputation, who did not want for talent, and who had inspired the Russians with confidence', but who, in comparison with FML Schmitt, 'neither possessed his calmness, his prudence, or his firmness'. Further, Stutterheim extolled his 'great personal courage' but felt he 'too easily abandoned his own opinions, to adopt those of other people'.[5] Langeron, however, viewed Weyrother in a very different light. He considered his abilities questionable, but not his character: 'harsh, coarse, insolent, filled with the opinion of his own merit, carrying his self-esteem to appalling excess'.[6] The tsar, lacking in military knowledge, now placed his complete confidence in Weyrother, a confidence not shared by all at headquarters, including Bagration and Miloradovich, who had also served under Suvorov in Switzerland: on one occasion, they had attempted to follow a route through the Swiss mountains prescribed by Weyrother, only to find that it did not exist. Nevertheless, Weyrother settled down to his task, confidently announcing there could be no more than 40,000 Frenchmen before them.

Yet this was supposition. The Allies lacked detailed knowledge of the current state of the French army, despite it being on Austrian lands.[7] On the day of the council of war, Count Stadion, the Austrian ambassador to St Petersburg, now with the army, and the ubiquitous FML Gyulai, set out from Olmütz for Napoleon's headquarters at Brünn. Sir Arthur Paget, also at Olmütz, expressed his concern as to the nature of their mission. In response, he was assured that the two men went to Brünn to observe the actions of Haugwitz, the Prussian foreign minister, who was due there any day to present Prussia's ultimatum. Paget, however, saw another purpose to their embassy. He expected a decisive battle to take place within the next few days and, 'Should the Allies gain the victory Count Stadion will be upon the spot to animate and second Count Haugwitz, should the reverse be the case he is no doubt destined to sign such a peace as I tremble to think off.'[8] Napoleon, unimpressed by their presence in his camp and considering them little more than spies, ushered them away to Vienna and a meeting with his foreign minister, Talleyrand.

It was imperative now for the emperor that the Allies did not withdraw, and while unaware at that moment of the direction Allied planning was taking, it was in his interest to display an apparent weakness. By this he hoped to encourage the Allies to give battle and abandon any plans they may have for retreat. Napoleon held only about 52,000 men close to him around Brünn, but he knew that when he gave the order he could draw Bernadotte and Davout rapidly towards him at short notice.

On 25 November, the day the Allies originally planned to advance, Napoleon sent an emissary towards Russian headquarters to open communications with the tsar. For this purpose he chose his aide, GD Savary, a master of intelligence work, Schulmeister's employer and the man who carried out the execution of the duc d'Enghien that had so appalled the Russian court. While the letter he carried contained little more than platitudes and an expression of goodwill towards Alexander, Savary used his time carefully in the Allied camp to observe and monitor the situation and attitude of the Allies. The tsar received Savary courteously, as did Constantine, but after a long interview, Savary could not fail to note the belligerent attitude of the officers of the imperial entourage and their influence over the tsar. Savary returned to Napoleon with a letter from Alexander in which he expressed his desire 'to see the peace of Europe re-established with fairness and on a just basis'. Yet as Russia did not acknowledge Napoleon's coronation, imperial protocol decreed that the letter be addressed to 'The Head of the French Government' and not 'Emperor'. This angered Napoleon, but the air of hostility perceived by Savary suited his purposes, suggesting that the Allies were inclined to fight.

Napoleon sent Savary back to request a 24-hour truce and a personal meeting with the tsar. The time would prove useful in drawing the outlying formations of his army towards Brünn. The Russians detained Savary overnight at their outposts and the tsar did not receive him until the morning of 29 November, by which time the Allies were two days into their advance and pushing back the French outposts. Alexander declined the offer, instead sending his great favourite, Prince Peter Dolgorukov, in his place. Napoleon advanced to meet Dolgorukov at the outposts of his army and walked with the prince, ensuring he should see only what the emperor wanted him to see.

Dolgorukov observed what he believed was an army nervous and unprepared for a major battle. Much has been made of the subsequent discussions between Napoleon and Dolgorukov. While the Russian prince was probably the most outspoken and arrogant of the tsar's aides, it suited Napoleon to play along submissively at first and then later claim indignation at the way the Russian envoy dictated to him. Faced with proposals for peace from Dolgorukov, which contained nothing new, Napoleon finally tired of the game and dismissed Dolgorukov with the words, 'Well then, we shall fight'.[9] Dolgorukov returned to Allied headquarters brimming with confidence, convinced that Napoleon feared a confrontation and would retire before the advance of the Allied army. This was just the news Alexander wanted to hear. Others with greater military experience doubted Dolgorukov's interpretation of the situation. As these discussions concluded, the Austro-Russian army marched slowly towards Austerlitz and Napoleon issued orders for the concentration of his army.

The Allied army left Olschan at 8.00am on the morning of 27 November. Now Kutuzov's regiments found themselves intermixed with those of Buxhöwden's army, forming five columns, numbered one to five from the right, with a separate advance guard. It advanced astride the Olmütz-Brünn road with I Column on the right, reaching towards the mountains that rose in the north. With a lack of detailed knowledge of the French position, this offered the possibility of turning the French left if an encounter took place on the road. To shield this initial movement, Prince Bagration, now commanding the Army Advance Guard, received orders to maintain his position before Wischau, allowing the army to close up behind him undetected. Kutuzov issued strict orders for march discipline to be maintained, but it is clear from documents issued from headquarters that many regiments allowed their wagons to disrupt the advance.[10] The army ended the day extended over 8 miles between the villages of Prossnitz and Prodlitz.

The following morning Bagration formed his advance guard into three columns: the centre column advanced along the road directly on Wischau, while the others swung out to left and right to envelop the town. Two French cavalry regiments stood in the town, commanded by Général de brigade Treillard, with another two behind it in reserve. Général de brigade Sébastiani sat with a regiment of dragoons some 3 miles to the south at Huluboschan. Treillard's instructions were to withdraw on the approach of the enemy, but surprised by Bagration's sudden advance, a squadron was cut off and after a spirited resistance the isolated Frenchmen surrendered to the Russian infantry, while four squadrons of Russian hussars took up the pursuit of the retiring French cavalry. In response, Murat initially fed more squadrons into action but then, becoming aware of the approach of a large cavalry force, he ordered them to withdraw. This force, commanded by General Leitenant Essen II, was led forward by the tsar in person. Caught up in the excitement of his first battle, Alexander then enthusiastically rode to the flank where, as Langeron remarked, he was exposed to a danger 'far more than appropriate for his rank'.

As soon as Napoleon heard of the Allied advance he ordered Maréchal Soult to draw in the detachments of IV Corps and concentrate towards Austerlitz. With every likelihood of battle increasing he now deemed the time right to order the concentration of the army. GD Caffarelli, standing with his division of III Corps south of Brünn at Pohrlitz, received orders to march by 1.00am the following morning and arrive at Brünn by 6.30am. From there his orders required him to advance along the Olmütz road: confirmation of his final destination would follow. In the meantime, with the rest of III Corps still on the road, Napoleon attached Caffarelli's division to Lannes' V Corps. Bernadotte, currently towards Bohemia watching Archduke Ferdinand, received orders to make all speed to Brünn, leaving Wrede's division of Bavarians to oppose Ferdinand alone. Orders were also despatched to Maréchal Davout, whose other two divisions were at Vienna and Pressburg, to march on Brünn where they were to arrive at the earliest possible moment. To all of them he expressed the feeling that a great battle would take place east of Brünn on either 29 or 30 November. In this he overestimated the speed of the Allies' ponderous advance.

By the evening of 28 November Bagration's advance guard occupied the town of Rausnitz, which he captured without loss following an attack by two battalions of the Arkhangelogord Musketeer Regiment.[11] All day the French had fallen back before him with little show of a determined resistance. The main army, following behind, occupied a position to the west of Wischau. The Russian officers who predicted that Napoleon feared battle were in high-spirits and 'this hope became the prevailing opinion at headquarters'.[12] The tsar was exhilarated after his first experience of action.

In Kutscherau, a village just over 4 miles south of Wischau, these territorial losses and gains had a great impact on the lives of the local population. The French first arrived on 22 November, 'a wild and haggard people', and took all the oats and hay they could find, along with the entire store of winter fodder belonging to the priest, Anton Meixner. Over the next three days they stole clothes, wine and horses. On 25 November GB Sébastiani arrived and restored order, although Meixner complained that he was required to provide Sébastiani and twelve officers with food and drink for the next three days. Then, on 28 November, as the French fell back, the Russians arrived in Kutscherau. Meixner likened them to a plague of locusts: 'No cellar was deep enough or lock strong enough for them not to be broken open and everything that they found removed'. The following day Buxhöwden arrived in Kutscherau with his entourage, complete with hunting dogs and women, who were of a type that Meixner felt he could not describe before 'the ears of decent people'. The Russian general assembled eleven coaches and the same number of wagons, ninety-six horses and 139 men, which the priest had to find means to feed that day. When all had departed the devastated village, Meixner was left to reflect, 'we have the right to consider that the Russians have not arrived here to force out the enemy but to bring us painful perdition and starvation ... what more could they have committed if they had appeared as the enemy?!'[13]

Napoleon appeared at the Posoritz post house that evening, and following a meeting with Murat, Soult and Lannes – during which Lannes and Soult almost came to blows – he gave the order for their men to fall back to new positions. In the very early hours of 29 November, the first day that Napoleon had considered battle possible, Soult withdrew his corps from Austerlitz, passed over the Pratzen Plateau and retired to positions behind the Goldbach stream. Lannes and Murat also moved their men to locations directed by Napoleon, closer to the Olmütz–Brünn road. Now the army occupied the area so closely scrutinised by Napoleon eight days earlier.

The Bosenitzerberg, which drew the emperor's attention at that time, now bristled with artillery and had earned the name 'Santon' from his soldiers. It is said that those veterans of the Egyptian campaign gave it the name in reference to the santons – hilltop chapels where the remains of holy men were interred – they had encountered in the Middle East. Yet Napoleon need not have hurried his men back: the five columns of the Allied army spent the entire day repositioning to the south of the Olmütz–Brünn road, to positions on the high ground between Huluboschan and Kutscherau, covering no more than 4 miles. However, Bagration did press forward with the advance guard, although only for 3 miles, to a position just to the west of the Posoritz post house, where he encountered French outposts occupying a hill close to Holubitz.

Although quickly reinforced, these outposts soon fell back when threatened by a Russian advance. Finally, under cover of darkness, the last remaining outposts melted away, back to the main body of the army behind the Goldbach. Some 3 miles to the south-east of Bagration, FML Kienmayer led his cavalry unopposed into Austerlitz. Despite this limited progress, the main body of the Austro-Russian army, which started the day only 12 miles from Napoleon's final battle line, ended the day no closer. While the Allies dithered, the French acted. Orders calling Davout to unite with the army at Brünn arrived in Vienna at about 3.00pm that day. Quickly forwarded to the corps commander at Pressburg, Davout immediately sent the order back to Vienna for GD Friant to lead his division north, while GD Gudin commenced the long march from Pressburg. Friant marched throughout the night, linking up with Bourcier's dragoon division on the way.

Also on 29 November Napoleon finally met with Haugwitz at Brünn. This much-heralded meeting lasted four hours, during which the emperor largely outmanoeuvred the Prussian minister. Then, as Haugwitz returned to his quarters at the end of this meeting, a message and carriage arrived. The letter advised him that as battle was imminent he should proceed immediately to Vienna, where Napoleon assured him he could continue the discussions with Talleyrand – who received instructions to do no such thing. And so Haugwitz, like Stadion and Gyulai before him, was pushed aside to allow Napoleon to concentrate fully on the approaching battle.

Friant and Bourcier continued their relentless march throughout the 30 November. By the evening they had reached Nikolsburg, 45 miles north of Vienna and only 25 miles south of Brünn. Bernadotte continued his march towards Brünn while Soult, Murat and Lannes completed their concentrations.

In the Allied camp matters were as disorganised as usual. The original dispositions dictated by Weyrother called for an advance that outflanked the French left. The lack of a determined defence in the early encounters with the enemy outposts convinced him that the French were determined to avoid conflict and draw back on the Brünn–Vienna road. On 29 November, therefore, he realigned the Allied army to the left of the Olmütz–Brünn road, from where it could now threaten the right of the French and cut the Vienna road. This shift to the left continued on 30 November, but rather than just a redeployment, Weyrother's directions included a redesignation of the column identities. The original II Column became the new III Column, likewise the old III Column was renamed IV Column and IV Column became II Column. As well as this change in column designation, officers and regiments also transferred between columns. These complex changes tested to the limit the ingenuity of the already overworked staff officers.[14]

As these stuttering moves unfolded, Kutuzov, although nominally commander of the Allied army, saw his authority increasingly marginalized. Langeron commented that he was 'commander-in-chief of the army, but commanded nothing'.[15] On one occasion, when Kutuzov asked the tsar for instructions regarding the order of march, Alexander responded, 'That does not concern you.' All direction now came from Weyrother, encouraging the tsar's young and opinionated followers to ridicule the aged general behind his back, referring to him as 'General Dawdler'. Yet Kutuzov was not alone in receiving such insults. Langeron adds that these same aides treated the Austrian generals and officers with similar contempt, with 'uncalled for jokes about the way they spoke and even on the uniforms of their allies. Even Kaiser Francis was not safe from these indecencies.'[16]

Langeron recorded the frustrations of a typical day during the advance towards the French:

> 'In the morning each general had to send to the four other columns to seek the regiments which were to compose his, and which, sometimes, were obliged moreover to march [5 or more miles] to reach him ... It was always ten or eleven o'clock before we could assemble. Often the columns cut across each other ... We arrived late, we scattered to seek food, we plundered the villages and disorder was at its height.'[17]

While Friant's division of Davout's corps marched 45 miles on 30 November, the Austro-Russian army managed to struggle across bad cross-country roads for 10 miles to take up a position between Niemschan, running through Hodiegitz, to Herspitz, about 3 miles east of Austerlitz, which Kienmayer continued to occupy. Bagration, with the Army Advance Guard, remained on the Olmütz–Brünn road close to the Posoritz post house, with outposts pushed forward to Holubitz and Krug, covering the junction where the road to Austerlitz branched off to the south. The Imperial Guard was furthest back at Butschowitz, around 4 miles to the rear.

During the day French outposts occupied the high ground of the Pratzen Plateau and had a perfect view of the leaden movements of the Allies. Napoleon also took the opportunity to observe the slow advance, relieved by its laboured approach, for all the time Bernadotte and Davout were drawing closer to the area he had chosen for battle.

This constant flow of soldiers marching across the rolling Moravian hills between Brünn and Olmütz did not take place in a landscape emptied of people. Of course some did abandon their homes to seek safety beyond the reach of the marauding armies, but others remained and saw their property and livelihood destroyed by friend and foe alike. Close to the great shallow lake at Satschan, in the villages of Menitz, Satschan and Telnitz, many villagers chose to stay. A local priest recorded their traumatic experiences:

> 'On 18 November, the entire Austrian army … led by Kienmayer, marched through Menitz and the rear sections of the army stayed in Menitz, Satschan and Telnitz for the night. This evening marked the beginning of our sorrows. Because our homes and barns were unable to house the army, they settled themselves into the streets and lit more than a hundred fires very close to the buildings, creating a bright day in the dark of night…It looked as though Menitz itself were engulfed in flames … The entire sky was aglow with a deep red colour. On this night alone the villagers lost a large part of their wood supply, straw, fences, gates and doors, used by the soldiers to feed their unquenchable fires. All through the night the only sounds heard were the breaking of the gates, doors and fences, and the cries of the anxious citizens.'[18]

On the following day the Austrians marched on towards Jirzikowitz, leaving a small hussar rearguard, but at 3.00pm these too rode off when the leading elements of the French army came into view:

> 'We witnessed the last Austrian soldiers disappearing behind Telnitz and immediately following them we could hear thunderous tramping and the distinct clatter of weapons and army songs of the French. Panicked citizens, who had never seen an enemy in their lives, ran to

and fro, wringing their hands in despair. In their anxiety, Menitz' citizens set forth toward the enemy in order to meet them and appeal to their enemy's compassion and grace ... In the meantime, the French forged onward from Menitz to Telnitz without interruption. When the enemy finally arrived at the fields near the edge of Telnitz they suddenly halted, stacked their muskets, and rushed, en masse, into Telnitz, Menitz and Satschan, charging into buildings and stealing anything they could lay their hands on: food, clothes, beds, furniture (tables, chairs), and so on, and used all of these acquired possessions to feed their fires. This violence continued all throughout the night. You could see nothing but the constant comings and goings of the enemy with their booty.'[19]

On the morning of 20 November the French left the villages and marched off towards Austerlitz, but for three days the villagers watched a constant stream of soldiers marching through Menitz and Telnitz. Then on 24 November a French regiment arrived and was billeted on Satschan and Menitz, staying for five days and increasing the suffering:

'It is not possible to sufficiently describe the horrors the inhabitants endured in those five days. They hardly had any basic material left with which to survive themselves, but were still expected to supply the soldiers with food and horse feed; any non-compliance would have led to the people being killed or burned out of their homes and towns. However, fortunately the local pond was full of fish and so they could comfortably supply the enemy with food. Day after day cattle were slaughtered, and as soon as they were butchered, the next immediate thought was where to find more cattle and food for the following day.'[20]

Then, during the night of 29–30 November, a French drummer beat the assembly and 'in five minutes the entire regiment disappeared'. They returned after an hour, but thirty minutes later:

'another commotion could be heard. From the chaos and agitated discussions of the officers, one could judge that something big was going to happen. Soldiers, in much disarray, packed their kits hurriedly, and with pale faces informed the inhabitants, "The Russians are coming."'[21]

And with these worrying words the French departed. In fact a short period of peace descended on the troubled villagers. A detachment of Austrian dragoons and Russian Cossacks rode into Satschan, raising the hopes of salvation for the inhabitants, but these were swiftly dashed:

'We abandoned all our previous sorrows and anxieties as soon as we saw the glistening white uniforms and heard our mother tongue spoken by an officer. We hoped that we would be delivered from the horror of our enemies. But the regiment galloped away again after an officer questioned us about the distance and strength of the enemy, about which we were not able to answer very accurately.'[22]

For the villagers, the horror of their situation would soon return.

While the Allies continued to edge forward slowly, Napoleon took the opportunity to tour the area on which he intended to fight once more. Riding with his marshals, Napoleon openly discussed his plans for the coming battle. He had cavalry outposts on the Pratzen Plateau and he could easily have occupied it with his whole army. From this strong position, he explained to them, he could defeat the Allies but considered that it would result in 'just an ordinary battle'. An ordinary battle meant that once he gained the upper hand the Allies would fall back, as they had done so many times before, forcing him to follow deeper into Moravia or more likely towards Hungary, where Archduke Charles could add massive reinforcements to his opponent's army. Napoleon needed a climactic battle, one that would bring the campaign to a sudden and final end. He informed his marshals that by giving up this dominant position he hoped to tempt the Allies forward. If they left this high ground to turn his right – for the confused manoeuvring of the Allies suggested this was their strategy – then he intended to draw them on before launching a sudden strike against the plateau to place himself in their rear and on their flanks. For this purpose he intended concentrating the main force of the army close to the Santon. This, he felt sure, would result in a crushing defeat for the Allies, leaving them 'without hope of recovery'.[23]

That evening Napoleon returned to his headquarters, now established on Zuran Hill just over a mile south-west of the Santon, above the village of Schlapanitz. Here he received the news he had been anxiously awaiting. Bernadotte, with I Corps, was encamped outside the gates of Brünn, only 6 miles from the battlefield. Then more good news followed. Marshal Davout arrived, far ahead of his men, but he was able to promise the emperor that the divisions of Friant and Bourcier would be within reach the following day. Napoleon could anticipate an army about 74,000-strong with which to oppose the 78,000 of the Allies, who were gradually drawing closer. Since the Austro-Russian army commenced its march from Olmütz, Napoleon's strength had increased by just over 40 per cent.

As the two armies settled down for the night, lying only 9 miles apart, it was time for Napoleon to plan his final dispositions for the battle that now appeared inevitable. The eagles of France, Russia and Austria were gathering for the kill.

Chapter 13

'To Make the Russians Dance'

'Let us go the emperor replied, I hope
that tomorrow evening things will be better.
And us also, almost all the grenadiers
said, because we are more than
willing to make the Russians dance.'*

Dawn on the 1 December heralded another cold, damp day. But if Napoleon expected to see the Austro-Russian army advancing towards him as he climbed the Pratzen Plateau, he was to be disappointed. That morning, Allied headquarters circulated orders for further changes in the composition of the attacking columns, and it was not until the early afternoon that they finally began to march towards the plateau. Alexei Ermolov, the Podpolkovnik of a Russian horse artillery battery attached to V Column, watched the columns advance in amazement:

'The columns were colliding and penetrating each other, from which resulted disorder ... The armies broke up and intermixed and it was not easy for them to find their allocated positions in the dark. Columns of infantry, consisting of a large number of regiments, did not have a single person from the cavalry, so there was nothing to help them find out what was going on ahead, or to know where the nearest columns, appointed for assistance, were and what they were doing.'[1]

However, not all the Allies spent the entire morning in inactivity. Kienmayer probed south of the Pratzen Plateau with his cavalry, pushing outposts towards Satschan and Menitz, villages bordering the great shallow lake. At 10.00am a cloud of Kienmayer's Cossacks disturbed a reconnaissance from Menitz by the

---

* Exchange between Grenadiers of 4ème Ligne and Napoleon on the eve of battle, *Mémoires du Général Bigarré*

Austerlitz - 2 December 1805
THE FRENCH PLAN

V CORPS

CAVALRY RESERVE

I CORPS

IV CORPS (Vandamme)

IV CORPS (St. Hilaire)

ANTICIPATED ADVANCE OF AUSTRO-RUSSIAN ARMY

IV CORPS (Legrand)

III CORPS

TO OLMÜTZ

TO AUSTERLITZ

Welleschowitz

Krzenowitz

Birnbaum

Rausnitz

Zbeischow

Littawa

Satalitz

Ottnitz

Posoritz Post House

Holubitz

Krug

Blasowitz

Staré Vinohrady

Pratze

Hostieradek

Augezd

Pratzeberg

Puntowitz

Girzikowitz

Kobelnitz

Punic Infantry

Sokolnitz

Satschan

SATSCHAN LAKE

Telnitz

MENITZ LAKE

Gadbach

Ottmarau

Schlapnitz

Kobelnitz

Maximiliansdorf

Turas

Chirlitz

Wernölitz

BRÜNN

Bellowitz

Welatitz

Santon

Bosenitz

Sarton

Golubach

Austerlitz - 2 December 1805
THE AUSTRO-RUSSIAN PLAN

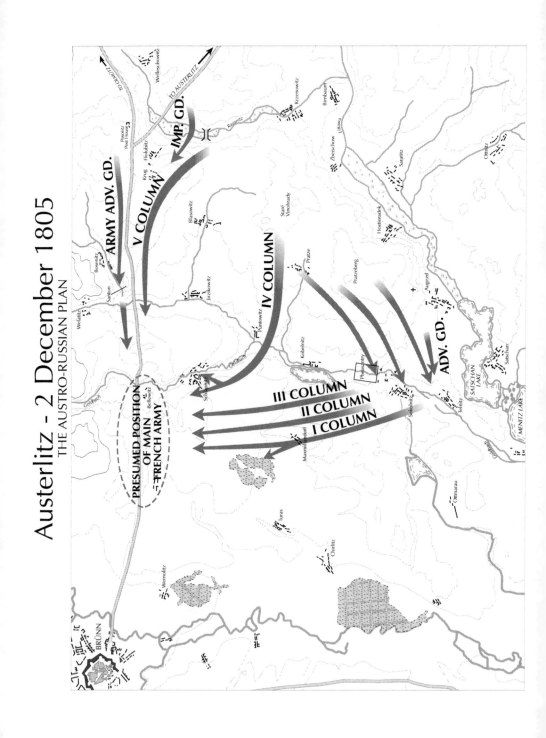

TO OLOMOUTZ

Weileschowitz

TO AUSTERLITZ

Posoritz Post House

Raunitz

Krzenowitz

Birnbaum

Holubitz

Krug

IMP. GD.

Littawa

Zbeischow

Sarantz

Ottnitz

ARMY ADV. GD.

V COLUMN

Blasowitz

Starè
Vinohrady

Hostieradek

Bosenitz

Pratze

Pratzeberg

Augezd

Sarton

Wielatitz

Jirzikowitz

IV COLUMN

Puntowitz

Kobelnitz

Puntowitz

ADV. GD.

SATSCHAN
LAKE

Satschan

Goldbach

Bellowitz

Schlapanitz

III COLUMN

Sokolnitz

Telnitz

MENITZ LAKE

PRESUMED POSITION
OF MAIN
FRENCH ARMY

II COLUMN

I COLUMN

Maximiliandorf

Goldbach

Turas

Ottmarau

Chiritz

Wernöditz

BRÜNN

French 11ème Chasseur à cheval. After much tentative manoeuvring by both sides, the Cossacks were eventually driven off and the French horsemen in turn retired to their bivouac at the extreme right of the French position.[2] Elsewhere outposts kept up an annoying exchange of fire throughout the morning.

The slow, deliberate movements of the Allied army observed by Napoleon convinced him it would now occupy the Pratzen Plateau as he had hoped. With this high ground secured, he anticipated the Allies forming a line from a position opposite the Santon in the north, running southwards along the plateau, to a point facing the village of Kobelnitz on the Goldbach. Before returning to his camp on the Zuran Hill, Napoleon toured through the army visiting many of his regiments and batteries, encouraging the men, for at last he felt certain that battle would follow the next day.

Once back at headquarters, Napoleon prepared his plan of battle based on the latest movements of the Allies, and at about 8.00pm he assembled his senior commanders to issue them with their orders and divulge his plans in detail. As he did so, the concentration of the French army on the left was complete. Suchet's division of V Corps stood across the Brünn–Olmütz road close to the Santon, extending towards the village of Jirzikowitz, with a detachment manning the Santon. Caffarelli's division, now attached to V Corps, drew up behind them. Bernadotte arrived with his corps during the day and fell in to the rear of Caffarelli. Murat, with the Cavalry Reserve, occupied a position behind this left wing of the army. Oudinot's grenadier division formed to the east of Zuran Hill, while the Garde Impériale occupied a position on the west side, between the hill and the village of Bellowitz. Two of Soult's divisions – Vandamme and Saint-Hilaire – formed on the hills behind Jirzikowitz and Puntowitz, with Vandamme to the fore. To cover all the ground south of Puntowitz, Soult's final infantry division – Legrand's – concentrated behind Kobelnitz with detachments extended in a thin string along the Goldbach stream to Telnitz, where the small battalion of Tirailleurs du Pô occupied the village.

The orders required Vandamme and Saint-Hilaire to have crossed the stream to their front by 7.00am and Legrand to occupy Kobelnitz. While Soult's corps took up these new positions, Suchet was to narrow his frontage by reforming his division, moving his right hand brigade behind his left brigade. Caffarelli would occupy the space freed up on Suchet's right. As Caffarelli moved forward, Bernadotte's men moved to occupy the ground he vacated, taking up a position with his left to the rear of the Santon. Oudinot's grenadiers were to move forward, placing their left behind Caffarelli's right. During the day, Davout rode back to rejoin his fatigued men, who continued on their extraordinary march, his new orders reaching him on the road. By the evening Friant and Bourcier made camp near the monastery at Gross Raigern. In forty-eight hours these men had marched a phenomenal 65 miles and, although almost half of the men dropped by the wayside unable to keep up the pace, the

4,000 men that remained were now only a little over 5 miles west of Telnitz, within touching distance of the battlefield.

Davout's orders required his men to be on the road again at 5.00am, marching to a position near the wood at Turas, some 3½ miles west of Kobelnitz, from where they could support Soult's weakly held right flank. At the conclusion of the meeting, all the marshals were instructed to return to headquarters at 7.30am in case enemy movements during the night necessitated significant changes. The result of these careful dispositions meant that much of the great concentration of the army took place hidden from prying eyes. While the left manoeuvred into position, strongly anchored on the fortified Santon, the far right, south of Kobelnitz, remained extended and weak, but it could expect to draw support in the morning from Davout.

Napoleon then explained his plan. He hoped to draw the Allies from the plateau, encouraging them to attack him along the line of the Goldbach, where he would attempt to delay them for as long as possible. Then, when the Allies had weakened their concentration on the plateau, he planned to launch his centre on a rapid advance against this high ground from where, once established, he could operate in strength against the rear and flanks of the Allies. Meanwhile, the left would advance and brush aside any opposition before wheeling to the right and completing the encirclement of the Austro-Russian army.

Even as Napoleon explained his intentions, riders passed amongst the army distributing a proclamation, announcing his basic plan to even the most lowly novice soldier. Reproduced on the emperor's mobile printing press, it informed his soldiers that they faced a Russian army determined to avenge the Austrian army of Ulm. But he assured them of the strength of their positions and added that 'while the enemy march upon my batteries, they will open their flanks to my attack'.[3] He urged them to 'carry disorder and confusion amongst the enemy', but asserted that should victory appear uncertain for a moment then he would join them in the front rank. But most importantly of all, he promised that victory would bring an end to the campaign and with it the reward of rest and peace. The proclamation did not reach Lieutenant Sibelet and the 11ème Chasseurs à cheval in their exposed bivouac behind Menitz until 1.00am. Unwilling to attract enemy attention to their position, an officer read it to the men by the light of a candle shrouded under a coat. Sibelet recorded that his men, inspired by the emperor's words, vowed to 'overcome or die'.

With the French army in position, seeking warmth, food and rest on another freezing night, the Allies were still stumbling up the steep eastern slopes of the Pratzen Plateau, searching for their appointed camping grounds in the dark. General Leitenant Dokhturov led his I Column – about 9,500 men – to encamp at the southern end of the heights, above the village of Augezd, detaching a battalion of *jäger* to occupy the village. General Leitenant Langeron took up a position between Dokhturov and the village of Pratze with II Column (some

Battle of Austerlitz - 2 December 1805
Positions occupied prior to the Austro-Russian Advance

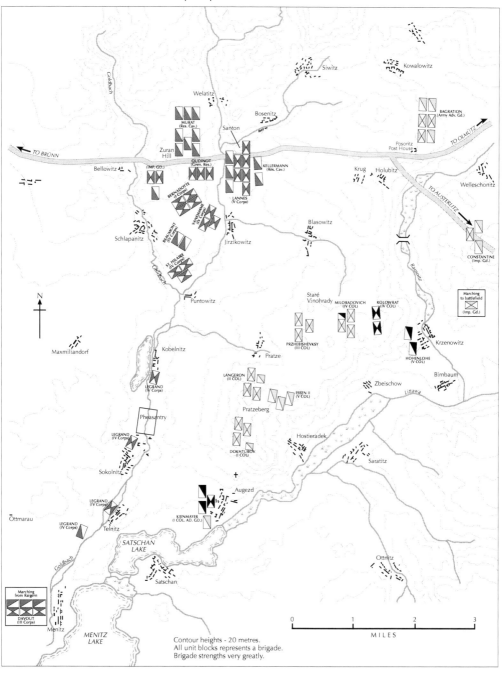

Contour heights - 20 metres.
All unit blocks represents a brigade.
Brigade strengths very greatly.

11,500 men). General Leitenant Przhebishevsky brought III Column – approximately 8,400 men – onto the heights to the right of Pratze. All three of these columns, forming the left wing of the army, came under the overall command of General Leitenant Buxhöwden and were composed of Russian troops.

FML Kienmayer's command, a mixed Austro-Russian formation about 5,500-strong, operated as an advance guard for I Column. As soon as the columns began to arrive in strength and occupy the plateau, Kienmayer headed south to post his men below the heights in front of Augezd, having been reinforced by five battalions of Austrian *grenz* infantry, transferred to his command during the day.

The IV Column, another mixed formation, under the joint command of the Russian General Leitenant Miloradovich and the Austrian Feldzeugmeister Kolowrat, advanced with about 14,500 men to camp on the plateau in the rear of III Column.

FML Prince Liechtenstein now commanded the main cavalry force, a mixture of Austrian and Russian regiments, some 5,300-strong. Although detailed to camp below the plateau in the rear of III and IV Column, in the confusion, part of the column spent the night on the plateau close to Langeron's II Column.

On the far right, Prince Bagration, commanding the Army Advance Guard – about 12,700 men – maintained his position across the Brünn–Olmütz road, but pushed his left beyond Holubitz towards Blasowitz, to offer flank protection to the march of the army.

The Imperial Guard, with 9,000 men, provided the army's only reserve and took up a position on hills to the north of Krzenowitz, in which village the Allied command set up its headquarters.[4]

From his position on the Zuran Hill, Napoleon's gaze followed the crest of the Pratzen from north to south. Now, all along the summit, the glow of camp fires revealed the position of the Allied army as it prepared for battle. Then, some distance away to the south, the sound of firing caused concern and he despatched a number of staff officers to investigate.

The firing came from Telnitz, some 6 miles away. After Kienmayer moved off the plateau to the position in front of Augezd he pushed the 3. O'Reilly Chevaulegers towards Telnitz to feel for any opposition. At the village they encountered the Tirailleurs de Pô. Taken by surprise the Italians offered a brief firefight in the dark before abandoning the village to the Austrian cavalrymen, who left a half-squadron garrison and returned to Augezd. Alerted now to what had taken place, Napoleon rode south with Soult and a small suite of officers and attendants to investigate for himself. This move against Telnitz had surprised Napoleon and he recognised a need to strengthen this southern end of the line. But before the party could return, they ran into one of Kienmayer's probing Cossack patrols. In that brief moment the life of

Napoleon hung in the balance and with it the outcome of the campaign. However, the small group evaded capture, although the horse of Napoleon's surgeon, A.U. Yvan, became stuck in the mud by the Goldbach and had to be pulled free before the whole group dashed back to the French lines: the coming battle alone would decide the destiny of Europe.

As he returned to his headquarters, Napoleon passed through the bivouacs of the army. Discovering the emperor in their midst, soldiers grabbed handfuls of straw from their rough shelters, and setting fire to them, attached them to poles culled from the surrounding vineyards. Holding them aloft to light his way they cheered his progress with cries of 'Vive l'Empereur!' Others took up the cry, adding to the fiery river of light that extended through the camps. This impromptu display of devotion by the army greatly moved Napoleon, coming as it did on the eve of battle and the eve of the first anniversary of his coronation as emperor.[5] This sudden eruption of light and commotion in the French lines startled the Allied outposts too. Yet far from being taken as an indication of the extent and concentration of the French army, many in the Allied camp saw it as confirmation of the rumours that were rife: that La Grande Armée was about to retreat.[6]

As the French army settled down again, Napoleon began to revise his orders in respect of what he had seen at Telnitz. The campfires he observed in front of Augezd and the attack on Telnitz suggested an Allied attack directed further to the south than originally anticipated. It would be necessary for Legrand to extend his division southwards to increase the security of the villages of Telnitz and Sokolnitz. Accordingly, in the early hours of the morning the 3ème Ligne attacked Telnitz, drove out the Austrian cavalry and recaptured the village. GB Merle's brigade formed to the north of Telnitz; the two single battalions of the Tirailleurs du Pô and Tirailleurs Corses covering Telnitz and the riverbank between Telnitz and Sokolnitz, with the two battalions of 26ème Légère ordered to march for the village of Sokolnitz. GB Lavasseur, with the final brigade of Legrand's division, occupied Kobelnitz and extended towards a large walled park north of Sokolnitz, known as the Pheasantry. This repositioning affected other formations too. Saint-Hilaire received orders to move his division from the second line and advance to a position on the right of Vandamme from where he was to prepare to cross the stream at Puntowitz. However, by the time he received the order at about 3.00am, a thick fog had descended on the valley and the division, unable to move, remained in position until morning.[7] Bernadotte, assigned to support Lannes, received orders to realign to the south, behind Vandamme's left.

The Allies, too, were busy finalising their plans. At 11.00pm, with the Allied army now established on the plateau, orders arrived directing the column commanders to assemble at Krzenowitz to receive orders for the following day. All except Bagration attended. At about 1.00am, when all were assembled, Weyrother arrived after an exhausting day in the saddle and spread a large and detailed map of the area between Brünn and Austerlitz on a table. According to Langeron he then:

> 'read us the arrangements in a raised voice and with a conceited air which was designed to show us his deep-seated belief in his own merit and in our inability. He resembled a high school master reading a lesson to some young school children: we were perhaps likely schoolboys but he was far from being a good teacher. Kutuzov, seated and half asleep since we arrived at his place, eventually did fall asleep completely before we left. Buxhöwden, standing, was listening and certainly understood nothing. Miloradovich kept quiet, Przhebishevsky stood at the back and Dokhturov was the only one who examined the map with any attention.'[8]

Weyrother described his plan in painstaking detail – in German – and waited patiently while a staff officer, Maior Toll, translated each section into Russian. In essence, he explained that the Allied army extended beyond the French right, so in by-passing it and occupying the villages of Telnitz, Sokolnitz and Kobelnitz, they could push onto the plain beyond. Then, advancing between Turas and Schlapanitz, they would throw the French back to the difficult hilly ground to the north. I Column was to attack Telnitz, II Column targeted the valley between Telnitz and Sokolnitz, and III Column Sokolnitz Castle. Once past the Goldbach, the columns were to wheel northwards with the head of each column in alignment. Moving last, IV Column was to pass to the right of Kobelnitz, align itself with the first three columns, and swing north towards Schlapanitz. Bagration was to hold his ground until he saw IV Column turn north, then he was to march straight ahead and engage the French left. However, Weyrother's plan presumed the main French strength to be occupying a position further back than it was, between Schlapanitz and Bellowitz. This lack of understanding of the French position is epitomised by the fact that Liechtenstein's cavalry column was instructed to push onto the heights 'between Schlapanitz and the Inn of Leschern'. This position lay close to the Santon and would place it but a mile from Napoleon's headquarters and within touching distance of Vandamme's division. The final component, the reserve formed by the Imperial Guard, was to advance to a position behind Blasowitz and Krug, to support Liechtenstein and Bagration.

Weyrother ended his instructions by stressing that the columns should commence their movement at 7.00am, an hour before sunrise, and emphasised that once they had secured their first objectives in the Goldbach valley, they were to align themselves with their neighbouring columns before wheeling northwards.

Having listened to everything Weyrother had to say Langeron spoke up: 'General, this is all very well, but if the enemy anticipate this and attack us near Pratze, what will we do? That scenario is not covered.' Weyrother replied: 'You know the audacity of Bonaparte; if he was able to attack us, he would have done it today.'

Langeron then referred to the great illumination seen in the French camps earlier and questioned its significance. In response, Weyrother assured him that it must either signal that the French were retreating or moving back to a new position. In either case, the Austrian chief of staff asserted, 'the orders remain the same.'[9]

It was 3.00am before Weyrother finished, at which point Kutuzov, who had taken no part in the meeting, finally stirred and dismissed the commanders back to their columns. But Kutuzov was no fool – it seems likely that he listened carefully to all that was said. He did not want to fight a battle now, and having been removed from the decision making process, he had no intention of being blamed for any defeat, which he sensed would follow. Only now could Maior Toll begin making a copy of Weyrother's orders in Russian. Around him a number of adjutants hovered impatiently while he completed his task: only then could they begin to recopy them for distribution to their columns.

Podpolkovnik Ermolov recalled that an officer arrived at his camp and handed a copy to General-Adjutant Uvarov. It ran for several pages:

> 'filled with difficult names of villages, lakes, rivers, valleys, and elevations and it was so complicated that it was impossible either to understand or remember them. He was not allowed to copy them, because a lot of other officers had to read it, and there were very few copies. I have to admit that after I listened to this disposition I had as little comprehension of it as if I was not aware of its existence; the only thing that I understood was that we were supposed to attack the enemy tomorrow.'[10]

But Ermolov was one of the lucky ones: some officers did not see the orders until about 8.00am, and by then the battle was already underway.

Langeron visited his outposts at a little after 4.00am and recorded that the 'deepest silence reigned everywhere, the darkness was impenetrable and I could discover nothing'.[11] Across the Goldbach, in the French lines, Général de brigade Paul Thiébault was preparing his division for the coming battle. His men gathered 'in the greatest silence under a clear and freezing sky'.[12] But during the early hours of the morning a thick winter's fog settled in the valley of the Goldbach, drawing a veil all along the entire French front line, behind which the army completed its arrangements unobserved by the Allies.

FML Kienmayer, the Austrian commander of I Column's advance guard, was first to move on the morning of 2 December, his task, to clear the village of Telnitz for the advance of Dokhturov's main body. He knew the lie of the land well following his recent reconnaissance patrols, and with his outpost having been thrown out of Telnitz, he expected it to be vigorously defended.

The small village on the eastern bank of the Goldbach was surrounded by vineyards and ditches, making it well-suited for defence, and it lay sheltered behind a small hill interposed between it and Kienmayer's men.

At 6.30am, in the pre-dawn darkness, Kienmayer advanced from Augezd, probing tentatively forward with the 1. Szeckel-Grenzregiment. These tough soldiers from Siebenburgen (now Transylvania in Romania), on the turbulent frontier of the Habsburg Empire, had only joined Kienmayer's command the previous day, under Generalmajor Carneville. The leading battalion closed on Telnitz with the regiment's other battalion in support. Detachments of French light cavalry (GB Margaron's brigade, including Lieutenant Sibelet's 11ème Chasseurs à cheval) were observed towards Menitz and on the high ground west of Telnitz. To oppose these, Kienmayer sent a detachment towards Menitz and formed the 4. Hessen-Homburg-Husaren to the right of the *grenz* infantry and the 11. Szeckel-Husaren to their left as protection against cavalry attacks. The 2. Szeckel-Grenzregiment stood further back in reserve with a single battalion of the 7. Brod-Grenzregiment from Slavonia.

In front of them, defending the hill shielding Telnitz, and in the ditches that surrounded the village, waited the weak battalion of the Tirailleurs du Pô, possibly supported by elements of the Tirailleurs Corses. These two battalions of foreign troops, from Italy and Corsica, would experience a long and distinguished career in the French army, but for now the ravages of campaign had taken their toll and between them they mustered less than 900 men. However, behind them a battalion of 3ème Ligne hastily prepared the village for defence, while the remaining two battalions of this regiment stood behind the village in support. In all, some 2,500 infantry, supported by about 1,000 light cavalry as well as artillery, waited for Kienmayer's attack.

Against these men the single *grenz* battalion, about 600-strong, advanced in silence. It was still dark as they approached the hill, led forward by Oberst Knesevich, but as they came into view, the *tirailleurs* lining the crest opened a devastating fire. Soldiers were falling all around and the supporting cavalry suffered too, but they maintained their position on the flanks. It came as a rude awakening to those who anticipated only light opposition along the Goldbach.

With casualties mounting, the battalion of 1. Szeckel fell back, seeking what cover it could in the vineyards. Seeing the attack grind to a halt, Kienmayer ordered the supporting battalion of the regiment forward. Twice these battalions advanced together up the hill and both times a murderous defensive fire repulsed them. The entire success of the Allied battle plan now depended on I Column leading the way across the Goldbach, so Kienmayer ordered Majorgeneral Stutterheim to lead a new attack. This time the 1. Szeckel succeeded and the *tirailleurs* fell back to occupy positions along the stream towards Sokolnitz. Only now did the Austrians realise the extent of the task confronting them as below, barricaded in the village, the 3ème Ligne awaited their assault.

Kienmayer ordered Carneville to bring forward the other three battalions of *grenz* infantry to support the attack. The Austrians now committed some 3,000 men to the attack on Telnitz, but as the reserve moved forward, they passed through the bodies of hundreds of casualties from the initial attacks. A number of attacks rolled forward and one almost reached the village, causing the defenders to commit their reserve: stubbornly fighting for every wall, tree and ditch, the French infantry threw the Austrians back.

It was now about 7.30am and the battle had been underway for about an hour, but to Kienmayer's surprise, the main body of Dokhturov's I Column was still not in sight. The two Szeckel regiments, supported by the Brod battalion, continued to make fresh attacks on the village, but they lacked the urgency and determination of their earlier forays. Then, out of the lifting early morning gloom, the head of Dokhturov's column came into view. It had finally emerged from the chaos and confusion which reigned on the plateau, as each of the allied columns struggled to assemble their men in the dark prior to their advance on the Goldbach.

Kienmayer sent a message to Buxhöwden, overall commander of the left wing, requesting urgent assistance. General Leitenant Fedor Fedorovich (Friedrich Wilhelm) Buxhöwden, a 55-year-old Estonian, had joined the army as a cadet officer at fourteen. He married well and through his wife's connections, had entered the Russian court, making quick promotion through the officer ranks. Langeron, who served under him and had an axe to grind, later described his commander as, 'the perfect emblem of stupidity and self-importance,' adding that he was a 'rather good subordinate officer … but as a general no one was more incapable of being commander-in-chief.'[13] However, Buxhöwden responded promptly to Kienmayer's plea and hurried forward General Maior Löwis' brigade: a single battalion of 7. Jäger and all three battalions of the New Ingermanland Musketeer Regiment. The *jäger* advanced straight up the hill to join the Szeckel infantry, while the musketeers formed a reserve behind them on the level ground. Together, the *jäger* and two of the Szeckel battalions stormed down on Telnitz, followed by the other three *grenz* battalions. The sight proved too much for the battered 3ème Ligne, who abandoned Telnitz before they could be overwhelmed and regrouped just over half a mile back on a rise by the road to Ottmarau.

Kienmayer quickly ordered his cavalry to push on beyond the village and probed towards a low plateau occupied by Margaron's cavalry. The two mounted bodies skirmished but neither side gained any advantage. Buxhöwden remained immobile some distance back, with Dokhturov and his two remaining infantry brigades. Holding this position he peered northwards searching for any sign of II and III Column: a necessary condition before contemplating an advance beyond the Goldbach.

Buxhöwden was not the only one awaiting developments. A mile away, across the frozen lake in Satschan, some of the villagers gathered and watched nervously from the church tower as the battle for Telnitz developed:

'We were terrified by the noise of a very raucous fight between advance guards on the fields over Telnitz and Augezd ... There were more and more shots, and when dawn finally broke, the first cannon shot hummed from Augezd Hill, by the small Chapel of St Antonin, and after that, a second shot rang out, followed by yet a third. After this, very intense gun fire started, so loud and rapid you could not separate one shot from another, and cannon shots thundered in brief succession. The ground shook and the tower itself seemed to tremble with us. We all turned pale and looked to each other silently, because we were unable to speak with the fear we were feeling. Finally, when the bright day began, it was possible to see many deep rows of soldiers, who were running against each other on the fields between Telnitz and Augezd. Eventually, smoke and dust completely clouded the horrifying theatre that surrounded us, and one could only hear the thundering of cannons, the clatter of muskets, and the war cries of the soldiers.'[14]

Up on the Pratzen Plateau the situation in the camps was indeed chaotic. Having arrived after dark and grabbed what rest they could, the column commanders attempted to form up their men before daybreak, prior to marching them towards destinations they could not see, and for which many officers still had no orders. At about 6.00am Langeron, commanding II Column, discovered the Russian cavalry of V Column amidst his men. They had misunderstood their orders and should not have even been on the plateau. Amongst the milling mass of cavalry and infantry Langeron located General Leitenant Shepelev and informed him that he should be $1\frac{1}{2}$ miles to the north. In response, Shepelev assured Langeron that Prince Liechtenstein had ordered him to this position, adding that if in the wrong, he would move at daybreak, as he did not know where to go in the darkness.[15]

The black winter sky began to lighten just before 7.00am. At this signal Langeron prepared II Column to move off the plateau and descend towards the Goldbach. Langeron formed his men behind 8. Jäger, the only unit under his command to have battle experience. Following the *jäger* came a company of pioneers, then Olsufiev's infantry brigade (the Vyborg, Permsk and Kursk Musketeer Regiments) with Kamenski I's infantry brigade (Ryazan Musketeer and Phanagoria Grenadier Regiments) forming the rear of the column. Just as 8. Jäger began to move off, the Russian cavalry that had appeared on the plateau an hour earlier recognised their mistake, and having reformed, began to march off, cutting right through II Column. Langeron halted his men and stood with

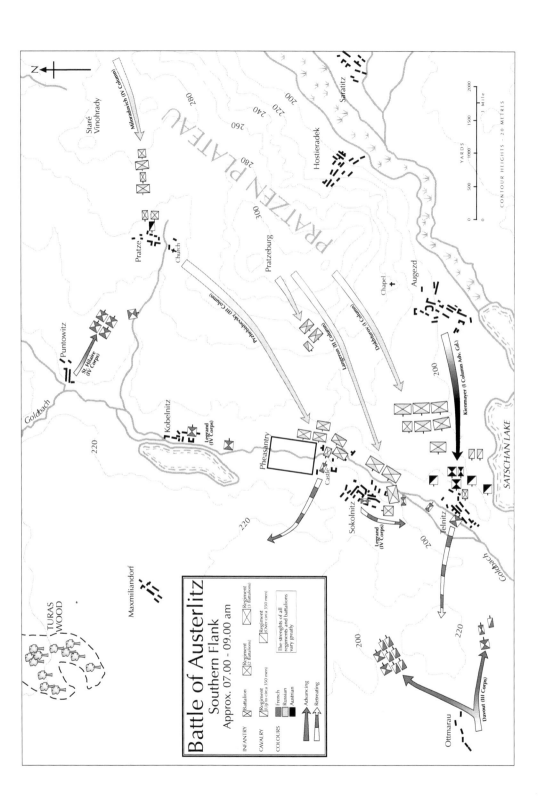

Battle of Austerlitz
Southern Flank
Approx. 07.00 – 09.00 am

INFANTRY   ☒ Battalion   ☒ Regiment (2 Battalions)   ☒ Regiment (3 Battalions)

CAVALRY   ▨ Regiment (Up to circa 350 men)   ▨ Regiment (Over circa 350 men)

The strengths of all regiments and battalions vary greatly

COLOURS   French   Russian   Austrian   Advancing   Retreating

CONTOUR HEIGHTS – 20 METRES

YARDS

1 Mile

PRATZEN PLATEAU

Staré Vinohrady

Miloradovich (IV Column)

Saratitz

Hostieradek

Pratze

Church

Pratzeburg

Przibischevsky (III Column)

Langeron (II Column)

Dokhturov (I Column)

Chapel

Augezd

Kienmayer (I Column Adv. Gd.)

Puntowitz

St. Hilaire (IV Corps)

Goldbach

Kobelnitz

Legrand (IV Corps)

Pheasantry

Castle

Sokolnitz

Legrand (IV Corps)

Telnitz

SATSCHAN LAKE

Goldbach

TURAS WOOD

Maxmiliandorf

Ottmarau

Davout (III Corps)

increasing impatience for about an hour as the cavalry moved slowly through his formation: then, deciding enough was enough, he pushed his men straight through their mounted comrades, thus adding to the confusion.

These delays meant Langeron was already roughly an hour behind schedule when he finally moved forward at around 8.00am. But Kamenski's brigade, bringing up the rear of the column, again found their path blocked by the cavalry, who presumably did not take kindly to Langeron's actions.

As his column moved slowly down from the plateau, Langeron observed I Column holding a position on his left while Kienmayer's advance guard cleared Telnitz. Drawing level with I Column, Langeron rode over to speak to Buxhöwden, who was only 300 paces away. He advised the commander of the army's left wing that there was no sign of III Column yet, which should have appeared on his right by now. III Column, commanded by General Leitenant Przhebishevsky, another foreign officer in Russian service who Langeron felt 'was not a distinguished general and had set his sights too low to be useful, but was a brave and honest man', had also suffered disruption at the hands of the cavalry. Having cleared Langeron's camp, the horsemen progressed through that of Przhebishevsky, north-east of Pratze village.

With no sign of III Column, Langeron sent forward 8. Jäger to skirmish with French light troops he could see near Sokolnitz, while artillery from both sides bombarded the village. Finally, at about 8.30am, III Column came into view, having made slow progress through the confines of Pratze and across ploughed fields that further retarded their march. All but two of these battalions had marched to Braunau and back. As these two columns began their march Sokolnitz was only lightly defended but, even as II and III Columns prepared to attack, the two battalions of 26ème Légère ordered from Kobelnitz were taking up their positions. The first battalion moved into the smouldering village while three companies of the second occupied the castle – in effect a large fortified country house – and its grounds, some 600 yards to the north. The remaining companies of the second battalion drew up on rising ground west of the castle, alongside two artillery pieces.

With support in sight, Langeron curtailed his artillery bombardment, and even though Kamenski's brigade had still not joined him, he set his column in motion, aligning his right on Sokolnitz. Leading with the 8. Jäger and the Vyborg and Permsk Musketeers, II Column encountered stiff opposition along the Goldbach right up to the edge of Sokolnitz, suffering many casualties in the process. The first battalion of 26ème Légère in the village – taking advantage of any cover it could find – opened a heavy fire on Langeron's leading troops, and instead of marching between Telnitz and Sokolnitz as directed by his orders, Langeron allowed himself to be drawn to attack and clear the village.

Further to the north, Przhebishevsky approached the castle, sending a battalion of 7. Jäger out to his right to protect his flank and hopefully make contact with IV Column, which should by now have been moving down from the plateau towards Kobelnitz. To clear the castle, he ordered General Maior Müller III to advance with his brigade, the remaining battalion of 7. Jäger and three battalions of the Galicia Musketeers: in all about 2,000 men swarmed across the muddy banks of the Goldbach towards the castle, anxiously watched from behind the walls and outbuildings by around 250 men of the 26ème Légère.

Despite their experience, there was little the soldiers of this tiny garrison could do in the circumstances, and they withdrew before the Russians were able to surround them. The retiring light infantry fell back on the main body of their battalion west of the castle, and once they had cleared the field of fire, the two artillery pieces opened up with canister on the disorganised mass below them. This fire added to the disorder, and when Müller fell severely wounded this confusion increased. At this moment the 2/26ème Légère charged forward and drove the bewildered Russians back.

Przhebishevsky, who until the day before had served under Langeron in II Column, knew neither his men nor officers, but rode forward in an attempt to rally them. In this he was successful and then called forward General Maior Strik, with the Butyrsk Musketeer Regiment, to take local command. Strik handled his men well and threw the 26ème Légère back to the high ground once more. Then, making another push, he drove the battalion off the slopes completely and took the two artillery pieces. The 2/26ème fell back to the north-west, towards Maxmiliandorf. Then, while Strik began to reorder his men, Przhebishevsky formed the Narva, Azov and Podolsk Musketeer Regiments as a reserve under General Leitenant Wimpffen, east of the Goldbach and close to the walled Pheasantry.

While the fighting around the castle intensified, Langeron launched his men into Sokolnitz. Two battalions of 8. Jäger and the Vyborg Musketeers stormed the village from the south, while the Permsk and Kursk Musketeers waited in reserve on the eastern bank of the Goldbach. Here, by the bridge, the stream widened and became a difficult obstacle. The battalion of 26ème Légère in the village fought stubbornly, but already outnumbered almost 3-to-1 by the determined Russians, their position became even more vulnerable when part of III Column entered the northern end of Sokolnitz. With casualties rapidly mounting and the Russians closing in on all sides, the 1/26ème abandoned the village and took flight southwards, in the direction of Telnitz. It was now around 9.00am and I, II and III Columns had achieved their initial goals.

But Weyrother's plan had anticipated little or no opposition at this stage, with the formations advancing in column and only deploying into battle formation once across the Goldbach. Instead, Langeron and Przhebishevsky needed to commit over 5,000 men to clear the determined 1,500 men of the 26ème Légère from Sokolnitz. To the south, Kienmayer and Dokhturov used almost 4,000 troops to drive approximately 2,000 men of 3ème Ligne and the weak battalion of the Tirailleurs du Pô from Telnitz. In effect – adding the

Tirailleurs Corses to the defenders along the Goldbach – 4,000 French had delayed the march of some 28,000 Allied troops for about an hour.

Even though the Goldbach now appeared secure, both Langeron and Przhebishevsky cast concerned glances towards the vast empty space on their right, where IV Column should have been, and of which there was still no news. Although there was little opposition in front of I Column, Buxhöwden refrained from ordering it forward. His orders were specific: each of his three columns should align on one another, and for the moment, II and III Column needed to reform after the battle for Sokolnitz before they could press on. It was the high water mark of the battle for the Allies.

While Napoleon awaited the arrival of his marshals at headquarters at 7.30am, the sound of gunfire from Telnitz confirmed his assumptions on Allied strategy were correct. At the same time the army shuffled into their final positions. Descending from the high ground and destined to lead the attack, Soult's two divisions passed through the villages of Puntowitz (Saint-Hilaire) and Jirzikowitz (Vandamme). Once in position, they stood silently on the eastern bank of the stream, eagerly awaiting the order to attack, their presence shrouded from the enemy by the fog and campfire smoke that blanketed the valley.

As Napoleon discussed his plans, reports began to arrive with news of the movements of the Allied army. Although some fog still clung to the Pratzen Plateau, a stream of messages revealed that those troops camped near Pratze overnight were marching toward Sokolnitz, and confirmed that fighting was already underway around Telnitz. Napoleon waited: his plan called for an assault on the plateau denuded of troops.

Then, close to 8.00am, the sun rose clean above the heights. It was an extraordinary sunrise – one that many observers later recalled in their accounts – which climbed slowly in the sky, 'as pure and radiant as in the brightest days of spring'. Then the fog on the heights began to disperse and the assembled officers peered into the glaring light, searching for any sign of enemy formations.

A report arrived soon after, finally confirming that the Allies had abandoned the plateau. It was the news Napoleon desperately hoped to hear. He dismissed his officers back to their men, keeping an ADC from each at headquarters who would carry the word when each corps was to commence its attack. But Maréchal Soult remained with the emperor. Soult, the 36-year-old commander of IV Corps, was extremely ambitious – as well as selfish, avaricious, and difficult to get along with – and also brave. He had excelled in the organisation and training of his corps at Boulogne, and Napoleon had entrusted to him the largest corps of La Grande Armée.

With one of Soult's divisions – Legrand's – already engaged along the Goldbach, the responsibility of carrying out the emperor's great plan fell to the marshal's other two divisions. Turning to Soult, Napoleon asked: 'How long will your troops take to ascend the Pratzen Plateau?' Soult, considering that Saint-Hilaire now occupied a position in front of Puntowitz, only about $1^{1}/_{2}$ miles from Pratze, replied confidently 'Twenty minutes at the most.' 'In that case,' Napoleon pondered, 'let us wait another quarter of an hour.' The time was approaching 8.30am.

However, contrary to the information Napoleon had received, the plateau was not clear of Allied troops. Out of sight on the eastern edge of the plateau, above Krzenowitz, IV Column still manned its camp. Under the joint command of the Russian General Leitenant Miloradovich and the Austrian Feldzeugmeister Kolowrat-Krakowsky, the column was strong in numbers but wanting in strength. All the Russian battalions had endured the long march to Braunau and the Austrian troops were a mixed bag. They included only one full regiment, the rest a gathering of individual battalions, many scraped together for the aborted defence of Vienna with only a few weeks training under their belts. Kutuzov attached his own headquarters to this column and in accordance with Weyrother's plan it was not to move until all three columns forming the left wing were well underway. Until III Column cleared its front, opening the route towards Kobelnitz, there was little for it to do. Due to the disruption caused by the Russian cavalry, Przhebishevsky's III Column marched late and had only just moved off the plateau when Tsar Alexander and Kaiser Francis arrived with their extensive entourages. Although neither monarch had attended Weyrother's meeting, they received copies of the plan and Alexander fully expected the march to have commenced at 7.00am as specified and to find the plateau clear of Allied troops. The presence of IV Column still in camp with stacked arms, as well as the presence of Kutuzov himself, surprised Alexander greatly. As Kutuzov approached the imperial party, the tsar, unaware of the delays experienced by II and III Column, demanded: 'Mikhail Larionovich,[16] why do you not advance?' 'I wait,' answered Kutuzov, 'until all the troop columns are united.' The tsar retorted: 'We are not on the field of exercise where one awaits the arrival of all the troops to begin the parade.' 'Sire,' responded the old warrior, 'it is precisely because we are not on the exercise field that I do not begin … Unless you order it![17]

Already out of favour with the tsar and unprepared to oppose his will, Kutuzov, gave the command for IV Column to take up their muskets, assemble and prepare to march towards Pratze. The time was probably a little after 8.30am. As the column got underway, unknown to them, Miloradovich's weak and weary Russian battalions and Kolowrat's largely untried Austrian recruits were on a collision course with Soult's experienced and battle-hardened veterans.

Meanwhile, back along the Goldbach the situation was also about to change dramatically.

The Allied attacks along the Goldbach had, after a struggle, met with success and Buxhöwden's wing of the army prepared for the next stage of the plan, to execute the great right wheel against the flank of La Grande Armée. Patches of fog still swirled along the valley as the men regrouped, but there was a distinct absence of urgency. Buxhöwden offered little direction other than ordering two artillery batteries to form up on a spur of high ground overlooking the Goldbach between Telnitz and Sokolnitz, while he settled down to wait. He passed the time drinking heavily.

In complete contrast, 5 miles west of Telnitz at Gross Raigern, urgency was definitely the order of the day. After their marathon march from Vienna it took a little longer than usual for Maréchal Davout to get his depleted corps (Friant's infantry division, Bourcier's dragoon division and with 1er Dragon Regiment operating separately) ready to march on the morning of 2 December. However, sometime between 5.30am and 6.00am they started on the road running north-east towards Turas. About 2 miles into the march, at the village of Rebeschowitz, Davout received a message from Napoleon, sent in the early hours of the morning, redirecting him towards Sokolnitz to take command of the right. Accordingly, Davout redirected his command eastwards. He had not progressed far when a second message reached him from Général de brigade Margaron, commanding the light cavalry between Sokolnitz and Telnitz. Margaron called for support for the 3ème Ligne, which was losing its grip on Telnitz. The sound of gunfire was clearly audible and Davout did not hesitate to send the 1er Dragons and GB Heudelet's brigade (108ème Ligne and the detached *voltigeurs* of 15ème Légère) to their aid, while the rest of his command pressed on towards Sokolnitz.

After these delays and redirections it was about 9.00am when Heudelet approached within cannon range of Telnitz. Corporal Blaise of the 108ème recalled that his regiment:

> '…began to encounter a great number of wounded of [3ème Ligne]. At this moment they made us double forward. Thus I was prevented from biting into a leg of goose which I had ready on top of my knapsack. I had intended to eat it there and then, knowing full well that I would scarcely have the leisure later in the day.'[18]

This sudden appearance of fresh and determined French troops caused consternation amongst the Allies. Kienmayer got off a few rounds with his artillery but the great cloud of smoke they produced further reduced visibility, already limited by patches of fog, completely obliterating the French advance from view. Then, emerging from the fog and smoke, Heudelet appeared, rushing towards Telnitz with around 900 men in two columns. The right hand column burst into the village and threw back the 7. Jäger, which in turn threw a battalion of *grenz* infantry into utter confusion. Fleeing from this unexpected onslaught, they fled in great disorder back on to the New Ingermanland Regiment. Generalmajor Stutterheim, who witnessed the rush, was unimpressed with what followed. He observed that this regiment: 'ought to have supported them; but retreated in a manner, which combined with the fog, threw a part of the column into confusion.'[19]

In their enthusiasm to close with the Russians, the right hand column pursued the fleeing allies beyond the confines of the village, while the left hand column, having advanced against an unfordable stretch of the Goldbach, veered towards a bridge on their left. Determined not to miss out on the chance 'to come to grips with the vaunted enemy infantry', these men rushed for the bridge, ignoring the pleas of their officers, and became greatly disordered in their attempt to cross the stream.

For Heudelet, the hero of Davout's victory over Merveldt at Mariazell in November, things were about to go wrong. Nostitz, detained by Murat during the battle at Schöngrabern, was back with the army. Observing the French struggling to reform, he ordered two squadrons of the 4. Hessen-Homburg-Husaren to attack. Under Oberst Mohr, the hussars charged into the disordered ranks of the left column. Battle-hardened by the constant rearguard actions during the retreat from Braunau, the Austrian hussars slashed their way into the French infantry, causing mayhem. Casualties quickly mounted, and at the same time, the battalion of Brod Grenzer advanced with fixed bayonets towards the right column with Oberstleutnant Desullenovich at their head. The over-extended battalions of 108ème Ligne poured back over the Goldbach, leaving many prisoners behind, while the *voltigeurs* of 15ème Légère covered their retreat. Most veered towards Sokolnitz in an attempt to escape pursuit, but as they did so they unexpectedly ran into a battalion of infantry advancing towards them through the fog. Almost at once the 108ème Ligne were assailed by musketry. All was confusion: the battalion firing on the 108ème was not Russian or Austrian, but the 1/26ème Légère, recently driven from Sokolnitz by Langeron's II Column. An officer of the 108ème, recognising they were under attack by friendly troops, desperately waved the eagle standard of his battalion until the mistake was recognised and firing ceased. But by now the shaken 108ème were in no condition to take any further part in the battle and retired towards Turas.[20]

Telnitz was once again in Allied hands. This time Kienmayer pushed his *grenz* infantry over the stream beyond Telnitz and Stutterheim followed with his cavalry (3. O'Reilly-Chevaulegers and a handful of 1. Merveldt-Uhlanen), as did Generalmajor Moritz Liechtenstein with 11. Szeckel-Husaren, and took up a position west of the Goldbach. Dragging their battalion artillery with them the Russian musketeer regiments of Bryansk, Vyatka and Moscow advanced too, as did 7. Jäger, once they reformed after their earlier scare. However, Buxhöwden still did not intend advancing further until II and III Column were ready to push beyond Sokolnitz, despite the only opposition in front of him being the recuperating battalions of 3ème Ligne, the 1er Dragons and Bourcier's dragoon division, all some way off. In the meantime, Buxhöwden contented himself drawing up the Kiev Grenadier Regiment and the musketeers of Yaroslavl, Vladimir and New Ingermanland behind the two artillery batteries overlooking the Goldbach between Telnitz and Sokolnitz.

While the guns at Telnitz fell silent, except for the occasional long-range artillery exchange, matters flared up again at Sokolnitz. Sometime after 9.00am the remaining two infantry brigades of Friant's division arrived before the village. After their gruelling march from Vienna, only the toughest and most resilient of his men remained. Determined to stifle any major advance westwards by the Russians, Friant ordered GB Lochet to lead his brigade against the village, spearheaded by the 800 men of the 48ème Ligne. With their *voltigeur* company to the fore, led by Lieutenant Pleindoux, the 48ème threw themselves at the south-west corner of Sokolnitz and their impetus carried them right into the village, driving the Russians before them. To their left, the 700 men of 111ème Ligne dashed forward in support and also smashed their way into the village, where they pushed back 'a huge mass of leaderless men who were advancing in disorder'. Friant's last brigade, commanded by GB Kister (15ème Légère, reduced to about 300 men by various detachments, and 33ème Ligne with about 500 men), moved to a position on high ground north of Lochet in reserve. Although hopelessly outnumbered by the Russians, the sheer aggression of the attack had their masses milling about in confusion for a moment. However, Langeron reacted quickly and fed the formed battalions of the Permsk Musketeers into the village, as well as one battalion of the Kursk Regiment, retaining the other two battalions as a reserve. This attack drove the 111ème out of the village and cornered the 48ème in the houses and barns at the southern end. Once free from direct attack, the 111ème rallied while the 48ème battled on for all they were worth as the fighting became vicious, desperate and bloody.

To ease the pressure on Lochet's brigade, Friant ordered Kister's men into battle. The 15ème Légère charged into the north-west corner of the village as the 33ème Ligne advanced into the space between the village and the castle. Przhebishevsky reacted by throwing two battalions of the Narva Regiment into the mix. Accounts of the fighting tell of individual battle-maddened French soldiers attacking overwhelming numbers of Russians with the bayonet, and of desperate struggles as both sides fought for the possession of treasured eagles and standards. The Russians probably had about 9,000 men bottled up within the confines of Sokolnitz and its immediate area, struggling to get to grips with Friant's 1,600 to put a stop to his waspish attacks. But no sooner had this new round of fighting got underway than Langeron received some disturbing news. An officer arrived from Podpolkovnik Balk, who commanded two squadrons of the St Petersburg Dragoons and a detachment of the Isayev Cossacks attached to II Column, and informed him that French columns were marching towards

Pratze and the plateau. Langeron listened but could not credit this information. He later wrote:

> 'Knowing that the fourth column of Generals Miloradovich and Kolowrat was to be on this side and not receiving any order from Kutuzov, I believed that [Podpolkovnik] Balk had mistaken the Austrians for the enemy, though the direction that he saw them taking appeared extraordinary to me. I ordered him to make a more exact reconnaissance and to advise me of what he could see.'[21]

Almost immediately, however, another rider arrived, bearing an urgent message from Count Sergei Kamenski, commander of Langeron's long overdue brigade. With shocking brevity it confirmed Podpolkovnik Balk's intelligence and informed the incredulous Langeron that the French were on the plateau; that he had turned his brigade to oppose them; and was facing 'very strong masses'.[22]

While Langeron absorbed this shocking news he must have pondered one crucial question – where was IV Column?

Chapter 14

Storming the Plateau

'Withdraw us, my General! …
If we take a step back, we are lost.'*

The delays caused by the repositioning of the Russian cavalry did not just affect the advance of the infantry columns on the Pratzen Plateau. Liechtenstein's V Column of cavalry was required to fill a two-mile gap in the Allied formation, from the northern slopes of the plateau to Prince Bagration's Army Advance Guard. The Austrian cavalry, commanded by FML Hohenlohe, began to move towards the appointed position between Blasowitz and Krug on time, but with a mere 1,000 men distributed in three regiments, they occupied little ground. Following his orders, Grand Duke Constantine moved the Russian Imperial Guard from its bivouac on high ground north of Krzenowitz and descended into the valley of the Rausnitz stream before taking up a position on high ground east of Blasowitz. Here it was intended to form a reserve for V Column and Bagration's Army Advance Guard. When Constantine took up his position he observed movement ahead of him near Blasowitz, which he presumed to be Liechtenstein's men. A discharge of artillery fire in his direction brought him quickly to reality: his Imperial Guard, the only reserve formation of the entire Allied army, was already occupying the front line.

To the right rear of Constantine, Prince Bagration held the main body of his command astride the Brünn–Olmütz road near the Posoritz post house, with outposts ahead of the main force. Bagration's orders were to hold his position until the left wing of the army gained ground. He expressed unhappiness at his passive role, and having digested Weyrother's plan in the early hours of the morning, felt sure the army was heading for defeat.

---

* Colonel Pierre-Charles Pouzet, 10ème Légère, to Général de division Saint-Hilaire.

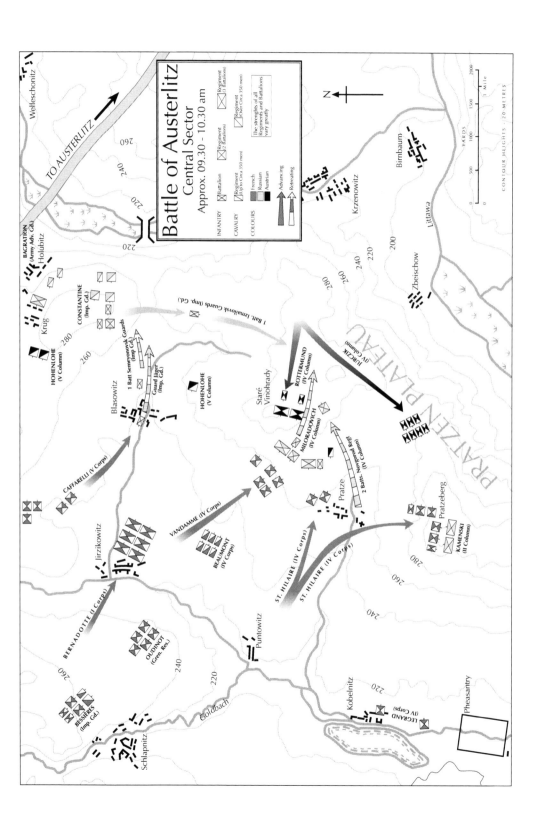

Battle of Austerlitz
Central Sector
Approx. 09.30 - 10.30 am

INFANTRY | ☒ Battalion | ☒ Regiment (2 Battalions) | ☒ Regiment (3 Battalions)
| ☒ Regiment (Up to Circa 350 men) | ☒ Regiment (Over Circa 350 men) |

The strengths of all Regiments and Battalions vary greatly

CAVALRY | Regiment

COLOURS | French | Russian | Austrian

Advancing | Retreating

CONTOUR HEIGHTS - 20 METRES

TO AUSTERLITZ

WELLESCHONITZ

BAGRATION (Army Adv. Gd.)
HOLUBITZ

KRUG

HOHENLOHE (V Column)

CONSTANTINE (Imp. Gd.)

1 Batt. Semenovsk Guards (Imp. Gd.)

Guard Jäger (Imp. Gd.)

HOHENLOHE (V Column)

BLASOWITZ

1 Batt. Izmailovsk Guards (Imp. Gd.)

Staré Vinohrady

ROTTERMUND (IV Column)

JURCZIK (IV Column)

MILORADOVICH (IV Column)

PRATZEN PLATEAU

CAFFARELLI (V Corps)

JIRZIKOWITZ

VANDAMME (IV Corps)

BEAUMONT (IV Corps)

Pratze

2 Batts. Novgorod Regt. (IV Column)

BERNADOTTE (II Corps)

OUDINOT (Gren. Res.)

ST. HILAIRE (IV Corps)

ST. HILAIRE (IV Corps)

Pratzeberg

KAMENSKI (II Column)

BESSÈRES (Imp. Gd.)

Puntowitz

Goldbach

Schlapnitz

Kobelnitz

LEGRAND (IV Corps)

Pheasantry

KRZENOWITZ

BIRNBAUM

LITTAWA

ZBEISCHOW

Up on the plateau, following Kutuzov's meeting with the tsar, General Leitenant Mikhail Miloradovich, the 34-year-old joint commander of IV Column, issued the orders for the leading Russian elements of the column to move off.

Miloradovich was the grandson of a Serbian asylum seeker who came to Russia to escape Turkish oppression. His father amassed a fortune while rising through the Russian civil ranks and became very powerful in the process. As an officer in the Izmailovsk Guards, Miloradovich came to the attention of Grand Duke Constantine, the two becoming friends, and by the age of twenty-seven he had risen to the rank of major general. However, he squandered his father's fortune, and according to Langeron, was conceited, thoughtless, insolent, and knew little of military matters beyond the parade ground. Langeron also considered that Miloradovich felt a strong desire to be the first in everything, whether 'in battle, a ball or an orgy'.[1]

As the leading battalions marched off, Miloradovich took few precautions for the security of his column. Marching so close behind Przhebishevsky it was logical that the route ahead must be clear of the enemy. Maior Karl Toll, who had spent a sleepless night ensuring Weyrother's plan was translated and despatched to the column commanders, now rode ahead of IV Column towards Kobelnitz, accompanied by a single Cossack rider. Some distance behind Toll marched two battalions of the Novgorod Musketeer Regiment and the grenadier battalion of the Apsheron. Two artillery pieces and two squadrons of the Austrian 1. Erzherzog Johann-Dragoner accompanied them, all under the command of Podpolkovnik Monakhtin. These leading units were earmarked to occupy Schlapanitz, on which the rest of the Allied army was to pivot.[2] Behind this advance guard, Miloradovich followed with the rest of the Russian troops of IV Column: nine battalions formed in two brigades commanded by General Maior Grigory Berg and Sergei Repninsky. Then, behind the Russians, FZM Johann Karl, Graf Kolowrat-Krakowsky, a 57-year-old Bohemian nobleman with forty years' military experience, led forward the Austrian contingent: the brigades of Generalmajor Rottermund and GM Jurczik. In this relaxed manner these final formations prepared to abandon the Pratzen Plateau.

Back at Napoleon's headquarters on Zuran Hill, the emperor waited for the news that the Allies had abandoned the plateau. Then, after his discussion with Maréchal Soult, he released the commander of IV Corps to lead the divisions of Saint-Hilaire and Vandamme against the vacant heights.

Soult galloped off to Puntowitz, where Saint-Hilaire's division stood, having already passed through the village. Although only just over a mile from Pratze, it had remained invisible to Przhebishevsky's III Column as it marched through the village en route for Sokolnitz, hidden in the fog and smoke, which hung heavily in this section of the valley floor. Soult well understood the importance of his orders and rode up and down the division calling on individual regiments to echo former glories. A triple issue of army brandy further enhanced their enthusiasm for the fight. With his men now fortified in mind and body, Louis Saint-Hilaire, the brave and talented 39-year-old divisional commander, ordered his men forward, leading with the two battalions of 10ème Légère, the single unit forming GB Morand's brigade. Morand's orders were to move onto the high ground to the right, or south side of Pratze village. The brigade of GB Thiébault followed Morand with two battalions each from 14ème and 36ème Ligne. Varé's brigade (two battalions each of 43ème and 55ème Ligne) marched in reserve, but once on the plateau, they were to form a link with Vandamme's division. As the division emerged from the gloom of the valley into the sunlight, the leading men saw the tail of Przhebishevsky's III Column disappearing towards Sokolnitz, completely unaware of the presence of this French force behind them. However, tempting though this target was, Saint-Hilaire continued towards Pratze, leaving the task of facing III Column to Legrand's division, which was defending the line of the Goldbach. Ahead of him all that now appeared to stand between his division and their goal were two riders emerging alone from Pratze: Maior Toll and his Cossack companion.

Toll presumed that these shadowy men in the distance must be a part of III Column that had lost its way. Then the crack of a musket and a puff of smoke focused his attention and he realised with horror that this was no wayward Russian column, it was a major French attack and he was directly in its path. Toll and his comrade turned quickly and galloped back to the plateau. Warned by the breathless major, Monakhtin hurriedly led the two battalions of the Novgorod Musketeers forward. He placed one on the high ground on the south side of Pratze and moved the other through the village and turned southwards over a bridge that crossed a wide, steep-sided stream running down to the Goldbach. Taking advantage of the ground, he concealed this battalion from the French. The Apsheron grenadier battalion acted as a reserve in the village with the 1. Erzherzog Johann-Dragoner further back supporting the left.

Soult's original orders were for Saint-Hilaire to bypass the village, in order to prevent him being drawn into a potentially time-consuming battle for its control, but during the advance Soult received some spurious information that Pratze was only lightly defended by the Allies. Consequently, he ordered Saint-Hilaire to sweep it clear as he advanced: in response, the 1/14ème moved against the village. Not expecting any significant resistance, the battalion approached the village without detaching skirmishers. As it approached Pratze in line, Colonel Mazas discovered the wide stream bed to his right. Then, without warning, the battalion of the Novgorod Regiment appeared from its concealed position 'and poured such a murderous fire at almost point-blank into him that in their surprise and alarm the entire 1/14ème broke and fled'.[3]

Observing the mayhem ahead of him, Thiébault immediately organised his other three battalions to remove this threat to his brigade, while Colonel Mazas rallied his battalion. At the same time, the 10ème Légère, keeping well-clear of

Pratze, crossed lower down the stream and continued to climb the slope towards the high ground south of the village – the Pratzeberg – its summit about 1,200 yards from the church. The cold early morning air then resounded with cries of 'Vive l'Empereur!' as the remaining 2,400 men of Thiébault's brigade advanced. With 2/36ème on the left, heading for the southern part of the village, supported by 1/36ème, and 2/14ème on the right marching towards the bridge and stream, these men closed on Monakhtin's advanced battalions.

Just over 1½ miles away to the south, General Maior Kamenski marched down the slopes of the Pratzen Plateau towards Sokolnitz at the head of Langeron's missing brigade. Some movement near Pratze caught his attention and he brought his brigade to a halt. In front of him he could see I, II and III Columns all engaged along the Goldbach, but this movement towards Pratze was puzzling. The closer he looked, the more worrying the situation became. The sound of gunfire breaking out near Pratze suggested the disturbing scenario of a French attack rolling towards the plateau and into the undefended rear of the Allied army. Kamenski quickly dashed off a warning note to Langeron, his column commander, at about 9.15am, and then turned his brigade back towards the high ground he had just vacated.

The 2/14ème Ligne dashed forward, changing from column to line as it rapidly advanced. Unfazed by the musketry of the Novgorod battalion behind the stream, the 2/14ème threw itself into the steep-sided watercourse and scrambled up the opposite bank to attack the Russians with the bayonet. The 2/36ème also stormed across the stream and entered the southern end of Pratze, which consisted only of the church and a couple of houses. Following in reserve, the 1/36ème opened fire on the defenders of the village but did not follow across the stream. Aware of the growing storm to the front, Miloradovich sent General Maior Repninsky forward with the grenadier battalion of the Novgorod Regiment towards the south of Pratze, to support the two musketeer battalions. But by the time he arrived both battalions were already in disordered retreat and fled past him, having been thrown back by Thiébault's aggressive assault.

Alexander was now close at hand, and he personally attempted to rally the two fleeing battalions, which rushed on without even recognising their tsar. He never forgave the regiment. Repninsky, who had advanced in a supporting role, now found himself in the front line, engaged in a vicious firefight with 2/36ème.[4] While this action took place on the south side of Pratze, Kutuzov and Alexander, to their horror, saw another large French formation heading towards them from the north. This was Vandamme's division, marching towards Staré Vinohrady (the old vineyard), the high point on the northern extent of the Pratzen Plateau, just over a mile north-east of Pratze village. Encouraged by this forward movement, Varé's brigade, temporarily detached from Saint-Hilaire's division, rushed forward towards the north side of Pratze and engaged two Russian battalions near the village (possibly the grenadier battalions of the Novgorod and Apsheron Regiments). These battalions, assaulted on two sides and already disrupted by the fleeing Novgorod musketeer battalions fell back on the main body, the Novgorod grenadiers were 'almost destroyed'. Repninsky remained wounded on the field, struck down by three musket shots. Keenly aware of their predicament, Kutuzov and Miloradovich hurried the remaining Russian battalions to occupy the high ground to the north of Pratze to face this onslaught.

Some distance behind Miloradovich, the Austrian brigades commanded by FZM Kolowrat were making slow progress through the vineyards. They had spent the night camped furthest back and had first to ascend part of the way on to the plateau. Aware of the escalation of firing to the front, a certain Hauptmann Tell of IR49 Kerpen went forward to ascertain what was happening. He swiftly returned with the news that the French were attacking on both sides of Pratze and closing like a pincer on IV Column. Then orders arrived from Kutuzov for Kolowrat to deploy to the left to prevent the French attack succeeding in claiming the Pratzeberg. It was a desperate decision because Kutuzov knew that half of the Austrian infantry were new recruits with limited training, but he had no choice if he was to have any chance of saving the situation and deny the plateau, the key to the battlefield, to the French. The surviving accounts express something of the confusion that existed on the plateau. Whether Kutuzov intended all the Austrian infantry to march for the Pratzeberg, or just a portion of it, is unclear. Certainly, Jurczik headed off southwards with his brigade: but whether all his battalions followed is uncertain. Rottermund's brigade, with its strongest component concentrated in the full six battalions of IR23 Salzburg, remained at the northern end of the plateau and moved forward to occupy a position on the Staré Vinohrady to the rear of the Russians but extending beyond the right of Miloradovich's new line. Austrian accounts mention battalions becoming separated from their brigades as they were rapidly pushed into battle.

As the surprised Austrians moved off, shocked by this sudden change of circumstances, Vandamme, supported by Varé's brigade, was closing menacingly on the plateau. His men, advancing steadily without firing, gradually narrowed the gap. Behind Vandamme's division, anyone still with the presence of mind to look beyond the immediate danger would have seen the ominous sight of the leading division of Bernadotte's I Corps passing through Jirzikowitz and reforming outside the village. The situation was clearly critical and the tsar sent off a request to Grand Duke Constantine to despatch a battalion of Imperial Guard infantry to the plateau.

Encouraged by Vandamme's advance, Varé's brigade began to threaten the left flank of the Russian line, causing Miloradovich to order General Maior Berg to take the Little Russia Grenadiers, supported by the grenadier battalion of the Apsheron Regiment to drive them back. The rest of the Russian line, the

Smolensk Musketeer Regiment and two musketeer battalions of the Apsheron Regiment, faced Vandamme. The fighting between Varé's Regiments (43ème and 55ème Ligne) and Berg's men was both desperate and stubborn. The Russians launched at least two bayonet charges, during one of which the Apsheron grenadier battalion, led by Kapitan Morozov, captured two French artillery pieces, later retaken.[5] The 55ème also repulsed an attack by the two squadrons of Austrian dragoons attached to IV Column before Vandamme's relentless march finally came to a halt about 100 paces from the Russian line. With Bernadotte able to offer support if needed, he formed his division in one line, maximising his firepower, and 'opened a fire of musketry which became general, and very destructive'.[6] One musket ball seared across Kutuzov's cheek as he stood a short distance behind the front line, causing a bloody wound. As soon as the tsar heard of this, he sent Dr James Wylie, his personal physician, forward: but as he rode up Kutuzov dismissed him saying, 'Thank His Majesty, assure him that my wound is not dangerous,' then waving an arm towards the French he added, 'that is where it is mortal'.[7] Away to the south, the danger to the Allies was mounting too.

While Thiébault cleared the Russian advance guard from its positions around Pratze, the 10ème Légère, supported by three artillery pieces, skirted the village and marched towards the Pratzeberg, the highest point on the southern extent of the plateau. As Général de brigade Morand led the men forward up the slope under their regimental commander, Colonel Pouzet, they found themselves in a dramatic race for the summit with Kamenski's brigade of II Column. Recognising the danger developing behind him, on his own initiative, Kamenski had turned the brigade and marched back to the plateau with the Phanagoria Grenadier Regiment and Ryazan Musketeers, about 3,800 men in all. Against them, the 10ème Légère could muster some 1,500. Forming the Phanagoria Grenadiers on the right and the Ryazan Musketeers on the left, Kamenski advanced directly against the 10ème. The single French regiment opposed this onslaught as best it could, but with the Russian line threatening to overwhelm its right flank and get around its left, it began to fall back.

The men of the 10ème were in great danger of being surrounded when help arrived, Saint-Hilaire leading forward the 1/14ème at the run, having rallied after their failed attack on Pratze. Wasting no time, Colonel Mazas placed his battalion in the front line to the right of the 10ème and prevented the Ryazan Musketeers from turning the flank. More help was on the way too. The two battalions of the 36ème were ordered to abandon the attack on Pratze and advance with all speed to support the 10ème, leaving 2/14ème to drive away the retreating Russians.

At about the same time General Leitenant Langeron arrived on the heights and he could not believe what he saw. On receiving Kamenski's message he handed temporary command of the fighting around Sokolnitz to General Maior Olsufiev, and went to see for himself what was happening. He did not intend being away for long. When he got there he found the French occupying the bivouac area that II Column had left only a couple of hours earlier and Kamenski involved in a full-scale battle. He approached the Phanagoria Grenadiers and noticed some of the men ducking to avoid artillery fire. Langeron noted that perhaps only 10 per cent of the regiment had ever been in battle before but he shouted to them: 'Raise your heads, remember that you are Russian grenadiers!' and then unwisely found himself drawn into the battle too.

Langeron recalled that in an effort 'To impose on the French and to animate the courage of our soldiers, and besides, not believing the enemies as strong as indeed they were ... I resolved to march forward.' The attack coincided with the arrival of 1/36ème, which entered the line to the left of the 10ème. The Russian line moved forward in a 'furious attack', their deep battle roar 'Oorah! Oorah!' resonating in the air as the French line fell back before them. In the attack, 'the first battalion of the Phanagoria Regiment, commanded by an excellent officer, Maior Brandt, who was wounded, advanced so close to the French that they took two guns.'[8] But the French were not to be outdone. Major Perrier, at the head of the newly arrived 1/36ème, inspired his men by his coolness and great courage before he crashed to the ground, felled by two bullets. Then Adjudant-Major Labadie of the 1/36ème grabbed the battalion's eagle standard and advanced on the Russians shouting: 'Let brave men follow me!' Arming themselves with muskets, captains Raoul and Duhil threw themselves immediately in front of the eagle to defend it, rallying the French line and pushing the Russians back again.[9]

Thiébault now rushed up from Pratze with the two remaining battalions of his brigade and three guns. But sometime around 10.00am, before he could push them into the line, a movement of unidentified troops was detected approaching from the north-east, which both the French and Russians observed with great concern. Langeron could not make out who they were, but to him they appeared to be in retreat. He sent an officer to discover their identity and found to his relief that they were Jurczik's Austrian battalions, ordered towards Pratzeberg by Kutuzov.

At the same time, Saint-Hilaire and Thiébault, positioned closer than Langeron to this new force, watched through their telescopes as the sound of their military music grew louder, until an officer closed to within shouting distance and cried, 'Do not fire; we are Bavarians.'[10] Both Saint-Hilaire and Thiébault viewed this information suspiciously but could not open fire and risk killing their allies. With his divisional commander's approval, Thiébault pivoted the line back on 1/36ème until it stood at right angles to the 10ème and 1/14ème. Then he aligned 2/36ème to the left of the first battalion with the three guns between them and positioned 2/14ème on the extreme left in column to face this potential threat. Just as he finalised these dispositions he welcomed the fortuitous arrival of a battery of six 12pdr guns, the reserve artillery of IV Corps. Three guns were placed on both flanks of the 36ème and he quickly masked all nine guns with squads of infantry. With his troops in place Thiébault crawled forward to take a closer look at these 'Bavarians', joined on the way by Morand. The two officers advanced about half way and as Thiébault studied them closely: 'an officer belonging to those regiments was joined by one who I saw come from Kamenski's brigade. They talked for a minute, and then each went quickly back to whence he came.'[11]

It was Langeron's man that Thiébault saw. Convinced that they now faced a new hostile threat, the two French officers returned to their men, Thiébault ordering the commander of the newly arrived reserve artillery to double-load his guns, much to his dismay, and stockpile rounds by his guns for rapid fire. Meanwhile, Kamenski and Morand, their lines now about 300 paces apart, kept up an exchange of artillery fire while their men prepared for the next attack. Once their attempted ruse was uncovered, the Austrian units swung into position to launch an attack against Thiébault's three battalions. Despite their inexperience, the leading Austrian battalions 'made their attack on the enemy with coolness and intrepidity'.[12] Ahead of them Thiébault ordered his men to hold their fire and allowed the Austrians to gradually close the gap, having instructed the gunners to sight their guns at about 40 yards. With final instructions for his men to aim at the cross belts of the advancing infantry and at the centre of formations, to avoid wasting shots, Thiébault recalled that he:

> 'let the formidable masses approach within range and then with my nine guns suddenly unmasked, the whole line poured in the most destructive fire ... Imagine my satisfaction when I saw each discharge cutting great square holes in the regiments ... and these regiments ... dispersing in fleeing masses.'[13]

In another version, Thiébault described the effect of his close-range fire as: 'entire lines fell with every blast. These troops which, with the help of their ruse, hoped to reach us unharmed, tried in vain to spread out: it was no longer possible. Retreat was their only hope of survival.'[14]

However, despite their limited training and experience, these beleaguered Austrian battalions did not disintegrate. Instead they rallied and reformed further to the south, closer to Kamenski.[15] But Kutuzov remained unimpressed. He later wrote: 'Indeed this reserve corps took the position which was assigned to them, but withdrew themselves with the first discharges of the enemy and completely uncovered the left flank of the column [Miloradovich's].'[16]

The distance between Morand's half of the French force and Kamenski now closed to less than 200 paces and Langeron described the moment that the 10ème Légère and 1/14ème:

'began a very sharp musket fire, very well directed and extremely murderous. Our soldiers replied with a less accurate independent fire: I desired to put an end to this and commence battalion volleys, but I was never to succeed there, in spite of the efforts of count Kamenski and those of [Podpolkovnik] Bogdanov, who, with sword raised, passed across the front of the soldier's muskets.'[17]

While Saint-Hilaire stood with Thiébault and Morand on the Pratzeberg, isolated from the rest of the French army, back on the north side of Pratze, Vandamme had finally overcome Miloradovich's opposition.

Vandamme's methodical advance towards the Russian positions brought his 7,600 men ever closer to Miloradovich's line, and the addition of Varé's brigade – about 3,200 men – provided the French line with a great numerical advantage. The Russian component of IV Column amounted to less than 5,000 men and from his twelve battalions, two from the advance guard had already dispersed, while the great losses suffered by a third battalion meant it could no longer be considered an effective force. The four battalions led forward by General Maior Berg towards Pratze continued to fight hard for a while, but after Berg was wounded their determination rapidly evaporated. Stutterheim commented that Berg's troops 'had lost that confidence in themselves, without which nothing is to be done in war'.[18] Without direction this part of the Russian line gave way and fell back, leaving Miloradovich with just five battalions. The Russian commander did his best to inspire his men, galloping about wildly, although some less charitable observers suggested his posturing was ineffective and merely designed to draw him to the tsar's attention.

Despite his best efforts, the strength of Vandamme's force, with GB Candras' brigade (46ème and 57ème Ligne) leading the attack, was too much. Although the Russians inflicted heavy casualties on the approaching brigade it continued to advance undaunted until deploying within 60 paces of their line, when it 'unleashed a devastating fire that consumed the Russians'. These last five battalions gave way and the colonel of the 46ème recalled that: 'With a shout of "Vive l'Empereur!" the regiment resumed the advance and passed over the debris of the enemy'.[19] With stories of the actions of Russian wounded at Schöngrabern well-known throughout the French army, none were left alive in their wake. Reporting later on the collapse of his command, Miloradovich recalled that:

'the tiredness of the men, shortage of ammunition, the difficult position and heavy firing by the enemy on all sides, brought the soldiers, who were up until this point fighting hard, into disorder during their retreat.'[20]

Kutuzov added a little more in his summary of the action to the tsar:

> 'Though this IV Column was the weakest of all (made up of troops weakened by the retreat from Braunau), it however defended with courage and maintained its position for a long time, keeping up a very sharp fire; but when the Generals Berg and Repninsky were wounded and thereby their brigades remained without command, the disorder set in.'[21]

The Russians had defended their front line for perhaps forty-five minutes, from the moment Thiébault sent his first battalion against Pratze to the retreat of Miloradovich's command. The time was now around 10.00am.

The Russians' spirited defence had, however, gained enough time for IV Column to set up a second defensive line. With its right resting on Staré Vinohrady and the left extended southwards, GM Rottermund's Austrian brigade formed a solid line, while Jurczik's brigade headed south to prevent the French capturing the Pratzeberg. Behind Rottermund's line Miloradovich was able to halt his fleeing men and rally them on the battalion of Izmailovsk Guards that had just arrived on the plateau, in response to the tsar's earlier order.

Even as Candras was driving off the Russians to his front, Vandamme's other two brigades, those of generals Schiner and Ferey, were closing on the newly formed Austrian line. At about this time – approximately 10.00am – the northern extreme of the battlefield, astride the Brünn–Olmütz road, also thundered into life.

The late arrival of V Column cavalry into their assigned position between Blasowitz and Krug resulted in Grand Duke Constantine finding his Imperial Guard, considered the army reserve, occupying the front line on high ground east of Blasowitz at around 9.30am. It was not immediately obvious that this was the front line, as Constantine could see movement near Blasowitz that he naturally considered to be Austrian troops. And so he contented himself with forming up the Guard. In the first line he placed the Preobrazhensk and Semeyonovsk Regiments with an artillery battery in the centre, and the Izmailovsk Regiment and Guard Jäger battalion in the second line. Each of the seven battalions also had two pieces of artillery with them. At the rear of the infantry he formed two regiments of cavalry: the Guard Hussars and Horse Guards. Some distance further back were the Chevalier Garde and the Guard Cossacks, and a long way to the rear the Guard Grenadier Regiment, forming the rearguard of the army.[22]

No sooner had Constantine completed his arrangements than a cannon ball smashed into the Preobrazhensk Guard, ripping away a file of the regiment.

Suddenly it was clear: the troops near Blasowitz were not allies at all, they were French. Constantine recognised his exposed position and took immediate action to remove this threat. He ordered the Guard Jäger to advance, drive off the opposition and occupy Blasowitz. As they attacked this force, composed of artillery and light troops sent forward from GD Rivaud's division of Bernadotte's I Corps, it melted away. With Blasowitz seemingly secure, Constantine grew concerned by the increasing noise of battle from the plateau and pushed forward a battalion of the Semeyonovsk Guards to support his *jäger*, positioning them just to the rear of the village. About this time the order arrived from the tsar on the heights for reinforcements, and in response, Constantine despatched a battalion of the Izmailovsk Guards. In less than thirty minutes the Imperial Guard infantry on the heights east of Blasowitz reduced from seven to four battalions. However, Prince Liechtenstein was now hustling his tardy cavalry into position between Blasowitz, Krug and Holubitz. It was not a moment too soon, for about two miles to the west Lannes, with V Corps, and Murat, with the Cavalry Reserve, had set their men in motion.

Lannes' men were drawn up with their left resting on the Santon and extending southwards across the Brünn–Olmütz road. On the left stood Suchet's division, with 34ème and 40ème Ligne forming the first line, and 64ème and 88ème Ligne the second. Lannes detached the 17ème Légère from the division to defend the Santon and its approaches, thereby shielding the left of V Corps. To Suchet's right, Caffarelli aligned his division. The 17ème and 30ème Ligne formed the first line with 51ème and 61ème Ligne the second. The 13ème Légère was tasked with protecting the right flank of the corps. GD Walther's dragoon division was held in reserve.

Murat's cavalry consisted of two divisions of heavy cavalry, two of light cavalry and an additional light cavalry brigade. The two heavy cavalry formations, commanded by Général Nansouty and d'Hautpoul, formed behind Lannes' corps. Kellermann's light cavalry division took up a position on Lannes' right, while the remaining light cavalry (Treillard's division and Milhaud's brigade) floated on the left.

Napoleon considered that Lannes and Murat would face little opposition on the northern flank. He had not anticipated any strong formations remaining in the sector of the battlefield when the Allied army swung its full weight against his right. As such, they were to hold their position until Soult was established on the plateau, then they were to sweep forward and cut off the Allies' retreat towards Olmütz. To Napoleon's surprise, Lannes and Murat were about to face the dogged and aggressive Prince Bagration.

The orders for Bagration's command specified he should not advance until the columns on the left made significant progress. However, the growing sound of battle and reports from his advanced left flank (6. Jäger and five squadrons each from the Mariupol and Pavlograd Hussars) around Holubitz warned him of the strong French presence building to the west.[23] He therefore left his position on the high ground near the post house and advanced to a position close to the road junction that led to Austerlitz. His right extended onto the high ground north of the road towards Kowalowitz, with his left resting on Krug and Holubitz. As his men drew up, Bagration arranged them for battle. He left the battle-weary 6. Jäger holding Krug and Holubitz, screened by Cossack detachments drawn from three regiments. The Elisavetgrad Hussars, the first of Adjutant-General Uvarov's cavalry regiments to arrive, took up a position to protect Bagration's left flank.[24] North of Holubitz, Bagration arranged his infantry in two lines, the Old Ingermanland and Pskov Musketeers in the front line, with the Arkhangelogord Musketeers behind. The remaining five squadrons of Pavlograd Hussars formed to the right of the line with 5. Jäger and five squadrons of the Mariupol Hussars occupied a position further out towards Kowalowitz. Behind the main body Bagration formed his reserve: five squadrons of the Tsarina Cuirassier, five of Tver Dragoons, and three squadrons of St Petersburg Dragoons.

With the news that Soult had gained a foothold on the Pratzen Plateau, Napoleon issued the order for Lannes to commence his forward move around 10.00am. With Kellermann's light cavalry screening the infantry, Lannes began to edge forward. For the Guard Jäger occupying Blasowitz, the most forward position in the northern sector of the battlefield, this was a worrying time. As well as Lannes' approach, Rivaud's division of I Corps was completing its disposition outside Jirschikowitz, from where it could threaten their position. Soon Lannes' would draw near to Blasowitz and inevitably attack the village before advancing again. And with his left flank protected by Bosenitz and his right by Blasowitz, Lannes would occupy a strong position, ideally suited to defence or offering a springboard from which to launch an assault on the Russian line.

Liechtenstein decided he needed to take action to stop Lannes' advance and ordered the Russian cavalry to form for battle. At the same time he sent the Austrian 7. Lotheringen-Küirassiere, with a cavalry battery, to a position between Blasowitz and the plateau to protect the open left flank of the *jäger*. To protect their right, the commander of V Column intended throwing his four Russian cavalry regiments at the French horseman shielding their infantry, but even before he completed forming his men for the attack the plan disintegrated. The Grand Duke Constantine Uhlans, an impressive regiment of lancers numbering almost 1,000 men, formed the head of this attacking force. However, instead of waiting until all regiments were in position, General Leitenant Essen II, the senior Russian cavalry commander, ordered General Maior Müller-Zakomelsky, commanding the lancers, to attack immediately, without waiting for support. This unexpected move forced the Russian artillery supporting the cavalry, which had opened on the French line, to cease firing. Seeing the Russian cavalry closing on his division Kellermann gave the order to retire. For a moment it appeared Kellermann was about to be crushed between the onrushing lancers and the solid wall of French infantry, but as the retreating horseman approached Caffarelli's division they: 'opened up their intervals as coolly as if they had been on a parade ground. Immediately Kellermann's cavalry passed through they closed up again and opened fire on the enemy.'[25]

Encouraged by the sight of Kellermann's cavalry falling back before them, the Grand Duke Constantine Uhlans pressed them closely, just catching the rearmost squadrons before they escaped through the French lines, leaving themselves confronted by the resolute front line of Caffarelli's division. The storm of musketry and grapeshot that ripped through the air at very short range decimated the lancers. They veered away from the carnage, leaving Müller-Zakomelsky badly wounded and perhaps as many as 400 men killed, wounded or dazed upon the ground. Also amongst the seriously wounded was Essen II who later died of his wounds.[26] The survivors fell back in great disorder to reform behind Bagration.

With the threat posed by the lancers removed, Kellermann's men returned to their position in front of the infantry. But before they were all in place, Liechtenstein's three remaining Russian cavalry regiments were now formed and General Leitenant Uvarov led forward the Elisavetgrad Hussars and Kharkov Dragoons, holding the Chernigov Dragoons in reserve. The Russian attack caught the French 4ème Hussards and inflicted numerous casualties before the other three regiments of Kellermann's division swarmed forward hacking and slashing all around the Russians. Then a brigade from Walther's dragoon division, commanded by GB Sébastiani, swung into the mêlée, causing complete confusion in the Russian ranks, forcing them to extricate themselves as best they could and fall back on the Chernigov Dragoons, but losing a number of men as prisoners.

Kellermann and Sébastiani also pulled back to reform. While both sides prepared to resume the cavalry contest, Bagration, following his orders to secure the high ground flanking the Brünn-Olmütz road – the Santon – began his attack. Far out on the right flank the 5. Jäger advanced rapidly towards Siwitz, supported by the Mariupol Hussars and a detachment of Cossacks. The *jäger* drove back the French outposts, but as they drew closer to the Santon, the captured Austrian guns placed on the summit opened on them. The *jäger*, with the Cossacks following, turned into the village of Bosenitz and pushed out the surprised occupants. There does not appear to have been any serious attempt to defend the village, with the Austrian history of the campaign describing the French encountered in the village merely as 'a mob of marauders'.

However, between the village and the Santon the 1/17ème Légère were drawn up. The *jäger* and five squadrons of Mariupol Hussars pressed forward forcing this battalion to fall back and defend itself against a number of determined cavalry attacks. But as it drew closer to the Santon, the artillery again belched forth and the 2/17ème Légère added to the weight of fire falling on the Russian attack. Against this volume of fire the advance stalled and then the mixed force began to retire back on Bosenitz. Sensing the moment had arrived, the 2/17ème Légère descended from the Santon and pressed towards the village. The attack by 5. Jäger had failed, and far from support, they withdrew through Bosenitz with the 17ème Légère swiftly reclaiming the village. The Mariupol Hussars did their best to protect the retreating *jäger* and Cossacks from the menace presented by the cavalry of Treillard and Milhaud, but eventually they were driven off and the threat to the French left completely removed.

While the battle for Bosenitz was being fought, the main cavalry contest resumed. A confusing series of charges and counter-charges followed, in which all Liechtenstein's Russian cavalry – as well as Bagration's horsemen – engaged Kellermann's and Walther's divisions. Podpolkovnik Ermolov, an eyewitness, watched this passage of the battle unfold but recorded that the situation was 'so strange that I could not form any connection between the different incidents'.[27] Regiments attacked, fell back, regrouped and charged again. But as Ermolov observed, 'In our cavalry, as in the rest of the army, the majority of actions were uncoordinated, without any consideration of support.'[28]

On the French side the attacks were far more unified, with cavalry, infantry and artillery all working in support of one another. In an attempt to bring an end to the constant stinging Allied cavalry attacks, Murat ordered forward his heavy cavalry: the *cuirassier* and *carabinier* regiments of Nansouty and d'Hautpoul. As these two divisions moved into position south of Caffarelli's infantry, Kellermann and Walther, with Murat in person, attacked the Russian cavalry again. And again the fighting was inconclusive: but with both sides tiring, the French began to pull back once more to reform, at which point Murat ordered forward Nansouty's division with d'Hautpoul in support. The timing was perfect, and leading with his two *carabinier* regiments, Nansouty smashed into the leading Russian unit, the Tver Dragoons. Against these fresh troops the dragoons crumbled and fell back, but the *carabiniers* continued and attacked Uvarov's Elisavetgrad Hussars and Chernigov Dragoons. Nansouty's second line – 2ème and 3ème Cuirassier – quickly joined in the mêlée and together they drove Uvarov's men back once more.

Nansouty now retired to reform his men behind Caffarelli's infantry, but as he did so a part of 3ème Cuirassier experienced some difficulty extricating itself from the Russian hussars. Taking advantage of this confusion, a Russian cavalry regiment attacked the 13ème Légère, holding the right-hand end of Caffarelli's line. However, the two battalions received the charge in line and blasted the Russian horseman at close-range. Then, as Nansouty reappeared, they galloped off to the protection of their own lines. The Russian cavalry facing Lannes and Murat was now seriously weakened, worn down by rising casualties and the constant uncoordinated efforts to stem the French tide.

Some time after 10.30, as the urgency of the Russian cavalry attacks waned, Lannes could see that Vandamme was pressing forward on the Pratzen Plateau and so ordered Caffarelli to recapture Blasowitz from the Russian Guard Jäger. He sent forward the 13ème Légère, with four companies leading the way as skirmishers, supported by 51ème Ligne. The Guard Jäger waited until the French moved into range and then opened a steady fire on them, which they were unable to penetrate. The French then attacked with the 1/13ème Légère, but as they pressed closer, Colonel Castex, commander of the regiment, fell dead and again the attack faltered. Finally, when the 2/13ème Légère joined the attack, the *jäger* were overwhelmed and poured back on the main body of the Guard, coming under fire from the 2/51ème Ligne as they retreated. The battalion of Semeyonovsk Guards, formed behind Blasowitz supporting the *jäger*, quickly attracted the attention of Caffarelli's victorious men and was forced back too.

While this attack had developed, Rivaud's division appeared to be ready to advance from Jirzikowitz, presenting a new threat to the flank of IV Column, already under great pressure on the plateau. In an effort to prevent this, Liechtenstein ordered Hohenlohe to take the Austrian 1. Kaiser-Kürassiere and 5. Nassau-Kürassiere over to a position south-east of Blasowitz to support 7. Lotheringen-Kürassiere. Then, with their brigade commander, Generalmajor Caramelli, at their head, the 7. Lotheringen charged towards Rivaud's infantry. Caramelli's horse was shot from under him during the advance, but the attack served its purpose, as it checked Rivaud's movement for a while. The Austrian cavalry launched other spoiling attacks on Rivaud's men, in an effort to keep them from entering the fray, but the horsemen soon attracted artillery fire from Vandamme on the Pratzen Plateau and were forced back out of range.

Up on the plateau, above the cavalry battles, Vandamme's assault continued to meet with success. After destroying Miloradovich's first line, Vandamme pressed on towards a second line formed by the Austrian brigade, anchored on the high point of Staré Vinohrady. Originally ascribed to GM Rottermund, the brigade was now commanded by Oberst Sterndahl of IR23 Salzburg. Rottermund in fact disappears from the accounts of the fighting on the plateau and may have been directed to command the troops attacking the Pratzeberg following Jurczik's wounding early on, while Kolowrat remained with Sterndahl on Staré Vinohrady. The main strength of this force was found in Sterndahl's six battalions of IR23 Salzburg, backed up by a battalion each from IR20 and IR24. While Miloradovich fought his losing battle with the attacking French, the Austrians completed their arrangements, forming their men in two lines with IR23 to the front.

Vandamme initially sent Schiner's single regiment brigade against the Austrian position, while his other brigades reformed. The two battalions of 24ème Légère broke down into skirmishers and swarmed towards the solid line formed by IR23, attempting to work around the flanks and disrupt the formation. However, even as the Austrians first took up their position, it appears the grenadier battalion, led by Oberstleutnant Hubler, pushed ahead of the rest of IR23 on the right, and became embroiled in a bayonet attack against Vandamme's men during their initial advance on Miloradovich's line. They succeeded in driving the French back but were attacked in turn by cavalry, probably from Boyé's brigade attached to IV Corps. The grenadiers, without support, suffered and it seems they lost a number of men as prisoners, led off towards Blasowitz. Despite the grenadiers' losses and mounting casualties in the firefight with 24ème Légère, the Austrian regiment, which started the battle with about 2,800 men, stood its ground. The powerful controlled volleys it poured back at the French kept their attackers at a respectful distance. After half an hour of these exchanges Vandamme pulled the 24ème Légère back – or IR23 pushed them – and prepared to make a concerted assault on the position.

Vandamme placed Ferey's brigade (4ème and 28ème Ligne) in the centre of his line, regrouping the 24ème Légère on the left and placing the 55ème Ligne from Varé's supporting brigade on the right. Varé's other regiment, the 43ème Ligne, remained close to Pratze, forming the link with Saint-Hilaire and Candras' brigade, which was still reforming after the battle with Miloradovich's men. In all, Vandamme ordered about 6,000 men against the Austrian line. Oberst Sterndahl plugged the gap in his line caused when the grenadier battalion became separated earlier in the action with the depot battalion of IR24 Auersperg. He now opposed Vandamme with a little over 3,000 men.

Vandamme moved forward under an intense barrage of artillery and musket fire, gaining ground in the centre and against the flanks of the Austrian line. Then, at a distance of about eighty paces, the whole French line unleashed its full firepower. Oberst Sterndahl did the best he could, but outnumbered, outflanked, and having already seen Miloradovich's Russians flee past, the line began to falter, then break. The regimental history of IR23 states their losses at twenty-seven dead, 160 wounded, 245 taken as prisoners and 797 missing, leaving 1,543 to escape from the plateau. Behind them, the battalion of IR20 (and possibly some troops separated from Jurczik's brigade) fell back in good order, preventing Vandamme inflicting even greater losses. The time was probably a little after 11.00am. Chaos was all around.

The tsar, bewildered by this dramatic turn of events, shouted desperate pleas of encouragement to his soldiers as they fled past him. He had hoped to lead his army to a great victory over Napoleon, but now his army was disintegrating before his eyes. Others, including Miloradovich, Kolowrat, Czartoryski and Weyrother, attempted to stem the haemorrhage of men from the front line, but to no avail. Even as the disaster unfolded, many Russian officers were already heaping the blame on the Austrian chief of staff, Generaleutnant Weyrother. Czartoryski later wrote: 'I also saw the unfortunate Weyrother, who had wandered from point to point and by bravely exposing his life strove to remedy the evil of which he had been one of the chief causes.'[29]

A final line of allies stood before Vandamme's victorious men: the battalion of Izmailovsk Guards, the rallied remnants from Miloradovich's Russian troops, possibly now joined by the battalion of IR20. The allies had lost much of their artillery, their horses, weak from lack of forage, unable to pull them through the sticky soil churned by the passage of thousands of men. Vandamme had no such problem and soon began to bombard this last line of defence. The determination of the Guard battalion alone could not hold the line intact. Miloradovich's battalions had already seen much close-quarter fighting over the previous two hours and now they had little left to offer. Once the main Austrian line broke, the resolve of this third position evaporated, and these last troops abandoned the high ground around 11.30, at about the time Miloradovich observed Constantine with the Imperial Guard leaving his position east of Blasowitz.[30]

From the confusion of this lost encounter Kutuzov later wrote:

> 'I realised in this moment that the force of the enemy, directed against our centre, was four to five times more considerable than ours and that it would end up, despite all the intrepidity of our troops, by breaking the line and seizing the heights (which would have given him the means of attacking the left wing of our army in the rear). I went there at once, in order to take the necessary measures to foil the enemy's plan.'[31]

As Kutuzov galloped away towards the southern end of the plateau, accompanied by Kolowrat and with Weyrother in attendance, the tsar found himself almost alone. Gone was the great entourage that rode with him to battle, despatched on urgent missions or swept away in the general confusion. His high hopes of victory fading fast, the tsar abandoned the plateau in the company of just his physician, an equerry, his groom and two Cossacks.[32]

Napoleon, still at his headquarters on Zuran Hill, far from the front line, sat at the centre of a web of communications. Reports and orders passed in and out keeping him constantly informed on the ebb and flow of battle. Everything he received appeared to assure him that the battle was generally following the path he had hoped for. Lannes and Murat were slowly pressing forward, exerting pressure on the unexpectedly strong force before them in the north. He had also not anticipated significant resistance on the Pratzen Plateau, but while Saint-Hilaire was embroiled in a tough battle south of Pratze village, the news of success from Soult's other divisional commander, Vandamme, was a great relief. Along the Goldbach, the combined effort of Legrand's division with Davout's hurriedly advanced men was proving even more successful than he had hoped for, as the great mass of Allies remained along the stream, unable to break out beyond the villages of Telnitz and Sokolnitz.

It was now time to take a closer view of the battle and oversee the next stage. Accordingly, Napoleon ordered the relocation of his headquarters to the newly captured height of Staré Vinohrady.

Chapter 15

'We Are Heroes After All, Aren't We?'*

While Vandamme's division dispersed the final remnants of IV Column from the plateau, Saint-Hilaire's battle for control of the Pratzeberg still raged. At about 11.00am Langeron, still personally involved in the fighting, received word from adjutants despatched from IV Column, advising him with stark simplicity of the collapse of this force. Langeron ordered these messengers to pass on the shocking news to Buxhöwden, who remained inactive about a mile away on the hillock overlooking the Goldbach. Having been away from the rest of his command, fighting in Sokolnitz, for an hour and a half, and with no sign of help coming from Buxhöwden, Langeron realised he must find reinforcements himself. Leaving Kamenski to continue the fight, Langeron galloped off back to Sokolnitz.

At around the same time Weyrother, Kolowrat and Kutuzov approached the Pratzeberg, following the defeat of the other half of IV Column, doing their best to encourage the Austrian troops. Kutuzov, accompanied by a staff officer, Prince Dmitry Volkonsky, then reached Kamenski's brigade just as it was in danger of being broken by a French attack, but Volkonsky rallied the Phanagoria Regiment by grasping their standard and leading them forward: order was again restored.

As Langeron headed off to find reinforcements, the Austrian battalions recovering from their attack on Thiébault's line reformed within reach of Kamenski's brigade. Their brigade commander, Jurczik, anchored his position on a small rise, where he concentrated some of his artillery. Major Mahler brought his battalion of IR49 Kerpen to the rise and drew the battalion of IR58 Beaulieu in to protect the flank. At the same time he moved two guns to a position from where they could enfilade the French line, which brought their fire to a halt for a while. Jurczik applauded his actions shouting, 'Bravo! Major

<hr />

* Captured Russian cavalry officer to Lieutenant Octave Levasseur, of the French horse artillery, 2 December 1805.

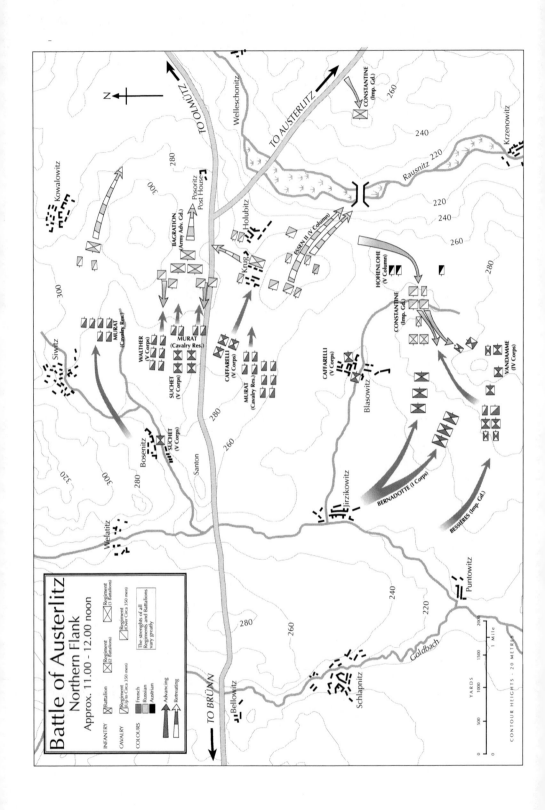

Battle of Austerlitz
Northern Flank
Approx. 11.00 - 12.00 noon

INFANTRY

CAVALRY

COLOURS
French
Russian
Austrian

Advancing
Retreating

Regiment
(Battalion)

Regiment
(2 Battalions)

Regiment
(3 Battalions)

Regiment
(Lower Circa 350 men)

Battalion

Regiment
(Up to Circa 350 men)

Regiment
(2 Battalions)

The strengths of all
Regiments and Battalions
vary greatly

N

TO OLMÜTZ

TO AUSTERLITZ

TO BRÜNN

Kowalowitz

Welleschonitz

Krzenowitz

Rausnitz

CONSTANTINE
(Imp. Gd.)

260

240

220

220

240

260

280

Holubitz

Posoritz
Post House

BAGRATION
(Army Adv. Gd.)

ESSEN II (V Column)

Krug

HOHENLOHE
(V Column)

CONSTANTINE
(Imp. Gd.)

VANDAMME
(IV Corps)

MURAT
(Cavalry Res.)

WALTHER
(V Corps)

SUCHET
(V Corps)

MURAT
(Cavalry Res.)

CAFFARELLI
(V Corps)

MURAT
(Cavalry Res.)

CAFFARELLI
(V Corps)

Blasowitz

Siwitz

Bosenitz

SUCHET
(V Corps)

Santon

Welatitz

BERNADOTTE (I Corps)

Jirzikowitz

BESSIÈRES (Imp. Gd.)

Puntowitz

Bellowitz

Schlapnitz

Goldbach

300

280

300

320

300

280

260

280

260

240

220

240

280

260

300

CONTOUR HEIGHTS · 20 METRES

YARDS

0   500   1000   1500   2000

1 Mile

Mahler!'[1] Shortly afterwards Jurczik fell to the ground, fatally wounded by a French musket ball. He died two weeks later.

Once the Austrian battalions had recoiled from the French artillery, Thiébault joined his men with the rest of the division and together they attacked Kamenski's brigade, driving them back and capturing a number of limbered Russian guns as well as retaking their own previously lost guns. Their impetus took them right to the summit of the Pratzeberg, and it was only with some difficulty that the officers managed to control the ardour of their men and halt the line. In fact, the infantry had now left their supporting artillery behind and with no word from Maréchal Soult or imperial headquarters, Saint-Hilaire felt his isolation keenly.[2] Recognising the urgent need to drive the French off the plateau, and aware of their current exposed position, the Allies prepared to make:

> 'a general and desperate attack at the point of the bayonet. The Austrian Brigade, with that under General Kamenski, charged the enemy; the Russians shouting, according to their usual custom; but the French received them with steadiness, and a well-supported fire, which made a dreadful carnage in the compact ranks of the Russians.'[3]

But the Russians pressed on. Thiébault, close to the centre of the action, watched as the Russians:

> 'charged on all sides, and while desperately disputing the ground, we were forced back. It was only by yielding before the more violent attacks that we maintained any alignment among our troops and saved our guns ... Finally after an appalling melee, a melee of more than twenty minutes, we won a pause; by the sharpest fire and carried at the point of the bayonet.'[4]

According to the notes kept by Thiébault, this 'twenty minute bayonet battle', claimed the lives of both Colonel Mazas, 14ème Ligne, and Thiébault's ADC, Richebourg. Thiébault was fortunate to escape injury himself when his horse fell to a Russian shot.[5] But as both sides recovered their breath, Général de division Saint-Hilaire rushed up to his brigade commanders, Thiébault and Morand, saying: 'This is becoming intolerable, and I propose, gentlemen, that we take up a position to the rear which we can defend.' Almost before he finished speaking, Colonel Pouzet of the 10ème Légère interrupted: 'Withdraw us, my General ... If we take a step back, we are lost. We have only one means of leaving here with honour, it is to put our heads down and attack all in front of us and, above all, not give our enemy time to count our numbers.'[6] Pouzet's stirring words did the trick, and reinvigorated, the French clung tenaciously to the ground they held, repelling all Russian attacks.

While the Russians doggedly continued to attack, the Austrian battalions were being pressed back, despite the best efforts of Weyrother and Kolowrat. Having reformed close to a small rise, supported by their artillery, the battalions reformed and engaged the 36ème in a firefight, halting an enemy advance with volley fire. However, the French recovered and attacked again, driving IR58 Beaulieu back. Mahler attempted a counter-attack with his battalion of IR49 Kerpen and that of IR55 Reuss-Greitz but reported coming under 'a very severe fire' that caused many casualties. With his left flank now exposed to attack due to the repulse of IR58, his position was becoming extremely dangerous. However, he managed to keep his men together and prevented them from falling back for a while with the help of his adjutant, Fähnrich Jlljaschek. Moreover, by maintaining volley fire, he was able to remove his wounded safely to the rear.

But elsewhere, the Austrians were gradually being forced back. Mahler started the battle with only 312 men in his battalion and was now reduced to around eighty, through casualties and men lost as prisoners. There was little more his tiny force could achieve and as the battalion of IR55 on his flank began to retreat he ordered his men away down the eastern slopes of the plateau.[7]

The odds were now stacked against Kamenski's resolute brigade as more French troops approached the Pratzeberg. Released by Vandamme, the 43ème Ligne moved to rejoin Saint-Hilaire's division and Boyé's brigade of cavalry (5ème and 8ème Dragons) was also on its way to add their support. The weight of French numbers now began to tell on the Russian line. On his left, the threat of an attack on his open flank by the French dragoons forced Kamenski to wheel back the extreme left-hand battalion of the Ryazan Musketeers. Having soaked up all the preceding Russian attacks, Saint-Hilaire, judging that the time was right, ordered the French line forward, in what turned out to be the decisive charge. This time Kamenski's men had little left to offer as the French poured forward over 'ground strewn with the dead', leaving no wounded Russians in their wake, capturing the Russian battalion artillery and retaking the highpoint of the Pratzeberg. Yet even in this moment of victory on the Pratzeberg the Russians inflicted another notable casualty: Saint-Hilaire was wounded and forced to retire to Puntowitz to have his wound dressed.[8]

Having arrived back at Sokolnitz, Langeron sent for General Maior Olsufiev, who was fighting in the village and informed him of the need to send reinforcements to the plateau. The only troops immediately to hand were the two battalions of the Kursk Musketeers, held in reserve just outside Sokolnitz. With no time to lose, Langeron directed these to the plateau. He then attempted to extract his other battalions from the village but only succeeded in pulling back 8. Jäger and the Vyborg Musketeers. The remaining battalion of Kursk Musketeers and the Permsk Musketeer Regiment, now so completely entangled with III Column and its battle for the village, could not be withdrawn. But even as the two Kursk battalions began their march, unknown to them, they were marching to their destruction.

Kutuzov recognised that any further resistance by Kamenski's brigade, after two hours fighting, would lead to their total destruction, so he ordered the retreat. Abandoning the plateau, they descended the south-eastern slopes to the valley of the Littawa, where they reformed. All along the valley other Allied units that had been driven off the plateau took up defensive positions or retreated to better ground. Before he left the plateau, Kutuzov despatched a hurried note to Buxhöwden, who still had not moved, ordering him to extract his three Columns from their bottleneck and retire. Soult's two divisions were complete masters of the Pratzen Plateau, having swept away Allied IV Column along with Kamenski's brigade of II Column by the sheer determination of their attacks. The time was probably around noon when, into this killing ground, marched the two lone battalions of the Kursk Musketeers, sent from Sokolnitz.

Believing the troops ahead of them to be Russian, they approached confidently but as they closed, Thiébault turned his exhausted men to face them and another firefight exploded. At the same time, Lavasseur's brigade of Legrand's division (IV Corps), which was occupying Kobelnitz, marched southwards presenting a possible flank threat to the Kursk battalions. To combat this move, the Podolsk Musketeers, part of III Column reserve, advanced to oppose them. Even without this intervention, the French troops on the Pratzeberg were in overwhelming numbers and soon began to surround the isolated Kursk battalions, who fought on for a while before collapsing amidst massive losses.

The victorious Thiébault, now mounted on his third horse – a small grey liberated from a captured Russian artillery limber – surveyed the destruction all around him. His own brigade had lost about a third of its strength, while another of his regimental commanders, Houdard de Lamotte of the 36ème Ligne, joined the growing list of wounded.

While this final struggle to clear the Allies from the Pratzen Plateau had reached its climax, elsewhere on the battlefield matters were also coming to a bloody conclusion.

Grand Duke Constantine, at the head of the Imperial Guard, had received no orders since a request arrived for him to send a battalion of infantry up onto the plateau. Since then his Guard Jäger had fallen back from Blasowitz, along with a supporting battalion of Semeyonovsk Guards. With only limited military experience, Constantine considered his options. To his right, masses of French infantry and cavalry were pressing aggressively towards Bagration, while to his left the Austrian cavalry, which had offered some protection on that flank, were withdrawing, having temporarily held back the advance of a massed infantry formation (Rivaud's division of Bernadotte's I Corps). Further to the left, up on the plateau, he could see that the French were driving back at least part of IV Column. Having surveyed the position, Constantine elected to pull back to his left rear (south-east), towards the Austrian cavalry and hopefully a junction with a reforming IV Column somewhere near Krzenowitz. At around 11.30am he turned his force, deploying the Guard Jäger as a flank guard.

In fact, he had not moved very far when he realised that the French troops previously held in check by the Austrian cavalry were now slowly advancing towards him. Up until now, Bernadotte had shown a marked reluctance to move forward since he crossed the stream at Jirschikowitz earlier that morning. Napoleon sent his aide, de Ségur, to ensure that Bernadotte carried out his orders, but the imperial messenger found the commander of I Corps agitated and anxious. Bernadotte indicated the Austrian cavalry to his front and bemoaned the fact that he had no cavalry of his own with which to oppose them, begging de Ségur to return to Napoleon and obtain some for him. De Ségur did as he requested but Napoleon had none to offer. However, now that the Austrian cavalry had withdrawn, Bernadotte cautiously advanced his corps, Rivaud edging slowing forward between the plateau and with Blasowitz to his left front, while Drouet led his division onto the lower slopes of the plateau in support of Vandamme.

Aware now of this forward movement, Constantine halted the Guard and faced them to confront this new threat. Behind him, the single bridge over the Rausnitz stream represented a very dangerous bottleneck. To gain time for his crossing, Constantine decided to strike a blow at the advancing French in an attempt to halt their advance. Forming the two Guard fusilier battalions from both the Preobrazhensk and Semeyonovsk Regiments for the attack, he held back the battalion of Izmailovsk Guards in reserve and organised the cavalry in a supporting role. Hohenlohe's three Austrian cavalry regiments took up positions protecting the left and right rear of the Russian Guard: 5. Nassau-Kürassiere to the left with 1. Kaiser and 7. Lotheringen-Küirassiere to the right. The four battalions leading the attack advanced with much confidence, roaring 'Oorah! Oorah! Oorah!' and when still 300 paces from the opposing French line, they broke into a run that their officers were unable to control. Although facing a withering barrage of musketry, the Russian guardsmen did not halt and smashed straight through the first line of massed skirmishers, pushing them back onto a formed second line of infantry, which they attacked with the bayonet. These too gave way, but although elated with their success, the Russian attack ground to a halt and when French artillery opened up on them they began to fall back in disorder.[9] But the threatening presence of the Russian Guard cavalry prevented any attempt at pursuit and kept Rivaud's division firmly anchored to the spot.

Up on the plateau, Maréchal Soult studied the ground, now that Vandamme had cleared Miloradovitch's men from his front. He noticed the movement of a large body of troops from high ground near Blasowitz towards the Rausnitz stream, imagining them some of Lannes' men moving to cut off the Allied retreat, but then, near Krzenowitz they turned and headed west. The movement puzzled him and he ordered Vandamme to send a battalion out to the left flank of the division to observe it. Selecting 1/4ème Ligne, Vandamme sent their commanding officer, Major Auguste Bigarré, at their head to investigate, detailing his own ADC, Vincent, to accompany him. The undulations of the plateau hid the lower ground from view and Bigarré had advanced about 1,200 yards when Vincent, who preceded him with a few scouts, came galloping back and warned him of the presence of a large body of enemy cavalry. Bigarré instructed the battalion to move to its left and then returned with Vincent to see the enemy formation for himself. As he approached the vantage point, five squadrons of Russian cavalry began to accelerate towards his battalion that now moved into view. Bigarré and Vincent galloped back to the battalion and hurried it into square to receive the inescapable charge.[10]

The Russian Guard cavalry had kept a watchful eye on their infantry as it fell back from the French lines, which presented a formidable obstacle to a cavalry attack. But then, descending from the plateau, a lone infantry battalion appeared. As the cavalry moved towards this tempting target, the battalion scrambled into square formation. The cavalry halted at what Bigarré described as long musket range, and instead of charging, unmasked a battery of six guns, which opened canister fire on the square, creating havoc in the packed ranks. Observing this from the high ground, Vandamme ordered the two battalions of 24ème Légère forward to support the 1/4ème, but they were too late, for the cavalry was already on the move.

Considering that the artillery had done enough damage to the square, two of the five squadrons of Horse Guards charged. The leading squadron rode into a hail of musketry and veered away, but the second squadron reached the square before the men had time to reload and smashed their way in, hacking and slashing at the infantry, who defended themselves furiously. The squadron swept right through the square, turned and rode back though it again.

Two previous bearers of the 1/4ème's eagle standard already lay dead on the ground: now, gripped desperately by the battalion's sergeant major, a soldier of twelve years' experience named Saint-Cyr, it was under attack again. Three horsemen surrounded him and hacked it from his grasp leaving him with five sabre wounds to the head and right hand.[11] By now the 1/4ème had collapsed and those still standing were fleeing back towards the plateau leaving about 200 dead and wounded on the ground. The two squadrons of Horse Guards retired eastwards to reform. Even before the battalion disintegrated, the 24ème Légère arrived, advancing in line. The remaining three Horse Guard squadrons spurred forward, and despite receiving a close range volley, smashed through the thin infantry line and sent them reeling backwards too. In the confusion and panic that followed, a soldier of the 1/4ème picked up a fallen eagle standard of 24ème Légère believing it to belong to his battalion and carried it to safety. It was now perhaps around noon as Napoleon arrived on the Pratzen Plateau to oversee the next moves.

No sooner had he arrived than those accompanying him observed a great dark mass of men coming towards the plateau in some disorder. Maréchal Berthier commented, 'what a splendid crowd of prisoners they are bringing back for you.' But Napoleon was not so sure and ordered one of his aides, Général de brigade Jean Rapp, to investigate. Leading two squadrons of the Chasseurs à cheval of the Garde Impériale, supported by a squadron of the Grenadiers à cheval and a half squadron of the Mameluks, Rapp advanced down from the plateau towards the site of the Russian Guard cavalry attacks. As soon as he cleared the plateau he saw that:

> 'The cavalry was in the midst of our squares and was cutting down our soldiers. A little to the rear we could see the masses of infantry and cavalry which formed the enemy reserve. The Russians broke contact and rushed against me, while four pieces of their horse artillery come up at the gallop and unlimbered. I advanced in good order, with brave Colonel Morland on my left, and [Chef d'Escadron] Dahlmann to my right. I told my men: "Over there you can see our brothers and friends being trodden underfoot. Avenge our comrades! Avenge our standards!"'[12]

Rapp led his Guard cavalry straight towards the Russian Horse Guard squadrons that had just cut up 24ème Légère. The Russians, disordered by their attack on the infantry, turned away and galloped off after a brief struggle leaving the *chasseurs à cheval* to ride on into the ranks of the reforming Preobrazhensk and Semeyonovsk Guard battalions, as these infantrymen defended themselves with the bayonet. The French cavalry soon received support from the half squadron of Mameluks, who slashed their way into the ranks of the Preobrazhensk battalions, currently dispersed as skirmishers in the vineyards and already engaged with Rapp's *chasseurs*. But now Rapp's formations were disordered and Constantine took the opportunity to send in the leading three squadrons of the Russian Chevalier Garde to break their attack and free his beleaguered infantry. The charge met with success, causing Rapp to withdraw and reform while allowing the Russian battalions to draw back. But their respite was brief, as the rest of the French Garde Impériale cavalry now joined Rapp. The great cavalry battle – Imperial Guard against Imperial Guard – that followed is difficult to recount in much detail from the accounts that survive. Indeed one observer, Coignet, a soldier in the Grenadiers à Pied of Napoleon's Guard, described how: 'For a quarter of an hour there was a desperate struggle, and that quarter of an hour seemed to us an age. We could see nothing through the smoke and dust.'

The Russian Guard cavalry drawn from the Horse Guards, Chevalier Garde and Guard Cossacks mustered about 1,800 men – the Guard Hussars appear not to have become directly involved in the fighting. Against them the French Garde mustered about 1,100 men, from the Chasseurs à cheval, Grenadiers à cheval and Mameluks. Although short on numbers, the well-disciplined French cavalry were able to withdraw from the fighting and fall back on their nearest infantry formations, reorganise and re-enter the fray in formed bodies. The Russians did not have this luxury, as their own Guard infantry battalions were caught up in the mêlée and unable to fire for fear of shooting their own horsemen. It became clear that the French were gaining the upper hand and Russian casualties mounted alarmingly, particularly in the Chevalier Garde. In particular, the fourth squadron of this elite formation was all but destroyed – only eighteen men reputedly making good their escape – and its wounded commander, Prince Repnin-Volkonsky, captured and presented to Napoleon.

Russian reports claim that the Chevalier Garde lost sixteen officers, 200 men and 300 horses killed and wounded. The Guards battalions extracted themselves from the maelstrom and fell back on the support of the Izmailovsk battalion, then all continued back towards Krzenowitz. The battered Russian cavalry also broke off the engagement and fell back too, their retreat protected by the Guard Hussars who hovered threateningly to the north, and the stand made by Hohenlohe's three Austrian cavalry regiments. The belated appearance above Krzenowitz of the three battalions of Russian Guard Grenadiers, numbering almost 2,000 men, but suggesting to the French the arrival of a new strong Russian formation, limited any further significant advance in this direction.

While the great cavalry battle to their front delayed Rivaud's movements further, Drouet had finally led his division up onto the plateau to the rear of Vandamme. The retreating battalion of 4ème Ligne, which had fled back onto the plateau and streamed past Napoleon without stopping, eventually rallied when they rejoined Vandamme's division, and despite their recent traumas, took an active part in the latter stages of the battle, unaware they had lost an eagle.

With the Pratzen Plateau secured by the gradual arrival of Bernadotte's corps, Napoleon turned his back on the northern flank. It was now clear that his grand plan to swing Lannes and Murat unopposed into the rear of the Austro-Russian army had failed, but it was also clear that the attacks by Saint-Hilaire and Vandamme had split the Allied army in two. Leaving Lannes and Murat to drive Bagration back, Napoleon issued new orders that he hoped would lead to the destruction of the left wing of the Allied army, which still remained locked in the Goldbach valley.

On the extreme right of the Allied line, General Maior Prince Bagration, like Constantine, received no fresh instructions from army headquarters. His original orders, which he viewed with little enthusiasm, required him to hold his position until, becoming aware of progress by the Allied left wing, he was to advance directly ahead and, initially, capture the Santon. Accordingly, he had pushed forward at about 10.00am but encountered extremely strong and determined opposition from Lannes' V Corps and Murat's cavalry. His attempt on the Santon had failed and now the French cavalry had pushed his own horsemen back after a series of ferocious mêlées. The French had secured the village of Blasowitz and the Russian Imperial Guard appeared to be moving further away, cutting his last tenuous link with the rest of the army. Bagration abandoned any offensive plans and looked to the preservation of his command.

With the Russian cavalry driven back behind their infantry to reform once more, Lannes ordered his two infantry divisions forward: Suchet on the left, Caffarelli on the right. In the face of this advancing wall of infantry, Bagration ordered all eighteen guns of his battalion artillery to open fire, along with twelve from a horse artillery battery. The brunt of this bombardment fell on the 34ème and 40ème Ligne of Suchet's division and 30ème Ligne from Caffarelli's, while also mortally wounding GB Valhubert, who commanded a brigade in Suchet's second line.

With the French infantry brought to a halt by this concentrated firepower, Lannes drew all his available artillery together and focused on knocking out the Russian guns. The more powerful French artillery came out on top in this duel and after a deadly exchange, the Russian horse battery was forced to withdraw with mounting casualties, leaving just the Russian battalion guns to support the infantry against the increasing threat. Lannes pushed his infantry on once more but now Suchet's division became the target for a series of desperate cavalry charges by Bagration's reformed horsemen.

However, assailed by musketry, canister fire and then French cavalry countercharges, all they could manage was to slow this advance. Caffarelli's division, operating south of the Brünn-Olmütz road, encountered less opposition and pushed ahead of Suchet's men to threaten Bagration's left flank, secured on the villages of Krug and Holubitz. In fact, the garrison of these villages was not strong, both defended by the men of 6. Jäger under General Maior Ulanius – who had already suffered considerably at Schöngrabern – with recovering cavalry formations to their rear. Sometime around noon, GB Demont's brigade (17ème and 30ème Ligne) and part of Général de brigade Debilly's brigade (61ème Ligne), advanced determinedly against the two villages.

Up until now the *jäger* had managed to repulse any French cavalry showing an interest in their position, but heavily outnumbered by Caffarelli's infantry – and despite an initial stout resistance – French troops drove 6. Jäger out at the point of the bayonet. However, despite a lack of support, Ulanius did manage to extricate some of his men and reach safety.[13]

With the villages of Krug and Holubitz now in French hands, Caffarelli redirected 17ème and 30ème Ligne against the left flank of Bagration's threatened line. To oppose them the Russian commander sent his reserve infantry, the Arkhangelogord Musketeer Regiment, commanded by General Maior Nikolai Kamenski II. Although the French and Russian infantry were fairly evenly matched, the French were always able to bring up supporting cavalry and artillery to disrupt the Russian lines whenever their own infantry fell back to reform for a fresh assault. At times the Arkhangelogord Musketeers were under attack from all sides, and at one point faced a charge by d'Hautpoul's 5ème Cuirassier, suffering horrendous casualties in the process. This regiment, which marched into battle with about 2,000 men, later showed losses of 1,625.[14] Kamenski II had his horse shot from under him and only escaped capture when another officer gave up his own mount.

With Suchet's division pressing him more and more from the front, Caffarelli making inroads on his left flank and Murat's cavalry ready to exploit any opportunity, Bagration gave the order to retreat. Despite constant French cavalry attacks, the Russian infantry held together, supported by self-sacrificing charges by the exhausted Russian horsemen, and fell back steadily, abandoning the road to Austerlitz and reoccupying the high ground north of the Posoritz post house. However, this constant pressure eventually caused a split and the Russian cavalry of V Column, commanded by General-Adjutant Uvarov broke away. In his report Uvarov wrote:

> 'we continued to fight with fervour, from which the losses on both sides were substantial. At the same time artillery and infantry of the enemy, moving on my flanks, opened such a fire that even with all the courage of the regiments which were under my command, we had to retreat across the river situated behind us.'[15]

Podpolkovnik Ermolov of the horse artillery recalled the confusion that then prevailed:

> 'Our losses multiplied even more when the men crowded together at the very boggy stream, over which there were very few bridges, and it was not possible to cross it in any other way than via a bridge. Here our fleeing cavalry plunged in wading, and a lot of men and horses drowned, while I, abandoned by the regiments to which I was assigned, stopped my battery, attempting by the means of a short range action to stop the cavalry pursuing us. The first pieces of ordnance that I was able to release from the press of our own cavalry, making several shots, were captured, my men were cut down and I was captured as a prisoner. The division of General-Adjutant Uvarov, crowding at the bridge, had the time to look around and see

that it was running away from a force small in number and that the majority of the forces were concentrated on the heights and were not coming down into the valley. Those who pursued us were then forced to retreat and exterminated, and my freedom was returned to me shortly, when I was already close to the French line.'[16]

When Ermolov returned and crossed the Rausnitz stream he found Uvarov's command still in great disarray at the foot of the hill held by the Russian Guard Grenadiers. With them now stood the tsar, prompting Ermolov to observe that 'there were no confidants present, on his face there was a look of supreme grief, and his eyes were filled with tears.'

Bagration continued his withdrawal in the face of ceaseless French cavalry attacks and artillery bombardment, drawing back across the Brünn-Olmütz road onto high ground overlooking it between Welleschowitz and Rausnitz. The Pavlograd Hussars suffered at the hands of the French cavalry as they protected this final move, but their sacrifice gained enough time for Bagration to take up this new position. Lannes and Murat now advanced to occupy the position abandoned by Bagration north of the Posoritz post house and found themselves in possession of row upon row of Russian knapsacks. It was the habit of the Russian soldier to take off his knapsack before entering battle to allow more freedom of movement, leaving behind him all his meagre personal belongings.[17] But if the French soldiers expected to find luxuries and warm clothing they were disappointed. Captaine Lejeune, Berthier's ADC, reported that each bag contained only:

> 'triptych reliquaries, each containing an image of St Christopher carrying the infant Saviour over the water, with an equal number of pieces of black bread containing a good deal more straw and bran than barley or wheat. Such was the sacred and simple baggage of the Russians!'[18]

Bagration must have been wondering just how long he could continue to hold his force together against these constant French attacks when help arrived. Advancing down the road from Olmütz with all speed appeared an Austrian artillery officer, Major Frierenberger, at the head of a column of twelve guns. As he came level with Welleschowitz he turned off and positioned his guns on the high ground rising to the north of the road. The official Austrian account of the incident continues the story:

> 'The army he faced was a victorious one. It had deployed at the Posoritz post house, and was now in full advance, firing with its powerful artillery against whatever Russian troops and batteries came into view. The Austrian battery now opened up in its turn

against the main battery of the French and their leading troops. The Austrians shot with such extraordinary skill that they compelled the enemy to pull back their batteries in a matter of minutes. Some of the hostile pieces were silenced altogether, and the advance of the whole French left wing was held back.'[19]

The battle on the northern flank now ground to a halt. Lannes and Murat had expected an almost unopposed advance but became embroiled in a lengthy and costly duel that had lasted almost three hours. In the face of the resolute defence now offered by these fresh Austrian guns, with their own ammunition supplies almost completely expended and their cavalry exhausted, the two corps forming the French left wing halted, and like Bernadotte's I Corps, awaited developments elsewhere on the battlefield.

Granted this unexpected respite, the survivors of Bagration's Army Advance Guard and to the south, IV and V Columns, and the Russian Guard, did what they could to instil some sense of order in their greatly depleted ranks. These latter formations nervously occupied the eastern bank of the Rausnitz stream, anticipating a renewed French assault at any moment, but it never came. Napoleon saw a greater prize elsewhere.

Chapter 16

The Legend of the Lakes

'a horrible spectacle was seen ...
twenty thousand men throwing
themselves in the water and
drowning in the lakes.'*

Général de division Legrand and Maréchal Davout, fighting along the Goldbach, had performed far better than even Napoleon had hoped. Although heavily outnumbered their aggressive tactics had contained the Allied left wing, while Soult's IV Corps cleared the Pratzen Plateau. Having witnessed the defeat of the Russian Imperial Guard, Napoleon now issued new orders to Soult's corps and to Davout, as he switched his attention southwards. Saint-Hilaire's division was to descend from the plateau, march towards Sokolnitz and attack the rear of the Allied forces engaged there, supported by Candras' brigade from Vandamme's division. Lavasseur's brigade of Legrand's division was to advance on Saint-Hilaire's right. A brigade of the Reserve Grenadier Division, which had also made its way up onto the plateau, received orders to support the attack on Sokolnitz via Kobelnitz 'and ensure that not one escapes'.[1] Vandamme was to lead his division to the southern end of the Pratzen Plateau in an attempt to cut off the retreat of any Allied formations that escaped this crushing attack. Also joining this exodus to the south were two brigades of Beaumont's dragoon division, riding to reunite with Boyé's brigade. Napoleon sent Berthier's ADC, Lejeune, to Davout, asking him to renew his assault on Sokolnitz in conjunction with Saint-Hilaire's attack. Napoleon then set off himself towards the southern end of the plateau, riding through the debris of IV Column, followed by the Garde Impériale and the rest of the Reserve Grenadiers. It was about 2.00pm when Saint-Hilaire resumed command of his division, having had his wound treated, and ordered the march on Sokolnitz.

---

* 30th Bulletin of La Grande Armée, 2 December 1805.

In fact, Davout did not need an order from Napoleon to encourage him to attack Sokolnitz. Having regrouped and rallied the various formations at his disposal, he had just thrown them in once more as Saint-Hilaire's division began to descend from the plateau. The 33ème Ligne launched itself against the western entrance to the village, while 48ème Ligne attacked the south-west.

Langeron chose this moment to make one last effort to extricate the Permsk Musketeer Regiment and the remaining battalion of the Kursk Regiment. With General Maior Olsufiev at his side, Langeron led a single battalion of the Vyborg Musketeers back into Sokolnitz, the main street of which was now 'literally choked up with the dead and wounded of both armies, piled one on top of another, and it was all but impossible to ride over the heaps of mutilated bodies and weapons'.[2] They came under 'a dreadful fire' from French troops occupying the houses and were then attacked with the bayonet. With casualties mounting and no hope of reaching his men, Langeron reluctantly withdrew from the village. Forming the battalion guns of the Vyborg Musketeers into a battery covering the bridge at the exit of the village, he positioned 8. Jäger to their left and the Vyborg Musketeers to the right of the guns. It was enough to deter pursuit for the moment, and once all was in place, Langeron rode off to Buxhöwden, who remained firmly anchored to the hillock he had occupied since early morning.[3]

To the north of the village of Sokolnitz, Davout sent 15ème Légère and 111ème Ligne forward in clouds of skirmishers against the castle and the massive barns and outhouses of its complex. As this attack gathered pace from the west, Général de brigade Thiébault arrived at the head of 36ème Ligne from the east side of the castle, leading the approach of Saint-Hilaire's division, which extended to the right, or north, heading towards the Pheasantry. To their right, Lavasseur's brigade reformed after an encounter with the 700 men of the Podolsk Musketeers. After an exchange that lasted half an hour, Lavasseur's two regiments (18ème and 75ème Ligne), some 3,000 men, drove the Russian regiment back to the Pheasantry. Lavasseur now prepared to march on the walled Pheasantry, while behind him a brigade of the Reserve Grenadiers headed for Kobelnitz. Opposing them, Przhebishevsky's frontline troops extended over a wide area. Some, mixed up with Langeron's missing men, were defending the north end of Sokolnitz village, while others occupied the castle and outbuildings. Further to the north, Przhebishevsky extended his command into the Pheasantry, drawing the defenders mainly from the Butyrsk and Galicia Musketeer Regiments. General Leitenant Wimpffen remained on the east bank of the Goldbach, close to the Pheasantry with Przhebishevsky's reserve, the Azov Musketeer Regiment and a battalion of Narva, now rejoined by the Podolsk battalions. The sudden appearance of Saint-Hilaire's division descending on his rear caused Przhebishevsky immediate consternation. He attempted to send a message to Langeron and

Buxhöwden but found to his dismay that the advance of 36ème Ligne had cut his line of communication to the south.

Thiébault wasted no time in sending 36ème Ligne in to attack the castle and the surrounding buildings. As his men closed they encountered stiff resistance:

> 'The avenues, stables, barns, outhouses, the main manor, served them well for hideouts, and they fought up to the very end everywhere. They made a great slaughter there. All had to be beaten, man by man. I saw individuals defend themselves as if they were in the midst of their battalions. I saw others, badly wounded and ready to fall, load their weapon as coolly as on exercise.'[4]

While the 36ème Ligne closed in on the castle, with their two *voltigeurs* companies leading, the rest of Saint-Hilaire's division began to exert pressure on III Column reserve. The seven battalions of the reserve numbered only about 2,100 men in total, the Azov and Podolsk Regiments having lost heavily at Schöngrabern just over two weeks earlier, but Saint-Hilaire's men had already suffered heavy casualties on the plateau. The battalion artillery kept the French at a respectful distance but an attempt to break through to Sokolnitz village failed. Wimpffen, at the head of part of the Narva battalion, became separated from the rest of the reserve and found it impossible to clear a path through streets clogged by 'an appalling mob'. General Maior Selekhov attempted to pull the men out, and reunited with Przhebishevsky, who had been fighting in the defence of the village, headed back towards the Pheasantry, still resolutely defended by the men of the Butyrsk and Galicia Regiments. From here they hoped to break through the tightening French noose and head towards Kobelnitz where Przhebishevsky, who had no knowledge of developments on the plateau, hoped to find IV Column.[5]

Meanwhile, the isolated and bewildered Wimpffen, with his detachment of the Narva Regiment, saw a group of about twenty French horseman riding towards him. Wimpffen attempted to obstruct their path but the leading Frenchman – the ADC, Capitaine Lejeune, returning to Napoleon after carrying orders to Davout – rode straight into the crowd, thrust his sword into Wimpffen's arm and took him prisoner.[6]

The castle was now finally back in French hands after a stout defence by the Russian garrison. Amongst the prisoners was General Maior Müller III, wounded in the left thigh during one of the first assaults on the castle in the morning. With the castle captured, the 36ème Ligne, according to their wounded colonel, Houdard de Lamotte, continued to clear the surrounding buildings: 'In this way, Sokolnitz was taken and became the theatre of a horrible massacre of Russians that had held firm in the barns and in the houses: only death stopped them firing.'[7]

Thiébault then attempted to reform the 36ème Ligne but noticed that a group of about 120 men were detached on the right, firing ineffectively at a pair of Russian guns on high ground overlooking the castle. Thiébault brought their firing to a halt, but unable to find an officer to lead the men in a charge against the guns, he placed himself at their head and attacked. At a range of fifty paces the guns unleashed a storm of canister fire, which scythed down about twenty of his men and smashed Thiébault's shoulder and breastbone, but left him sitting dazed in the saddle. The charge pressed home and almost subconsciously he saw his 'men taking the battery and slaughtering all the gunners who had served it, then the Russian troops which supported it surrendered'.[8] Other disorganised groups of Russian soldiers tried to escape from the slaughter in Sokolnitz but they stood little chance.

Przhebishevsky's attempt to break out to the north was also doomed to fail. Supported by General Maior Strik and Selekhov, he pushed his desperate men past the Pheasantry, constantly under fire and with casualties falling all the time. On one flank, Lavasseur's brigade fired into this 'mass of men in confusion',[9] on the other, the 10ème Légère added to the destruction, while to their rear some of the 36ème Ligne joined the tightening cordon. Then, as the fugitive Russians drew closer to Kobelnitz, another formation loomed into view: GB Dupas' brigade of the Grenadier Reserve. With his forlorn command now forced towards Kobelnitz's frozen lake, Prebyshevsky realised the end was close. In his report sent to the tsar he recounted how they:

> 'were reduced to confusion by the vicious salvoes of canister which came in from three sides. We ran out of cartridges, and we had no hope of support. With all this we fought on against the enemy to the limit of our strength, according to the loyalty we owe to Your Imperial Highness.'[10]

Przhebishevsky's ordeal finally ended when Colonel Franceschi, at the head of about eighty men of 8ème Hussards, galloped into the milling mass of Russian infantry to demand and receive the surrender of the commander of III Column and his remaining men. In the final moments a few determined men tore regimental standards from their poles and wrapped them around their bodies in a last defiant gesture to prevent them falling into French hands. The total losses of III Column amounted to 5,280 or 70 per cent of their starting strength.[11]

Having left his men drawn up outside Sokolnitz, Langeron rushed off to speak to Buxhöwden, the overall commander of the Allied left wing. Langeron was now desperate, for it was clear the army was in a bad position. But when he reached Buxhöwden, he realised his commanding officer was drunk and his frustration and anger got the better of him:

'His face was crimson and he appeared to me to have neither his head nor even his reason. I told him what had happened on the plateau and that we were turned and surrounded by the enemy. He answered me rather coarsely: "My General, you see enemies everywhere." I replied to him, in truth, with little enough respect: "And you, Count, you are not in a fit state to see them anywhere."'[12]

Buxhöwden did not forget Langeron's insubordination and was to have his revenge later. But Langeron was not alone in condemning Buxhöwden's lack of activity. An Austrian staff officer who was present, Hauptmann Jurczik, 'dared to reproach Count Buxhöwden for his uncertainty and his inaction' with, as Langeron put it, 'even more force than me.'

Buxhöwden had, in fact, received the earlier order from Kutuzov to retire, but as it failed to spell out the total defeat of Allied forces on the plateau, he ignored it. He discussed the situation with Kienmayer and Stutterheim and decided to stay put and hoped to alleviate whatever the problem was by finally pushing back the French right. But now, with French formations flowing over the edge of the plateau, it was clear that the battle plan had gone badly wrong and it was time, belatedly, to save what he could of his command.

The only option apparent to Buxhöwden was to march back eastwards, passing Augezd, with the plateau on the left and the frozen expanses of Satschan lake on the right: beyond Augezd, across the Littawa stream, he presumed he would find IV Column. He issued orders to the closest regiments (the Vladimir, Yaroslavl and New Ingermanland Musketeers and Kiev Grenadiers) of I Column – those dubbed by Langeron as Buxhöwden's 'guard of honour' as so far they had not fired a shot – to prepare to march. Then for the protection of their open left flank, he ordered the artillery commander of I Column, Count Sievers, to reform his two twelve-gun batteries facing the plateau and extend them towards Augezd. The timing was opportune, for no sooner were the guns in position than Beaumont's dragoons appeared from the direction of Sokolnitz. Tempted by the sight of the retreating Russian infantry they began to advance, but a well-ordered fire by Sievers' guns forced the French cavalry away up onto the plateau.[13]

Increasing pressure building up against the men Langeron had left facing Sokolnitz had already forced them to give ground towards Telnitz. West of Telnitz, Kienmayer and Dokhturov realised the danger developing behind them and commenced pulling their men back through the village, by which time Buxhöwden was already leading the way to Augezd. Dokhturov ordered General Maior Löwis to organise a rearguard in and around Telnitz to delay any French pursuit, supported by Kienmayer's cavalry, while the *grenzer* infantry followed the remaining regiments of I and II Column in pursuit of those already making for Augezd.

After Napoleon had issued his orders for the redirection of the central part of the army, he rode to the southern end of the plateau. Once there, he followed the gentle downwards slope to the tiny Chapel of Saint Antonin, which nestled on a lower spur overlooking the village of Augezd and the frozen Satschan lake. Here he found Vandamme and Soult watching the Allied forces making their way eastwards. They recognised the need to close down this route to the Allies, for once they passed beyond the Augezd defile they were safe, but for the moment there was nothing they could do as they waited anxiously for the first of Vandamme's fatigued and wounded division to arrive. The first two Russian battalions were already emerging from Augezd when the leading unit of Vandamme's division finally arrived at the chapel. Soult, giving, as far as Thiébault was concerned, his first order since he launched his corps at the Pratzen Plateau early in the morning, ordered Vandamme to stop them.[14] Immediately a single battalion of 28ème Ligne bundled down the slope and cut the road leading from Augezd to Hostieradek: the trap was sealed. The time was close to 3.30pm.

Buxhöwden just missed escaping through Augezd before the French obstructed his path to safety. Then the rest of Vandamme's leading two brigades arrived, and despite the traumas already suffered by 4ème Ligne and 24ème Légère, at the hands of the Russian Horse Guards, they, with the remaining battalion of 28ème Ligne: 'rushed like a torrent down upon the village, in which a sharp fire of musketry at first took place, but which was of short duration, before they gained possession of the village.'[15]

The attack not only captured the village but 2/4ème Ligne also netted Polkovnik Sulima of the Moscow Regiment and two battalion standards, but the main body of the regiment managed to retreat back towards Telnitz.[16]

At the head of the following units, Buxhöwden veered away from danger and made a dash towards a 'rotten wooden bridge, covered with manure, and intended for the passage of cattle', which crossed over the marshy ground and a broad, deep stream feeding Satschan lake. Buxhöwden and his entourage led the way across but behind them an Austrian gun and limber proved too much for the weak structure, which collapsed beneath its weight, sealing this escape route too. Unconcerned by the fate of his men behind him, Buxhöwden rode on towards Austerlitz, leading just the two battalions that passed safely through Augezd, having exerted command over about 34,000 men at the commencement of the battle. A short while later Czartoryski, who was endeavouring to discover what was happening on the left wing, saw him approaching. Of this encounter Czartoryski wrote: 'The poor general had lost his hat, and his clothes were in disorder; when he perceived me at a distance he cried, "They have abandoned me! They have sacrificed me!" He continued his retreat, and I hastened to join the [tsar].'[17]

In desperation, the mass of men following Buxhöwden took the only other option and moved tentatively onto the frozen surface of Satschan lake. Some of the battalion artillery followed too, severely testing the strength of the ice as those fleeing slithered their way across. A French witness described this bleak white expanse 'blackened by the scattered multitude of fugitives'.[18] Vandamme's artillery had also now arrived close to the chapel above Augezd and immediately unlimbered and opened fire on the disorganised mass of Russians below. At the same time, Vandamme's successful capture of Augezd allowed his infantry to turn their attention to Sievers' Russian batteries. These gunners refused to abandon their guns and kept firing until overwhelmed by infantry emerging from Augezd and attacking their open right flank.

Back on the ice the inevitable happened. The sheer concentration of weight at first caused the ice to crack and then break, dumping the horrified Russian soldiers into the black icy waters. Fortunately the lake was shallow – rarely more than chest-deep – and once they overcame the initial shock, the men were able to struggle on. But soon, artillery fire directed on the lake made the horror more acute for those desperately wading through the freezing mud and water. For some, particularly the wounded, it proved too great an exertion and they slipped below the surface to a watery grave. Others, helped along by comrades, struggled on, while compassionate French soldiers waded in and hauled back those they could reach. Napoleon made much of this episode in his reporting of the battle, claiming 20,000 Russian soldiers drowned. This is pure propaganda. A few days after the battle the lake was drained. Discovered in the mud were 'Twenty-eight to thirty cannon, 150 corpses of horses and only two or three human corpses'.[19] Local estimates suggest as few as 200 men in total lost their lives crossing the Satschan lake; others up to 2,000: but not 20,000.

Langeron, with two of his adjutants and three officers of the Vyborg Musketeers gathered together a small group of soldiers close to the destroyed bridge. Chaos and confusion were everywhere. As the French approached, Langeron, having abandoned his horse, led this knot of men on foot, struggling through the wide expanse of marsh and stream beds to relative safety on the other side and followed the general line of retreat. The deterioration of the army greatly shocked Langeron: 'after the passage of the streams … No two men of the same company remained together, all were mixed up and confused: the soldiers threw away their guns and no longer listened to their officers, or their generals.'[20]

Seeing the fate that awaited those who ventured onto the ice, Dokhturov turned the units still on dry land and marched them back toward the rearguard near Telnitz. Here Dokhturov consulted with Kienmayer and decided that the only means of escape now open to them lay to the south, across a narrow causeway separating the Satschan and Menitz lakes, which would open up a route along the south side of the Satschan lake. Although it would only allow little more than two men abreast to pass, there was no other option. Kienmayer immediately rode ahead with the 4. Hessen-Homburg-Husaren and some Cossacks to secure this route by taking up a position on high ground between

Satschan and Ottnitz. From here, overlooking Augezd, the Austrian cavalry hoped to deter any French attempt to cross the streams and marshes to cut Dokhturov's retreat. The rest of Kienmayer's Austrian cavalry – 3. O'Reilly Chevaulegers and 11. Szeckel-Husaren – pushed forward a little to shield the rest of the army as it prepared to file away to the south. The *chevaulegers* formed the front line and the Sysoev and Melentev Cossack Regiments joined the force, hovering on their flanks.

This southward movement of the remaining Allied forces quickly attracted French attention. Consequently, a battery of Garde Impériale horse artillery established itself close to the northern bank of the lake and opened up on the Russians as they filed over the causeway. This concentrated target soon came under heavy bombardment, and when a howitzer shell hit an ammunition cart the resulting explosion prevented many following vehicles passing the spot. Fortunately for those following on foot, the ice of the Menitz pond – which held firm – proved their ally, allowing them to pass the burning obstruction and continue their march. Even so, as Stutterheim recalled, 'The Russian infantry, fatigued and exhausted, retired very slowly.'[21]

Determined to prevent this gradual escape of the Allies, Beaumont's dragoons advanced to engage the protective Austrian cavalry. Three French dragoon regiments attacked in a column of squadrons hoping to punch through the Austrians, who formed with their squadrons in line. The 3. O'Reilly Chevaulegers spurred their horses forward, and by the time the two forces met, the Austrian formation considerably overlapped both French flanks and was able to swing in onto the column and cause a great number of casualties. To bring help to their desperate comrades, another two dragoon regiments rode towards the struggling mass, but coming under heavy fire from a cavalry battery attached to the Austrian *chevaulegers*, they quickly found themselves in difficulty too. But the dragoons managed to break off the engagement and flooded back the way they had come, with the disordered Austrians in close pursuit.

Fortunately for the dragoons, one formed regiment of their division remained and this, the 21ème Dragons, launched themselves at the O'Reilly Chevaulegers and sent them scrambling back to rejoin the hussars and Cossacks. However, all the time more and more Allied troops were escaping across the causeway. Increasing French pressure on Telnitz had finally driven out the rearguard from the village and they too had joined the exodus to the south. Now the last of the infantry formations, the Moscow Musketeer Regiment, which had lost heavily at Augezd earlier, fell back to take up a strong position on a hill resting on Satschan lake south of Telnitz. Here they formed a final rearguard, protecting the causeway and offering support to the cavalry as they withdrew.

Unfortunately for GD Beaumont, Napoleon had watched the failure of his dragoons to break the Austrian resistance. An officer on Soult's staff, Saint-

Chamans, standing close by, observed the emperor 'in an evil temper': 'He caught sight of a staff officer who had accompanied the division. "Go back there", said the emperor, "and tell the general in command from me that he's no bloody good!"'[22]

While the O'Reilly Chevaulegers waited the order to retire they recovered quickly, despite being under fire, and advanced once more against the mass of dragoons, who were still reforming behind the 21ème Dragons. But as they approached the French line it parted to reveal another horse artillery battery of the Garde Impériale. Blasted at close range, the Austrian cavalry turned and fell back with their supporting units and artillery to the hill south of Telnitz held by the Moscow Regiment, allowing this, the last of the Allied infantry to retreat across the causeway. Despite coming under increasing artillery fire and suffering heavy casualties, the Austrian cavalry continued to hold this position, supported by their battery, which eventually managed to quieten the French fire. The cavalry held on to this exposed position until the last of the Russian infantry passed to safety, when they too peeled away and crossed the narrow causeway. As soon as they vacated the hill, French troops rushed forward to occupy it and their artillery continued to fire on the retreating cavalry until it moved out of range.[23] The last Allied troops had withdrawn from the battlefield. The time was between 4.00pm and 4.30pm, the sky had darkened, and the freezing drizzle that had fallen for a while turned to sleet mixed with flurries of snow.

As for the rest of the Allied army, except for Bagration's command, there was still much confusion. Kutuzov, after abandoning the Pratzen Plateau with the Phanagoria and Ryazan Regiments, remained in the Littawa valley close to Hostieradek until about 3.30pm, at which point he ordered them to fall back eastwards towards the road to Hungary. The tsar reached a point close to Austerlitz, where he met Miloradovich holding on with some of his men, and Weyrother who 'was tired out and in despair, and hastened away without making any attempt to excuse himself'.[24] From here, a little before 4.00pm, the tsar sent General Wintzingerode to Bagration with orders for him to withdraw on Austerlitz and 'maintain himself there as long as he could without exposing himself to disaster'.[25] This move meant abandoning the road to Olmütz and with it the baggage train of the army. Elsewhere, the Imperial Guard and Liechtenstein's V Column cavalry, the Russian and Austrian components operating independently, retired from their position close to Krzenowitz and fell back through Austerlitz. They left behind them a small mixed rearguard overlooking the Rausnitz stream, drawn from the Guard and Uvarov's cavalry, all under the command of Podpolkovnik Ermolov who still retained two artillery pieces.[26] These men finally fell back through Austerlitz around midnight when belated orders arrived recalling them. Their sudden appearance surprised Bagration, as he had no idea they had been out in front of his position.

Shortly after the tsar had ordered Bagration to Austerlitz, the sound of French soldiers cheering the arrival of Napoleon in their midst drifted on the wind to the tsar's melancholy group. The generals were dismissed to return to their men and lead them towards Hungary, and the tsar began his journey in the same direction, reaching the village of Hodiegitz at about 5.00pm. At the same time Kutuzov was in Wazan, only about 3 miles to the west, but in the confusion neither party could find the other, although the tsar did learn that Kaiser Francis was making for Czeitsch on the Hungary road with the Austrian battalions of IV Column.

Having received this information, the tsar decided to head for Czeitsch too, about 16 miles south of Hodiegitz. With his carriage lost, Alexander set out on horseback with a handful of aides and attendants and covered 8 miles to the village of Urchitz before stopping for the night in a lowly peasants' hut where he slept on a bed of straw. He suffered great intestinal pains during the night and at one point his doctor feared for his life, but he was well again by morning.[27]

The rest of the army, much of it in disorganised mobs, trudged on through the freezing night, through mud, rain and snow. The elated but exhausted French army did not pursue.

Chapter 17

'The Fate of Empires'

'A moment decides a battle,
an hour the result of a campaign,
a single day the fate of empires.'*

Darkness drew a shroud across the battlefield, covering the dead and the dying who lay in their thousands, nourishing the damp, chilled Moravian soil with their blood.

It would appear that total Russian losses in killed, wounded, prisoners and missing amounted to somewhere between 21,000 and 25,000, of which some 5,600 stragglers eventually rejoined the army. The estimate of total Austrian losses varies between 3,500 and 5,900 of which, no doubt, some later found their way back to the army. So, by taking the middle ground and allowing for the return of stragglers, total Austro-Russian losses may have been in the region of 21,000 men, from which French sources state there were 9,767 Russian and 1,686 Austrian prisoners.

The French gave their total losses at about 8,800 (Soult's three infantry divisions recorded losses of 4,239[1]), although it is reported that Bernadotte believed the figure to be nearer 12,000.[2] Therefore, when the guns finally fell silent, it is fair to believe that their deafening boom was replaced by the pitiful groans and pleas of at least 13,000 wounded men of all nations: the motionless bodies of another 5,000 remaining silent forever.

Yet it was not the level of casualties that decided the battle: in fact, there was little difference in the totals of killed and wounded on either side. The disjointed Allied command structure, reduced to fighting a series of individual unsupported battles, found itself completely outmanoeuvred by Napoleon's coordinated attacks across a battlefield on which he knew every rise and fall of the terrain.

---

* Count Alexander Suvorov (1729–1800), Russian Field Marshal.

Although it was now dark, Napoleon slowly toured the battlefield, receiving a rapturous greeting from his men whenever he came across a detachment huddled around their fires. La Grande Armée was in high-spirits and too intoxicated on the elation of victory to sleep. Podpolkovnik Ermolov, left behind with his small Russian rearguard near the Rausnitz stream, could not fail to hear their celebrations: 'I had to listen to music, songs, and happy shouting in the enemy's camp. They taunted us with the Russian cry of "Ooora!"'[3]

But away from these raucous celebrations Napoleon wandered amongst the piles of frigid corpses, posed in all the attitudes of death. He instructed his entourage to:

> 'remain silent, so that we could hear the cries of the wounded. Whenever he heard one of these unfortunates he went to his side, dismounted, and made him drink a glass of brandy from the store which followed him everywhere ... he remained extremely late on the battlefield; the squadron of his escort spent the whole night stripping the Russian corpses of their greatcoats, with which to cover the wounded.'[4]

All on the battlefield that night remarked on the bitter cold. Napoleon finally arrived at the Posoritz post house at about 10.00pm, where he intended to sleep. Before he settled down for the night he began to dictate a proclamation to the army, which opened with the words, 'Soldiers, I am pleased with you.' Then having recounted their exploits and victories and promising a return to France he ended: 'My people will greet you with joy, and it will be enough for you to say: "I was at Austerlitz", for them to reply: "There is a hero."'

While Napoleon composed these words of victory the battlefield remained a lonely place of death and despair.

After a remarkable day, Major Bigarré of the 4ème Ligne was making himself comfortable in a room in the shattered village of Telnitz when shocking news arrived. The eagle standard stacked outside with the arms of his first battalion was revealed as that of 24ème Légère, and an officer of the regiment had arrived to claim it. Bigarré rushed outside to see for himself and was distraught to find it was true. The 1/4ème Ligne had lost their eagle in the attack by the Russian Horse Guards and until now had not realised that the one they held was not their own. Accompanied by his adjudant-major, Bigarré immediately rode off to the scene of their disastrous engagement almost 6 miles away, picking his way through the gloom and the bodies of the fallen. Once he located the spot he painstakingly traversed the ground in a vain attempt to locate the lost eagle. Already in a highly emotional state, Bigarré then came across:

'a Russian Horse Guard … who, stretched out on his stomach, muttered French words of which I was to understand only these: "Princess Koniska, Petersburg, goodbye, always." While wanting to raise him to put him on my horse, he expired in my arms, gripping me so extremely with sorrow that my adjudant-major did well to separate me from him. This handsome young man … appeared to have received a blow of lance or sabre which had passed through his body, because his uniform was dyed with blood on both sides.'[5]

It was now about 11.00pm and the lateness of the hour and the cold of the night persuaded Bigarré to abandon his fruitless search and the dead Russian guardsmen. He returned to Telnitz, leaving the battlefield to the dead and dying, feeling 'inconsolable' at the loss of the eagle and expressing a feeling of 'death' in his heart.

The citizens of Satschan, who earlier had watched the battle develop from the church tower, had thought themselves spared the horrors of war. But when Dokhturov's men began to retreat in their direction at the end of the battle, panic set in. The village records tell that:

'a strange fear twisted itself around everybody. "Save yourselves!" could be heard everywhere. We ran down the tower, women grasped their children, men grabbed the elderly, and we all fled for cover … On 4 December, the enemy had departed from Menitz and Satschan, and their citizens crawled with fear and caution toward their houses. The first things we saw were our devastated dwellings, full of stiff corpses and emaciated dying people, some of whom were trying to push their wounded insides back into their broken bodies, and unable, with a final rasp, dying right in front of our eyes.'

Other returning villagers ventured out onto the battlefield to see the desolation and destruction for themselves. One man found:

'thousands of corpses stretched out on the ground one by one or in heaps. The expression on their faces was frightful to see. Hands, feet, dismembered bodies and trunks were scattered about. At one place a cripple stretched out his bloody hand and cried for help. Elsewhere we saw a soldier who had sunk up to his waist in mud and was half frozen.'

Yet, five days after the battle some wounded still lay unattended on the field. Capitaine Lejeune, working on a topographical survey of the area:

'came upon a group of fourteen Russians, who when wounded had
crawled close to each other for the sake of warmth. Twelve were
already dead, but two still lived, their hollow cheeks, furrowed with
the tears they had shed, bearing witness to the agony they had
endured … I at once fetched some peasants from Sokolnitz, and
made them carry the poor fellows to a place of security … One of
them, who knew but one word of French, kept on repeating,
"Monsieur, monsieur!"'[6]

At about 4.00am on 3 December FML Fürst Liechtenstein, commander of
Allied V Column, arrived at Napoleon's headquarters on the orders of the
kaiser to propose an interview and armistice between the emperors of Austria
and France. Napoleon was not averse to the idea but delayed it until the
following day: he felt there was much to gain by pursuing the defeated Allied
army and cornering it before discussing peace.

First, however, Napoleon needed to find the Allied army that had
disappeared into the darkness the previous evening. Bagration, commanding
the rearguard of the army had pulled out of Austerlitz overnight and retreated
down the road towards northern Hungary (now Slovakia) where he found
Kienmayer and his ever-present cavalry covering the retreat of the army at
Niskowitz, just over 3 miles south of Austerlitz. Bagration continued for about
another 3 miles before halting north of Urchitz.

Napoleon's cavalry patrols began searching at dawn on 3 December and
incredibly, considering the amount of equipment the retreating Allied army
abandoned on the road, could find no sign of them. Then Napoleon received a
report from Murat, which stated that he had received information that the
Allies had managed to cut back to the Brünn-Olmütz road during the night and
were falling back on the latter town. The information was wrong, but unaware,
Napoleon ordered Murat with the Cavalry Reserve and Lannes at the head of
V Corps off on a wild-goose chase to the north-east. They captured much
baggage but found no trace of the retreating Austro-Russian army. Only later
in the morning, when Napoleon moved to Austerlitz did he learn the truth: the
Allied army was retreating towards Hungary.

The emperor immediately recalled Murat and Lannes. Orders then
despatched to Soult, Davout, the Garde Impériale and Reserve Grenadiers
directed them toward the March river, the border with northern Hungary.
Gudin's breathless division of Davout's III Corps, which on the day of the
battle reached Nikolsburg after a marathon march from Pressburg, now found
itself the closest formation to the retreating allies.

Benefiting from this respite, the Allied army gradually regrouped during the
day, with all the Russian troops passing through Czeitsch and continuing
towards Göding on the border. Once he heard the French were in Austerlitz,
Kienmayer fell back to Saruschitz, from where he could support Bagration.

Other Allied formations that had not reached Austerlitz in time for the battle received instructions redirecting them on Göding. Merveldt, after his long cross-country journey following his defeat at Mariazell had gathered about 4,500 men about him at Lundenburg, about 14 miles south-west of Göding, while General Leitenant Essen I was at Napajedla with about 10,000 Russian troops, just over 30 miles east of Austerlitz.

At the same time, the Archdukes Charles and John were marching through Hungary with about 80,000 men and arrived at Körmond, 100 miles south of Göding on 6 December. And in Bohemia, Archduke Ferdinand stood menacingly, with some 10,000 men facing Wrede's 6,500 Bavarians. Ferdinand attacked on the day of Austerlitz, pushing the Bavarians back, but unaware of the outcome of the main battle, the Bavarians successfully fought back the following day. On 4 December both sides looked to recover, then on 5 December Ferdinand attacked again, pushing the Bavarian force back through Iglau to Budwitz, at which point both sides learnt of the armistice and fighting ceased.

The value of the advice given by Kutuzov and others to avoid battle, fall back and draw in reinforcements is clear to see. Perhaps by the middle of December the Allies could have called on an army of around 170,000 men in Hungary. But by 3 December both Francis and Alexander, as well as the army that had been at Austerlitz, had lost the stomach for the fight, as well as over half their artillery and vast quantities of military equipment. Francis wanted peace.

Kaiser and tsar met at Czeitsch at about noon on 3 December. Alexander told Francis, 'Act according to your own interests', for he intended to continue his retreat across the March to Hollitsch. Disappointed, Francis later wrote that this decision 'deprived us of very necessary support at the moment when we had to treat for peace'.[7]

The Russians arrived at Göding during the day and Kutuzov gave the order for the disordered companies, regiments and columns to be reformed. He also intended crossing the river but Weyrother rode up, and in the name of the tsar, ordered the army to remain and bivouac on the north bank with the river at their backs. Langeron commented bitterly that the order 'convinced many among us that he wanted to complete his work and deliver us to the French'.[8]

At about 2.00pm French troops approached Bagration's rearguard on the main road at Urchitz and skirmished for a couple of hours before he and Kienmayer fell back after dark over the Spáleny stream. Following his previous night spent in the humble surroundings of the Posoritz post house, Napoleon spent this night in the luxurious splendour of the Kaunitz Castle in Austerlitz. Here, surrounded by numerous captured enemy banners and standards, the trophies of war, he basked in the glory of the crushing defeat he had imposed on the armies of Austria and Russia. Never had Napoleon achieved such a crushing victory and so dominated a battlefield, but the errors committed by the Allies contributed much to the enormity of his triumph. He was able to muse, 'I fought thirty battles such as this one; but never one where victory was so pronounced and destiny so finely balanced.'

The next morning, 4 December, a suspension of arms took place, and at a little after 2.00pm, Napoleon and Francis, with Liechtenstein in attendance, met by a mill less than a mile north of Nasedlowitz, where the road crossed the Spáleny stream. The meeting lasted some two hours and by the end of it an armistice was agreed, coming into effect the following day, with the articles being finally signed on 6 December.

Napoleon returned to Austerlitz and Francis to Czeitsch, while two officers, Général de division Savary and Generalmajor Stutterheim, rode to Hollitsch to seek Alexander's acceptance of the terms. If he agreed, they were to ride on and locate Merveldt and Davout and inform them that hostilities were over. But there was still time for one more panic in the Allied camp.

During the afternoon, while talks progressed, Gudin's division and light cavalry from Davout's main body approached Göding. News of this French advance on the town brought orders for an immediate withdrawal. Langeron saw:

> 'The adjutants of the emperor and Kutuzov galloping by shouting: "Retire! Pass by the town and the bridge this instant!" etc. Everyone precipitated towards the gate, which was soon overburdened, fortunately we did not have wagons and we were no longer encumbered with our guns and caissons.'[9]

It was a tense moment but the Allies had one final card to play in the game of bluff that started back at the Tabor bridge. Merveldt sent a message to the advancing French troops, falsely claiming that a general armistice was already in place. When the news reached Davout he remained suspicious but Merveldt backed it up with a confirming note from the tsar. In these circumstances Davout ordered his men to stop and the relieved Russians continued to pass unmolested across the March river to Hollitsch.

Savary and Stutterheim reached Hollitsch at about midnight and gained an immediate audience with the tsar. They informed him of the terms of the armistice and he readily accepted: the Russian army would leave the Austrian states in the shortest possible time and return to Russia. The two envoys then rode off into the night to search out Merveldt and Davout, who they located in the early hours of 5 December: thus the last two belligerent forces in the field put down their weapons. The war was over, now it was a question of settling the peace.

Napoleon returned to Brünn on 7 December and by 12 December was back at the Schönbrunn Palace outside Vienna. The following day he met with Prussia's foreign minister, Haugwitz, whom he had dismissed from Brünn eight days earlier. Haugwitz had arrived to deliver Prussia's ultimatum, but now, due to the dramatically changed circumstances, he instead offered Napoleon his king's congratulations on the great victory.

Fully aware of the nature of Haugwitz's mission, Napoleon replied by suggesting that his master would not be speaking of friendship if the result of the battle had brought a different decision. Then Napoleon further discomforted Haugwitz by severely rebuking him for the Treaty of Potsdam between Prussia and Russia. Having knocked the Prussian minister off balance he drew him back by dangling the much-coveted territory of Hanover before him in exchange for the minor Prussian controlled lands of Ansbach, Cleves and Neufchâtel. With Haugwitz dazzled by the offer, Napoleon continued to pressurise him, adding that all existing Prussian treaties should be abandoned for one between Prussia and France: Prussia was to enact any economic sanctions against Britain that France decreed and Prussia's other foreign minister, Hardenberg, be dismissed from office. Increasing the pressure, Napoleon required Haugwitz to sign the agreement within a few hours, and on 15 December he acquiesced. The minister had arrived to deliver an ultimatum and departed having traded Prussia's honour. Later Prussian attempts to moderate the terms failed and when Haugwitz attended Napoleon in Paris in February 1806 to ratify the treaty, the emperor humiliated him again, adding further clauses that confirmed France's dominance.

With the tsar and his army marching back to Russia, and Prussia emasculated by the Treaty of Schönbrunn, Napoleon turned his attention to Austria. Talleyrand, Napoleon's able foreign minister and now Grand Chamberlain, had long since urged a policy of moderation towards Austria. He saw Austria as an opponent to Russian expansion when the presumed break-up of the Ottoman Empire occurred. By punishing Austria with the confiscation of Italian and German territory but sweetening the loss with Ottoman lands in the east, he hoped to embroil Austria and Russia even more, freeing France to turn once more to face her implacable enemy, Britain. Again, three days after Austerlitz, Talleyrand urged the emperor not to break up the Austrian monarchy, claiming, 'it is indispensable to the future safety of the civilized world.' But Napoleon had his own ideas of suitable punishment for Austria: he knew the Habsburg Empire was at his mercy and he intended to exploit it to the full.

On 23 December Talleyrand arrived at Pressburg to dictate Napoleon's terms of peace: it was not a discussion. The Austrian negotiators only extracted one concession, the reduction of a financial indemnity from 100 million francs down to 40 million (£2 million in 1805). Napoleon eliminated Austrian influence in Italy by claiming the lands of Venetia, Dalmatia and Istria, all bordering the Adriatic and appending them to the fledgling Kingdom of Italy, forcing Austria to acknowledge him as king. In Germany, Tirol and Vorarlberg were handed to Bavaria as a reward for her loyalty, while Baden and Württemberg were aggrandized by the addition of Habsburg lands in Swabia.

In all, the Habsburg Empire lost 2.5 million subjects. The electors of Bavaria and Württemberg became kings and the margrave of Baden a grand duke, with their sovereignty guaranteed by Napoleon. It marked the first steps in the formation of the Confederation of the Rhine, Napoleon's replacement for the ancient and decrepit Holy Roman Empire.

In return for this exclusion from Italy and severe limiting of her authority in Germany, Napoleon granted Austria the sop of Salzburg. The Austrian diplomats made a desperate plea for the retention of Tirol and Dalmatia without success and on 26 December they reluctantly signed the Treaty of Pressburg. For Napoleon it appeared a brilliant diplomatic triumph, but in Austria it bred a feeling of humiliation, then resentment, and eventually a determination for revenge.

La Grande Armée marched through Vienna at the beginning of its homeward journey, the first departures taking place on 9 January 1806 and the last units leaving twenty days later. Meanwhile, Maréchal Massena, having pursued Archduke Charles across northern Italy, headed south to conquer Naples. But despite the promises of Napoleon's bulletins and proclamations, the majority of the army did not return home. Due to the tense situation with Prussia, most of the army went into cantonments throughout southern Germany, in a great belt from the rivers Rhine and Main to the Danube.

There remained much ill-feeling amongst Napoleon's senior commanders and one, Maréchal Lannes, taking umbrage at his minor mention in the report of the battle, published in the Bulletin de la Grande Armée, decamped forthwith from Austerlitz and returned to France. Many of the others continued to bicker and spit at each other as Napoleon, with an eye to the diplomatic and political benefits to himself, later awarded the honours of victory. Murat, who had married Napoleon's sister Caroline in 1800, became grand duke of Berg and Cleves, while Berthier was awarded the principality of Neufchâtel, both territories appropriated from Prussia. Although Napoleon had cause to reprimand Murat twice during the campaign, he remembered his important scouting mission to Bavaria back in September and the capture of the Tabor bridge. However, it was the naming of Bernadotte as prince of Ponte-Corvo, a rich Papal enclave on Neapolitan soil, which raised the hackles of most of the rival marshals. Although clearly undistinguished in the campaign, Napoleon used the award politically to settle Bernadotte – who continued to show evidence of his republican origins – firmly in the imperialist camp.

The performance of Soult's IV Corps during the battle was remarkable. While Vandamme's division captured the northern end of the Pratzen Plateau and then, turning south, took Augezd and cut off the Allied escape route, Legrand's heavily outnumbered division maintained a desperate defence of the line of the Goldbach, supported by part of Friant's division of III Corps. But perhaps the performance of Saint-Hilaire's division is the most extraordinary. Having started the battle on the Goldbach facing east, they ended the battle back on the same stream facing west, having stormed the plateau, driven off the defenders of Pratze, captured the Pratzeberg and descended from the plateau to take Sokolnitz.

Yet of the whole army, it was a formation of IV Corps, 4ème Ligne that attracted Napoleon's displeasure. At a review in Vienna he harangued them for losing the eagle standard of their first battalion, despite the fact they had captured two Russian standards. He eventually replaced the eagle in Berlin in 1806.

Prussia, having failed to commit to the war in 1805, where she could perhaps have played a pivotal role alongside the armies of Austria and Russia, now found herself browbeaten into a humiliating treaty with France. But when Napoleon then offered Prussia's reward of Hanover back to Britain without any notice, Prussia finally balked. Despite forming an alliance with Russia, Prussia took to the battlefield against France alone in October 1806, resulting in a crushing defeat for her army at the twin battles of Jena and Auerstädt.

The Russian army began its long march home through northern Hungary and Galicia on 8 December. As well as receiving supplies from the Austrian authorities, the Hungarian population welcomed the defeated army and readily offered up what food they could spare. But this abundance soon dried up once the army crossed back onto Russian soil, when the rigours of the campaign and weather took hold, bringing disease to the army. Langeron recalled that a quarter of the army was struck down with what he called 'hospital fever': 'there was no hospital, nor hospital equipment prepared. The patients were piled up in certain houses and many became victims of the lack of care, medicine and even of food.'

Thus the curtain closed, bringing a wretched end to a miserable campaign for Russia's army. However, the inquests continued for some time. Despite blaming the Austrians for all that had gone wrong – for there was now no love lost between the two allies – there seemed a need to punish individuals. Many held Kutuzov to blame for not pressing his views determinedly enough on the tsar, but he vehemently denied any responsibility for the defeat for years to come.

Kutuzov remained out of the military front line for the next few years, with various governors' appointments, before returning to active command against the Turks in 1811. In 1812 Kutuzov was appointed commander-in-chief of all Russian forces and by his strategy of retreating before the French, as he had advocated in 1805, he wore down the French and eventually forced them out of Russia.

Both Buxhöwden and Miloradovich had the ear of Kutuzov and the tsar, convincing them of their loyal service, while Buxhöwden managed to heap the blame for his own failings at Austerlitz on the foreign officers under his command: Przhebishevsky (Polish) and Langeron (French). Langeron, invited to resign and sent to Odessa, served in the Army of Moldavia for five years before his rehabilitation in 1812. Two years later he marched into Paris at the head of his corps. Przhebishevsky, on his return to Russia, after being held prisoner by the French, faced a court martial on the erroneous grounds that he surrendered at the beginning of the battle. Although cleared of this charge, his case passed to the Council of State, which, looking for a scapegoat, found him guilty of numerous other charges including not securing his line of retreat, failing to maintain communication with the other columns and also failing to supply his troops with sufficient cartridges. Sentencing saw him demoted, reduced to the rank of a private for one month, and ordered to resign from his command. Langeron reports that Przhebishevsky was finally reinstated as lieutenant-general some ten years later.[10]

The two battalions of the Novgorod Musketeer Regiment that fled past Kutuzov and Alexander early in the battle did not escape punishment. As a mark of humiliation the officers wore their swords without sword knots while the lower ranks lost their swords completely and had five years added to their twenty-five-year term of service.

Russia remained unaffected by the Treaty of Pressburg and Napoleon hoped to draw the tsar into an alliance against Britain but he failed. Instead, Russia sided with Prussia, joining Britain and Sweden in a Fourth Coalition. The Russian army was too far away to assist Prussia when Napoleon attacked in 1806, and as a consequence, was obliged to maintain the struggle with limited Prussian support the following year. After a bloody draw at Eylau, the subsequent French victory at Friedland settled the war leading to a temporary alliance between France and Russia.

The condition Austria found itself in at the end of the war is clearly illustrated in a gloomy letter written a few days after the signing of the Treaty of Pressburg by Archduke Charles to his brother the kaiser:

'Austria faces a terrible crisis. Your Majesty stands alone at the end of a short but horrible war; your country is devastated, your treasury empty ... the honour of your arms diminished, your reputation tarnished and the economic well being of your subjects ruined for many years.'[11]

Austria now embarked on a period of military reform, with Archduke Charles at the helm. But the kaiser could never dismiss his feeling of suspicion towards Charles, leading to numerous court intrigues; which in turn affected the implementation of his reconstruction. Although experiencing much pressure to align the Austrian army with Prussia in 1806, Charles wisely avoided committing to the cause. In 1809 Austria rose again against Napoleon, burning to avenge her losses in 1805, but although repulsing Napoleon at

Aspern-Essling, defeat in the subsequent battle at Wagram forced Austria to sue for peace.

On the eve of the departure of the Russian army from Hollitsch the tsar dismissed GM Franz Weyrother, his Austrian chief of staff. Langeron felt that the tsar was 'finally disgusted' with him.[12] Burdened with the stress of defeat and suffering from the effects of the huge responsibility and workload that fell to him during the campaign, Weyrother became ill and withdrew to Brünn where he died a few weeks later, on 16 February 1806, aged fifty-two.

Also in February, FML Mack faced court martial for his capitulation at Ulm. The trial lasted until June 1807 and the resulting judgement stripped him of his rank, withdrew his Maria Theresa Order and sentenced him to two years imprisonment. On his release in 1808 Mack settled to life as a virtual recluse. Later, in 1819, after the dust had finally settled on a Europe ravaged by war, his rank was reinstated and his Maria Theresa Order restored at the request of Feldmarschall Schwarzenberg. At Ulm, fourteen years earlier, Schwarzenberg had been one of the officers who abandoned Mack, leaving him to his fate by riding out of the city with Archduke Ferdinand. Mack died aged seventy-six in 1828.

And what of Charles Schulmeister, Napoleon's 'Emperor of Spies'? He left Vienna on 14 January 1806 and returned home a rich man. He invested his fortune in a large château at Meinau near Strasbourg. But despite this wealth, Schulmeister craved the *Legion d'Honneur*, an award Napoleon denied him, saying, 'The only reward for a spy is gold.' Schulmeister rejoined Savary in the war against Prussia in 1806 where, besides carrying on an extremely effective espionage campaign, he succeeded, at the head of thirteen cavalrymen, in capturing the town of Wismer and its garrison of 500 men. In 1807, at the Battle of Friedland, Schulmeister received a wound from a bullet that cut across his forehead leaving a prominent scar. At the conclusion of the campaign, with his fortune further enhanced, Schulmeister returned to Meinau and invested the money in developing his estate. Savary called for Schulmeister again in 1809, when the rewards of the campaign enabled him to purchase another château and property in Paris, but he also entertained lavishly and spent unwisely, building up extensive debts. Then, in 1814, when the Allies drove Napoleon back into France, the Austrians issued an arrest order for Schulmeister and his two chateaux were ransacked by the Prussians, forcing him into hiding. After the Waterloo Campaign, Schulmeister was captured by the Prussians and imprisoned in the fortress of Wesel but bought his freedom at vast cost, the figure variously reported but at the least £1.4 million in current terms. Schulmeister remained under surveillance by the Bourbons until 1827, during which time he invested in a series of business enterprises that invariably failed, forcing him to sell off his properties one by one to ease the debts. Finally, in 1843, he sold off his last asset, the château at Meinau, leaving him penniless. Five years later, when Schulmeister had attained the grand age of seventy-eight, a former comrade, now the minister of finance, took pity on him. He arranged a tobacco kiosk concession for him in Strasbourg that granted him a small income for the next five years until his remarkable life came to an end in 1853, caused by a swollen artery of the heart. He outlived all the central characters of this story.

The Treaty of Pressburg destroyed the Third Coalition by withdrawing Austria from the war. The original plans of the signatories called for flanking attacks in Hanover and the Kingdom of Naples in which British troops would participate. Accordingly, Swedish and Russian troops arrived in Swedish Pomerania early in October and advanced on Hanover. In mid-November a British army joined them, having sailed from England two days after the receipt of news of Mack's surrender at Ulm. Prussia also sent troops into Hanover but the prevarication of Frederick William in joining the coalition caused confusion and prevented the pursuit of decisive action against French forces occupying Holland. When news arrived of Austerlitz and of the treaty concluded between Prussia and France, as well as that between Austria and France, Allied troops began to draw back from their forward positions. By February 1806 they were embarking for home.

At the same time the Anglo-Russian force detailed to land in the Kingdom of Naples arrived only belatedly, in early January 1806, and learning of Austerlitz abandoned the plan, re-embarking a few days later.

In London, the prime minister, William Pitt, had waited expectantly for the positive results from the coalition he had done so much to bring together and finance. The news that Napoleon had abandoned plans to invade Britain and was marching to face the armies of Austria and Russia brought him great relief, but this was followed by the shocking details of Mack's defeat at Ulm, which reached him on 3 November. However, the arrival of full details of the great naval victory of Trafalgar four days later lifted his mood again. On 9 November, at the Lord Mayor's banquet in London, guests fêted the prime minister as the 'Saviour of Europe'. In response he declared, 'Europe is not to be saved by any single man. England has saved herself by her exertions, and will, as I trust, save Europe by her example.' It was his last public speech.

Pitt had suffered from ill health all his life and now the stresses and strains of office were taking their toll on him, as were crippling debts and an addiction to port wine. On 7 December he left London for Bath, to 'take the waters', in the hope that it might benefit his constitution. It was here that he received the crushing news of Austerlitz. This, followed by the destruction of the coalition brought about by Austria's treaty with France and the failure of the Allied expedition to Hanover, conspired to weaken his spirit dramatically. He returned to his home in Putney Heath in London on 11 January. As he entered his house he pointed to a map of Europe and with great foresight announced, 'Roll up that map, it will not be wanted these ten years.' Two days later a meeting to discuss bringing the army home from Hanover seemed to drain him even further and a friend who visited on 15 January observed that 'his countenance is extremely changed, his voice weak, and his body almost wasted'. The following day he took to his bed and on 23 January, William Pitt, the implacable opponent of Napoleonic France and leading architect in the creation of the Third Coalition, died. His last words embodying the failure he felt in his heart: 'Oh my country! how I leave my country!'

In Paris, Napoleon stood victorious, casting his long shadow of dominance over Europe. But peace did not follow. Within a few short months he would again unsheathe that finally honed weapon, La Grande Armée, and cast it towards Prussia. It was the beginning of a sanguinary journey that was to last almost ten years: a journey that would cost the lives of many thousands of men, and finally end on the rolling, muddy fields of Waterloo.

Appendix I: Place Names

I have retained the original spelling of town/village names as they were known in 1805 and are familiar from the literature of the campaign. However, to allow readers to follow the campaign on modern maps I have provided a comparative list giving the current versions which replaced these mainly German names.

Old		New
Augezd	-	Újezd u Brna
Austerlitz	-	Slavkov u Brna
Bellowitz	-	Bedřichovice
Blasowitz	-	Blažovice
Bosenitz	-	Tvarožná
Brünn	-	Brno
Budweis	-	České Budějovice
Budwitz	-	Moravské Budějovice
Butschowitz	-	Bučovice
Czaslau	-	Čáslav
Czeitsch	-	Čejč
Deutsch Brod	-	Havlíčkův Brod
Frainspitz	-	Branisovice
Göding	-	Hodonín
Gross Raigern	-	Rajhrad
Herspitz	-	Heršpice
Hodiegitz	-	Hodějice
Hollitsch	-	Holíc
Holubitz	-	Holubice
Hostieradek	-	Hostěrádky-Rešov
Huluboschan	-	Hlubočany
Iglau	-	Jihlava
Jirschikowitz	-	Jiříkovice
Königsgrätz	-	Hradce Králove
Körmond	-	Komárno
Kowalowitz	-	Kovalovice
Kremsir	-	Kromeriz
Krug	-	Kruh
Krzenowitz	-	Křenovice

Kutscherau	–	Kučerov
Lundenburg	–	Břeclav
Marburg	–	Maribor
Maxmiliandorf	–	Dvorska
Menitz	–	Měnín
Nasedlowitz	–	Násedlovice
Neu Schallersdorf	–	Nový Šaldorf
Niemschan	–	Němčany
Nikolsburg	–	Mikulov
Niskowit	–	Nížkovice
Olmütz	–	Olomouc
Olschan	–	Olšany u Prostějova
Ottmarau	–	Otmarov
Ottnitz	–	Otnice
Pilsen	–	Plzen
Pohrlitz	–	Pohořelice
Pratze	–	Prace
Pressburg	–	Bratislava
Prodlitz	–	Brodek u Prostějova
Prossnitz	–	Prostějov
Raab	–	Gyor
Radziwilo	–	Radyvyliv
Rausnitz	–	Rousínov
Rebeschowitz	–	Rebešovice
Saruschitz	–	Žarošice
Satschan	–	Žatčany
Schlapanitz	–	Šlapanice
Stanitz	–	Ždánice
Telnitz	–	Telnice
Teschen	–	Český Těšín
Troppau	–	Opava
Urchitz	–	Uhřice
Wazan	–	Vážany nad Litavou
Welleschowitz	–	Velešovice
Wischau	–	Vyškov
Znaim	–	Znojmo

Appendix II: Order of Battle

LA GRANDE ARMÉE AT AUSTERLITZ

Commander-in-Chief: Emperor Napoleon

Chief of Staff: Maréchal Berthier

Total strength of army including staff – 74,500
Approx. 605 staff personnel, 58,135 infantry, 11,540 cavalry, 4,220 artillery and train, 157 guns.

Garde Impériale: Maréchal Bessières
Total strength approx. 3,885 infantry, 1,130 cavalry, 660 artillery and train, 24 guns.

Infantry of the Garde Impériale

Général de brigade (GB) Hulin	
Grenadiers à pied	(2 btns)
GB Soulès	
Chasseurs à pied	(2 btns)
Royal Italian Guard	
Colonel Lecci	
Grenadiers à pied	(1 btn)
Chasseurs à pied	(1 btn)

Cavalry of the Garde Impériale	
GB Ordener	
Grenadiers à cheval	(4 sqns)
Colonel Morland	
Chasseurs à cheval	(4 sqns)
Mameluks	($^{1}/_{2}$ sqn)

Grenadiers De La Réserve: Général de Division (GD) Oudinot and GD Duroc
Total strength approx. 4,650 infantry, 0 cavalry, 340 artillery and train, 8 guns.

Brigade: GB Mortières
1er Grenadier Régiment   (2 btns)
    (3 Grenadier coys and 3 Fusilier coys from both 13ème and 58ème Ligne)
2ème Grenadier Régiment   (2 btns)
    (3 Grenadier coys and 3 Fusilier coys from both 9ème and 81ème Ligne)
Brigade: GB Dupas
3ème Grenadier Régiment   (2 btns)
    (3 *carabinier* coys and 3 *chasseurs* coys from both 2ème and 3ème Légère)
4ème Grenadier Régiment   (2 btns)
    (3 *carabinier* coys and 3 *chasseurs* coys from both 28ème and 31ème Légère)
Brigade: GB Ruffin
5ème Grenadier Régiment   (2 btns)
    (3 *carabinier* coys and 3 *chasseurs* coys from both 12ème and 15ème Légère)

I Corps: Maréchal Bernadotte
Total strength approx. 10,900 infantry, 0 cavalry, 420 artillery and train, 22 guns.

1er Division: GD Rivaud
Brigade: GB Dumoulin
8ème Ligne   (3 btns)
Brigade: GB Pacthod
45ème Ligne   (3 btns)
54ème Ligne   (3 btns)

2ème Division: GD Drouet
Brigade: GB Frere
27ème Légère   (3 btns)
Brigade: GB Werlé
94ème Ligne   (3 btns)
95ème Ligne   (3 btns)

III Corps: Maréchal Davout
Total strength approx. 3200 infantry, 830 cavalry, 190 artillery and train, 12 guns.

2ème Division: GD Friant
Brigade: GB Kister
15ème Légère   (2 btns less the *voltigeurs*)
33ème Ligne   (2 btns)
Brigade: GB Lochet
48ème Ligne   (2 btns)
111ème Ligne   (2 btns)
Brigade: GB Heudelet
15ème Légère   (*voltigeurs*)
108ème Ligne   (2 btns)

Attached to III Corps from the Cavalry Reserve.
4ème Dragon Division: GD Bourcier
Brigade: GB Sahuc
15ème Dragons   (3 sqns)
17ème Dragons   (3 sqns)

Brigade: GB Laplanche
18ème Dragons	(3 sqns)
19ème Dragons	(3 sqns)

Brigade: GB Verdière
25ème Dragons	(3 sqns)
27ème Dragons	(3 sqns)

Attached (independantly) to III Corps from the 4ème Dragon Division of the Cavalry Reserve.
1er Dragons	(3 sqns)

IV Corps: Maréchal Soult
Total strength approx. 22,700 infantry, 2,650 cavalry, 1,320 artillery and train, 38 guns.

1er Division: GD Saint Hilaire
Brigade: GB Morand
10ème Légère	(2 btns)

Brigade: GB Thiébault
14ème Ligne	(2 btns)
36ème Ligne	(2 btns)

Brigade: GB Varé
43ème Ligne	(2 btns)
55ème Ligne	(2 btns)

2ème Division: GD Vandamme
Brigade: GB Schiner
24ème Légère	(2 btns)

Brigade: GB Ferrey
4ème Ligne	(2 btns)
28ème Ligne	(2 btns)

Brigade: GB Candras
46ème Ligne	(2 btns)
57ème Ligne	(2 btns)

3ème Division: GD Legrand
Brigade: GB Merle
26ème Légère	(2 btns)
Tirailleurs du Pô	(1 btn)
Tirailleurs Corses	(1 btn)

Brigade: GB Féry
3ème Ligne	(3 btns)

Brigade: GB Lavasseur
18ème Ligne	(2 btns)
75ème Ligne	(2 btns)

Light Cavalry Brigade
Brigade: GB Margaron
8ème Hussards	(3 sqns)
11ème Chasseurs à cheval	(4 sqns)
26ème Chasseurs à cheval	(3 sqns)

Attached to IV Corps from the Cavalry Reserve.
3ème Dragon Division: GD Beaumont
Brigade: GB Boyé
5ème Dragons   (3 sqns)
8ème Dragons   (3 sqns)
12ème Dragons   (3 sqns)
Brigade: GB Scalfort
9ème Dragons   (3 sqns)
16ème Dragons   (3 sqns)
21ème Dragons   (3 sqns)

V Corps: Maréchal Lannes
Total strength approx. 12,800 infantry, 1,130 cavalry, 500 artillery and train, 23 guns.

3ème Division: GD Suchet
Brigade: GB Claparède
17ème Légère   (2 btns)
Brigade: GB Beker
34ème Ligne   (3 btns)
40ème Ligne   (2 btns)
Brigade: GB Valhubert
64ème Ligne   (2 btns)
88ème Ligne   (2 btns)

Attached from III Corps
1er Division: GD Caffarelli
Brigade: GB Eppler
13ème Légère   (2 btns)
Brigade: GB Demont
17ème Ligne   (2 btns)
30ème Ligne   (2 btns)
Brigade: GB Debilly
51ème Ligne   (2 btns)
61ème Ligne   (2 btns)

Attached to V Corps from the Cavalry Reserve.
2ème Dragon Division: GD Walther
Brigade: GB Sébastiani
3ème Dragons   (3 sqns)
6ème Dragons   (3 sqns)
Brigade: GB Roget
10ème Dragons   (3 sqns)
11ème Dragons   (3 sqns)
Brigade: GB Boussart
13ème Dragons   (3 sqns)
22ème Dragons   (3 sqns)

Cavalry Reserve Corps: Maréchal Murat
Total strength approx. 5,800 cavalry, 380 artillery and train, 12 guns.

1er Heavy Cavalry Division: GD Nansouty
Brigade: GB Piston
1er Carabiniers   (3 sqns)
2ème Carabiniers   (3 sqns)
Brigade: GB La Houssaye
2ème Cuirassiers   (3 sqns)
9ème Cuirassiers   (3 sqns)
Brigade: GB Saint-Germain
3ème Cuirassiers   (3 sqns)
12ème Cuirassiers   (3 sqns)

2ème Heavy Cavalry Division: GD d'Hautpoul
Brigade: Colonel Noirot
1er Cuirassiers   (3 sqns)
5ème Cuirassiers   (3 sqns)
Brigade: GB Saint-Sulpice
10ème Cuirassiers   (3 sqns)
11ème Cuirassiers   (3 sqns)

Light Cavalry Brigade
Brigade: GB Milhaud
16ème Chasseurs à cheval   (3 sqns)
22ème Chasseurs à cheval   (3 sqns)

Attached to the Cavalry Reserve Corps from I Corps.
Light Cavalry Division: GD Kellermann
Brigade: GB Van Marisy
2ème Hussards   (3 sqns)
5ème Hussards   (3 sqns)
Brigade: GB Picard
4ème Hussards   (3 sqns)
5ème Chasseurs à cheval   (3 sqns)

Attached to the Cavalry Reserve Corps from V Corps.
Light Cavalry Division: GB Fauconnet
Brigade: GB Treillard
9ème Hussards   (3 sqns)
10ème Hussards   (3 sqns)
Brigade: GB Fauconnet
13ème Chasseurs à cheval   (3 sqns)
21ème Chasseurs à cheval   (3 sqns)

Artillery Reserve Park
Total strength approx. 410 artillery and train, 18 guns.

THE AUSTRO-RUSSIAN ARMY AT AUSTERLITZ

Supreme Commander at Austerlitz: Tsar Alexander I

Commander-in-Chief of Allied forces: General of infanterii
Mikhail Kutuzov

Chief of Staff: Generalmajor (GM) Weyrother

Austrian Commander: Feldmarschalleutant (FML) Prince Liechtenstein
Observing: Kaiser Francis I

Overall Commander of I, II and III Columns: General Leitenant (GL)
Buxhöwden

Total strength of Austro-Russian army excluding general staff – 76,410
Approx. 53,035 infantry, 14,450 cavalry, 7,875 artillery and train, 1,050 pioneers, 318
guns.

(Austrian army approx. 16,820 men: 11,420 infantry, 3,195 cavalry, 1,775 artillery and
train, 430 pioneers, 70 guns.)

(Russian army approx. 59,590 men: 41,615 infantry, 11,255 cavalry, 6,100 artillery and
train, 620 pioneers, 248 guns.)

Imperial Guard: Grand Duke Constantine
(Russian formation)
Total strength approx. 5,400 infantry, 2,600 cavalry, 980 artillery and train, 100
pioneers, 40 guns.

Guard Infantry: GL Maliutin
Brigade: GM Depreradovich I
Preobrazhensk Guard   (2 btns)
Semeyonovsk Guard   (2 btns)
Izmailovsk Guard   (2 btns)
Guard Jäger   (1 btn)
Brigade: GM Lobanov
Guard Grenadiers   (3 btns)
Guard Pioneers   (1 coy)

Guard Cavalry: GL Kologrivov
Brigade: GM Jankovich
Guard Hussars   (5 sqns)
Guard Cossacks   (2 sqns)
Brigade: GM Depreradovich II
Chevalier Garde   (5 sqns)
Horse Guards   (5 sqns)

Army Advance Guard: GL Bagration

(Russian formation)
Total strength approx. 7,875 infantry, 4,065 cavalry, 735 artillery and train, 30 guns.
(Reinforced by two Austrian batteries at latter stage of battle – 12 guns/approx. 295
personnel)

Brigade: General Maior (GM) Dolgorukov
5. Jäger   (3 btns)
Brigade: GM Ulanius
6. Jäger   (3 btns)
Brigade: GM Kamenski II
Arkhangelogord Musketeer Regiment (MR) (3 btns)
Brigade: GM Engelhardt
Old Ingermanland MR   (3 btns)
Brigade: GM Markov
Pskov MR   (3 btns)
Brigade: GM Wittgenstein
Pavlograd Hussars   (10 sqns)
Mariupol Hussars   (10 sqns)
Brigade: GM Voropaitzki
Tsarina Leib-Cuirassier   (5 sqns)
Tver Dragoons   (5 sqns)
St. Petersburg Dragoons   (3 sqns)
Attached to Army Advance Guard
Brigade: GM Chaplitz
Khaznenkov Cossacks   (5 sqns)
Kiselev Cossacks   (5 sqns)
Malakhov Cossacks   (5 sqns)

Advance Guard of I Column: FML Kienmayer
(Austro-Russian formation)
Total strength approx. 2,500 infantry, 2,400 cavalry, 300 artillery and train, 250
pioneers, 12 guns.

Brigade: GM Carneville (Austrian)
7. Brod-Grenzregiment   (1 btn)
14. 1 Szeckel-Grenzregiment   (2 btns)
15. 2 Szeckel-Grenzregiment   (2 btns)
Brigade: GM Stutterheim (Austrian)
3. O'Reilly-Chevaulegers   (8 sqns)
1. Merveldt-Uhlanen   (¹/₄ sqn)
Brigade: GM Nostitz (Austrian)
4. Hessen-Homburg-Husaren   (6 sqns)
2. Schwarzenberg-Uhlanen   (¹/₂ sqn)
Brigade: GM Moritz Liechtenstein (Austrian)
11. Szeckel-Husaren   (6 sqns)
Attached to Advance Guard
Sysoev Cossacks   (5 sqns)
Melentev Cossacks   (5 sqns)

I Column: GL Dokhturov
(Russian formation)
Total strength approx. 7,500 infantry, 250 cavalry, 1,600 artillery and train, 100 pioneers, 64 guns

Brigade: GM Löwis	
7. Jäger	(1 btn)
New Ingermanland MR	(3 btns)
Brigade: GM Urusov	
Yaroslavl MR	(2 btns)
Vladimir MR	(3 btns)
Bryansk MR	(3 btns)
Brigade: GM Liders	
Kiev Grenadier Regiment (GR)	(3 btns)
Moscow MR	(3 btns)
Vyatka MR	(3 btns)
Attached to I Column	
Denisov Cossacks	(5 sqns)

II Column: GL Langeron
(Russian formation))
Total strength approx. 10,100 infantry, 360 cavalry, 750 artillery and train, 100 pioneers, 30 guns

Brigade: GM Olsufiev I	
8. Jäger	(2 btns)
Kursk MR	(3 btns)
Permsk MR	(3 btns)
Vyborg MR	(3 btns)
Brigade: GM Kamenski I	
Phanagoria GR	(3 btns)
Ryazan MR	(3 btns)
Attached to II Column	
St Petersburg Dragoons	(2 sqns)
Isayev Cossacks	(1 sqn)

III Column: GL Przhebishevsky
(Russian formation)
Total strength approx. 7,560 infantry, 750 artillery and train, 100 pioneers, 30 guns

Brigade: GM Müller III	
7. Jäger	(2 btns)
Galicia MR	(3 btns)
Brigade: GM Strik	
Butyrsk MR	(3 btns)
Narva MR	(3 btns)
Brigade: GM Loshakov	
8. Jäger	(1 btn)
Azov MR	(3 btns)
Podolsk MR	(3 btns)

IV Column: GL Miloradovich and Feldzeugmeister (FZM) Kolowrat
(Austro-Russian formation)
Total strength approx. 12,100 infantry (3,180 Russian and 8,920 Austrian), 125 cavalry (Austrian), 1,865 artillery and train, 300 pioneers, 76 guns (40 Austrian and 36 Russian)

Advance Guard: Podpolkovnik (PP) Monakhtin
1. Erzherzog Johann-Dragoner	(2 sqns) (Austrian)
Apsheron MR	(1 btn)
Novgorod MR	(2 btns)
Brigade: GM Berg	
Little Russia GR	(3 btns)
Novgorod MR	(1 btn)
Brigade: GM Repninsky	
Apsheron MR	(2 btns)
Smolensk MR	(3 btns)
Brigade: GM Rottermund (Austrian)	
IR20 Kaunitz	(1 depot btn)
IR23 Salzburg	(6 btns)
IR24 Auersperg	(1 depot btn)
Brigade: GM Jurczik (Austrian)	
IR1 Kaiser Franz	(1 depot btn)
IR9 Czartoryski	(1 depot btn)
IR29 Lindenau	(1 btn)
IR38 Württemberg	(1 btn)
IR49 Kerpen	(1 depot btn)
IR55 Reuss-Greitz	(1 depot btn)
IR58 Beaulieu	(1 btn)

V Column: FML Johann Liechtenstein
(Austro-Russian formation)
Total strength approx. 4,650 cavalry (1,170 Austrian and 3,480 Russian), 600 artillery and train, 24 guns (6 Austrian and 18 Russian)

Austrian Cavalry: FML Hohenlohe
Brigade: GM Weber	
1. Kaiser-Kürassiere	(8 sqns)
(2 sqns detached to army HQ)	
Brigade: GM Caramelli	
5. Nassau-Kürassiere	(6 sqns)
7. Lothringen-Kürassiere	(6 sqns)

Russian Cavalry: GL Essen II
Brigade: GM Penitzki	
Grand Duke Constantine Uhlans	(10 sqns)
Brigade: GL Uvarov	
Elisavetgrad Hussars	(10 sqns)
Kharkov Dragoons	(5 sqns)
Chernigov Dragoons	(5 sqns)

Attached to V Column
Denisov Cossacks	(2½ sqns)
Gordeev Cossacks	(5 sqns)
Isayev Cossacks	(4 sqns)

Notes

Chapter 1
1 Sir Arthur Paget's despatches are located in the National Archives (formally the Public Records Office), FO 7/75.
2 *The Times*, 18 December 1805.
3 Ibid., 19 December 1805.
4 Ibid., 20 December 1805.
5 Ibid., 21 December 1805.
6 Palmer, p.53.

Chapter 2
1 Rose, I, p.418.
2 Ibid., p.424.
3 Furse, p.95, quoting, Alison, *History of Europe*, Chap. xxxiii, p.312.
4 Rose, I, p.46, quoting Hulin, *Catastrophe de duc d'Enghien*, p 118.
5 Rose, I, p.462.

Chapter 3
1 Kukiel, p.42.
2 Ibid., p.59.
3 Rose, II, p.11.
4 Rottenberg, p.74 (or page 97 of reprint).
5 Ibid., p.87 (or page 113 of reprint).
6 Economic Policy & Statistics, House of Commons Library, Research Paper 02/44, *Inflation: The Value of the Pound 1750–2001*. According to British government statistics £1.25 million in 1805 had the same purchasing power as £64m in 2001.

Chapter 4
1 *The Times*, 8 Feb. 1806. A full report of the July 1805 meeting in Vienna.
2 It is often stated that Kutuzov began his march 10 days later than expected by the Austrians due to a misunderstanding caused by the Austrians using the Gregorian Calendar and the Russians the Julian – which features a difference of twelve days after 1800. This is not true. Kutuzov's march was officially put back to 20 August following Wintzingerode's late departure from Vienna in July, then further unanticipated delays meant he did not start until 25 August.

Chapter 5
1 Maude, pp.79–80.
2 Rothenberg, p.84 (or p.111 in reprint).
3 Angeli, p.464.
4 Maude, p.132.
5 Furse, p.143.

Chapter 6
1 Maude, pp.160–161. Quoting an order from Napoleon to Murat, 4 October 1805.
2 Ibid., pp.141–142, quoted from Fézensac, Général Raymond–Aimery-Philippe–Joseph de Montesquiou, *Souvenirs Militaires*, Paris, 1863.
3 Ibid., p.167.
4 Ibid., p.202.
5 Ibid., pp.176–177, and Willbold, pp.26–28.
6 Willbold, p.28.
7 Ibid., p.31.

Chapter 7
1 Maude, pp.143–146.
2 Willbold, p.34.
3 Paget Papers, 1 November 1805. It should be noted that this well–known quote may be a little biased. It was written by Paget a few days after Ferdinand appeared in Vienna and gave his report to the kaiser. Mack's report was not published at this time.
4 Willbold, p.37.
5 Ibid., p.36.
6 Maude, pp.185–186.
7 Krauss, pp.294–296. The actual strengths of 106 battalions are given for 6 October 1805. The average appears to be about 550 men against an establishment figure of 800. IR20 Kaunitz admit to a total loss of 226 men at Günzburg.
8 Nine hundred prisoners given in Willbold, p.41, Maude, p.185 and Lieutenant L. Loy, *Historiques du 84e régiment d'infanterie de ligne 1684–1904* (Lille, 1905), pp.279–280.
9 Lieutenant L. Loy, *Historiques du 84ème régiment d'infanterie de ligne 1684–1904* (Lille, 1905), pp279–280. The 9ème Légère became the 84ème Regiment in 1854.
10 Furse, p.194.
11 Furse, p.191.

Chapter 8
1 Douay et Hertault p.67, and Willbold, pp.54–56.
2 Riesch's report in Willbold, pp.47–48. The geological conditions along this stretch of the river bank differ drastically from those further east and south of the river. When Col. F.N. Maude walked over this area while researching his book The Ulm Campaign, he found the soil here 'the most viscous and slippery mud it has ever been my misfortune to meet', extending east towards Albeck and south–west to Ulm. On the south bank however he found the ground much firmer, and 'though much water lay in pools, and the country roads were far from being bottomless, nor did it appear to me likely that they would become so even under such traffic as the marching of the Austrian and French troops.' This he discovered was due to the nature of the 'cretaceous rock, and layers of deep–sea mud…which poach up under

traffic into a viscid water–holding medium of the most aggravating description.'
Colonel Maude also recorded that his own walking pace was reduced to one mile an
hour in this area. Maude, pp256–258.

3 Maude, p.240.
4 Paget Papers FO7/75 Enclosure in correspondence of 1 Nov. 1805 and Angeli,
pp.477–488.
5 Willbold, p.90.
6 Maude, p.246 and Angeli, pp.486–487.
7 Douay et Hertault, p.72.
8 Angeli, p.479.
9 Seventy–one officers and 1,553 men were captured at Trochtelfingen. Maude,
p.239.
10 From the Journal of the Count of Neipperg, an Austrian Staff Officer. Part quoted
in Willbold, p.99.
11 Willbold, pp.99–100.
12 Paget Papers, FO7/75 Enclosure in correspondence of 1 Nov. 1805.
13 Willbold, p.56.

Chapter 9
1 Mikhailovsky, pp.83–84.
2 Douay et Hertault, pp.77–78. See also, Karl Ludwig Schulmeister, *Gazette of the
Napoleonic Alliance*.
3 Ibid., pp.79–82.
4 Paget Papers, Paget to Rt. Hon. Lord Mulgrave, 1 Nov. 1805.
5 In fact this was the work of Schulmeister. See Douay et Hertault, p.72.
6 Paget Papers, Paget to Lord Mulgrave, 1 Nov. 1805.
7 Kukiel, p.65.
8 *The Times*, 30 Nov 1805, from a letter written in Enns on 30 Oct.
9 Ibid., from a letter written in Ried on 25 Oct.
10 Douay et Hertault, pp.85–86.
11 Mikhailovsky, p.88.
12 Paget Papers, Paget to Lord Mulgrave, 1 Nov. 1805.
13 *The Times*, 30 Nov 1805, from a letter written in Vienna on 29 Oct.
14 Ibid., from a letter written in Enns on 31 Oct.
15 Paget Papers, Paget to Lord Mulgrave, 8 Nov. 1805.
16 Ibid.

Chapter 10
1 Mikhailovsky, p.95.
2 Egger, *Hollabrunn*, p.2.
3 Langeron, Letter from Kutuzov to Miloradovich, 26 July 1806, p.65.
4 Lejeune, I, pp.24–25.
5 Ibid., p.25.
6 Parkinson, p.65. Quoted from Bragin, M., *Kutuzov*, Moscow, 1944, p.23.
7 Mikhailovsky, p.92. Alexander Suvorov (1729–1800) revered Russian military
leader who held great faith in the use of the bayonet. He is quoted, 'The ball will
lose its way the bayonet never! The ball is a fool, the bayonet a hero!'
8 Ibid., p.93, Quoted from, Dumas, Count M., *Précis des évènements militaires*, Tome
XIII, p.503.
9 Mikhailovsky, pp.96–97.
10 Burton, p.62.

11 Egger, *Hollabrunn*, p.2.
12 Ibid., p.8, and Douey et Hertault, pp.95–97.
13 Angeli, p.336.

Chapter 11
1 Langeron, p.67.
2 Parkinson, p.71.
3 Masson, p.142.
4 Ibid.
5 Janetschek, p.27.
6 Duffy, p.70. Quoted from *Souvenirs Militaires d'Octave Levasseur*, Paris. 1914, p58.
7 Langeron, p.25.
8 Ibid., p.26.
9 Ibid., p.25.

Chapter 12
1 Langeron, p.27.
2 Stutterheim, pp.40–41.
3 Langeron, p.138. Langeron's notes are added to an account of the Battle of Austerlitz submitted by Kutuzov to the tsar.
4 Stutterheim, p.18.
5 Ibid., p.26 & p.36.
6 Langeron, p.28.
7 Stutterheim, pp.20–21.
8 Paget Papers, Paget to Lord Mulgrave, 25 November 1805.
9 Highly colourful accounts of this meeting appear in Savary and de Ségur. Another account, published in *The Times* of 7 February 1806 and attributed to Dolgorukov, gives another more restrained view of the discussions under the heading 'Refutation of certain misrepresentations which have been circulated with a malignant design'.
10 Kutuzov, p.210.
11 Ibid., p.213.
12 Stutterheim, p.53.
13 Janetschek, p.39.
14 Kutuzov, pp.216–217.
15 Langeron, p.159 note 12.
16 Langeron, p.158 note 9.
17 Langeron, p.32.
18 Richter, Gabriel. This account recorded in the Satschan school chronicles by Richter can be accessed on line in the History section of, http://www.austerlitz2005.com.
19 Ibid.
20 Ibid.
21 Ibid.
22 Ibid.
23 Duffy p.80, quoted from Ségur, II, pp.451–452.

Chapter 13
1 Ermolov, p.54.
2 Masson, pp.144–145.
3 This is the version issued to the army. In a subsequent version of the proclamation Napoleon reworked it to read 'while the enemy marches to turn my right, they open

their flanks to my attack.' The original version reflects the position as Napoleon saw it before he recognised how far to his right the Allied attack had swung.

4 Kutuzov, pp.216–217 and Stutterheim, pp.59–61.
5 There are different versions of this event, some suggesting it may actually have taken place early in the evening and a number of different units claim to have been the first to take up the burning brands.
6 Ermolov, pp.53–54.
7 Thiébault, Passage du Goldbach, p.11.
8 Langeron, p.33.
9 Ibid.
10 Ermolov, p.54.
11 Langeron, p.43.
12 Thiébault, III, p.456.
13 Langeron, p.10.
14 Richter, Gabriel. Available online at http://www.austerlitz2005.com.
15 Langeron, p.43.
16 Coloquial form of Illarionovich.
17 Mikhailovsy, pp.181–182.
18 Duffy, p.109.
19 Stutterheim, p.87.
20 This narrative of the battle for Telnitz is based on the accounts of Stutterheim, the history of the KK Grenz Infanterie Regiment First Szeckler Nr. 14 and Second Szeckler Nr. 15 and the account of Corporal Blaise of the 108ème Ligne.
21 Langeron, p.45.
22 Ibid.

Chapter 14
1 Langeron, p.12.
2 Kutuzov, p.225.
3 Thiébault, III, p.468.
4 *Spectateur Militaire*, June, 1847, p.6–7, Kutuzov, p.225.
5 Kutuzov, p.226.
6 Stutterheim, p.101.
7 Mikhailovsky, p.184.
8 Langeron, p.74.
9 *Spectateur Militaire*, June, 1847, pp.8–9.
10 Thiébault, III, pp.469–470.
11 Thiébault, III, p.471.
12 Stutterheim, p.103.
13 Thiébault, III, pp.471–472.
14 *Spectateur Militaire*, June, 1847, p.13.
15 Thiébault, III, p.474.
16 Langeron, p.144.
17 Ibid., p.75.
18 Stutterheim, p.105.
19 Bowden, p.361.
20 Kutuzov, pp.226–227.
21 Langeron, p.145.
22 Mikhailovsky, pp.190–191.
23 Kutuzov, p.220.
24 Stutterheim, p.93.

25 Duffy, p.124.
26 This version of the charge by the *uhlans* is based on that given by Langeron, p.53 and Kutuzov in Langeron, pp.146–147. However, Stutterheim (pp.94–95) maintains that the *uhlans* followed Kellermann's cavalry through the French battalions in an attempt to get at the second line of French cavalry. Assailed by close range musketry on all sides they withdrew with heavy casualties.
27 Ermolov, p.60.
28 Ermolov, p.56.
29 Gielgud, II, p.109.
30 Kutuzov, p.227.
31 Langeron, p.145.
32 Mikhailovsky, p.186.

Chapter 15
1 Mahler.
2 Thiébault, III, p.473.
3 Stutterheim, pp.104–105.
4 Thiébault, III, pp.474–475.
5 Thiébault, Thiébault Brigade, p.14.
6 Thiébault, III, p.475.
7 Mahler.
8 Thiébault, III, pp.475–476 and Thiébault Brigade, p.14.
9 Mikhailovsky, p.193.
10 Bigarré, pp.170–171.
11 Ibid.
12 Rapp, pp.60–61.
13 Langeron, p.56 footnote 28.
14 *The Kiwer*.
15 Kutuzov, p.222.
16 Ermolov, p.57.
17 Langeron, pp.146–147.
18 Lejeune, I, p.30.
19 Duffy, p.130–131.

Chapter 16
1 Dumas, available online at http://www.histoire–empire.org
2 Lejeune, I, p.38.
3 Langeron, p.76.
4 Thiébault, III, pp.479–480.
5 Mikhailovsky, p.200–201.
6 Lejeune, I, p.39.
7 Thiébault, Thiébault Brigade, p.20.
8 Thiébault, III, p.481.
9 Mikhailovsky, p.201.
10 Kutuzov, p.268.
11 Mikhailovsky, pp.200–201.
12 Langeron, p.47.
13 Langeron, p.51.
14 Thiébault, III, pp.508–509.
15 Stutterheim, p.121.
16 Bigarré, p.173 and Mikaberidze, pp.385–386.

17 Gielgud, II, p.110.
18 Ségur, II, p.473.
19 Furse, p.405.
20 Langeron, p.51.
21 Stutterheim, p.126.
22 Duffy, p.146.
23 Stutterheim, pp.126–127.
24 Gielgud, II, p.109.
25 Ibid., p.110.
26 Ermolov, p.58.
27 Palmer, p.111.

Chapter 17
  1 Thiébault, Thiébault Brigade, pp.22–23.
  2 Mikhailovsky, p.210.
  3 Ermolov, p.58.
  4 Rovigo, II, p.209.
  5 Bigarré, pp.174–175.
  6 Lejeune, I, p.43.
  7 Angeli, p.360.
  8 Langeron, p.60.
  9 Langeron, p.61.
10 Langeron, p.59.
11 Rothenberg, p.104 (or p.135 of reprint).
12 Langeron, p.61.

Select Bibliography

Bigarré, Général, *Mémoires du Général Bigarré*, Paris 1893 (Reprinted 2002).

Bowden, Scott, *Napoleon and Austerlitz*, Chicago 1997.

Burton, Lieutenant Colonel R.G., *From Boulogne to Austerlitz*, (reprinted Cambridge 2003).

Castle, Ian, *Austerlitz 1805: The Fate of Empires*, Oxford 2002.

Chandler, David, *The Campaigns of Napoleon*, London 1967.

Chandler, David, *Dictionary of the Napoleonic Wars*, London 1979.

Douay, Abel, and Hertault, Gérard, *Schulmeister: Dans les Coulisses de la Grande Armée*, Paris 2002.

Duffy, Christopher, *Austerlitz 1805*, London 1977.

Duffy, Christopher, *Eagles Over the Alps: Suvorov in Italy and Switzerland 1799*, Chicago 1999.

Egger, Rainer, *Das Gefecht bei Dürnstein-Loiben 1805*, Vienna 1986.

Egger, Rainer, *Das Gefecht bei Hollabrunn und Schöngrabern*, Vienna 1982.

Ermolov, Alexey, Zapiski, *Moscow 1865–68* (reprinted Moscow 1991).

Furse, Colonel George A., *Campaigns of 1805: Ulm, Trafalgar & Austerlitz*, London 1905 (republished Tyne & Wear, 1995).

Gielgud, Adam (ed.), *Memoirs of Prince Adam Czartoryski and his Correspondence with Alexander I*, 2 Vols., London 1888.

Grunwald, Constantin de, *Metternich*, London 1953.

Hausmann, Franz Joseph, *A Soldier for Napoleon: The Campaigns of Lieutenant Franz Joseph Hausmann, 7th Bavarian Infantry* (ed. John H. Gill, trans. Cynthia Joy Hausmann), London 1998.

Hollins, David, *Austrian Commanders of the Napoleonic Wars 1792–1815*, Oxford 2004.

Hourtoulle, F.G., *Austerlitz: The Empire at its Zenith* (trans. Alan McKay), Paris 2003.

Janetschek, Clemens, *Die Schlacht bei Austerlitz (2 December 1805)*, Brünn 1898

Krauss, A., *Der Feldzug von Ulm*, Vienna 1905.

Kukiel, M., *Czartoryski and European Unity 1770–1861*, Princeton 1955.

Kutuzov, M.I., *Sbornik Dokumentov*, Vol. 2, Moscow 1951.

Langeron, Alexandre, *Journal Inédit de la Campagne de 1805: Austerlitz* (also including accounts of Austerlitz by Stutterheim and Kutuzov), Paris 1998.

Lejeune, Général, *Mémoires du Général Lejeune*, 2 Vols. London 1897.

Macdonell, A.G., *Napoleon and His Marshals*, London 1950.

Manceron, Claude, *Austerlitz: The Story of a Battle*, London 1966.

Masson, Frédéric, *Aventures de Guerre 1792–1809*, Paris 1894 (reprinted 2003).

Maude, Colonel F.N., *The Ulm Campaign 1805*, London 1912.

Maycock, Captain F.W.O., *The Napoleonic Campaign of 1805*, London 1912.

Mikaberidze, Alexander, *The Russian Officer Corps in the Revolutionary and Napoleonic Wars, 1792–1815*, New York 2005.

Mikhailovsky-Danilevsky, A.I., *Opisanie Pervoi Voini Imperatora Aleksanda s Napoleonom v 1805-m Godu*, St Petersberg 1844.

Palmer, Alan, *Alexander I: Tsar of War and Peace*, London 1974.

Parkinson, Roger, *The Fox of the North: The Life of Kutuzov*, Abingdon 1976.

Rapp, Général, *Mémoires du Général Rapp*, Paris 1823.

Rose, J.H., *The Life of Napoleon*, 2 Vols., London 1924.

Rothenberg, Gunther, E., *Napoleon's Great Adversaries: The Archduke Charles and the Austrian Army 1792–1814*, London, 1982 (reprinted as Napoleon's Great Adversary, Staplehurst, 1995).

Rovigo, Duke of, (Général Savary), *Mémoires du Duc de Rovigo*, 7 Vols., Paris 1828.

Schönhals, C.v., *Der Krieg 1805 in Deutschland*, Vienna 1873.

Ségur, Général Comte de, *Histoire et Mémoires*, 8 Vols., Paris 1873.

Stutterheim, Major General, *A Detailed Account of the Battle of Austerlitz*, London 1807 (reprinted 1985).

Thiébault, Général Baron, *Mémoires du Général Baron Thiébault*, 5 Vols, Paris 1893.

Thompson, J.M., *Napoleon Bonaparte: His Rise and Fall*, Oxford 1963.

Uhlíř, Dušan, *Bitva Tří Císařů*, Brno 1995.

Willbold, Franz, *Napoleons Feldzug um Ulm*, Ulm 1987.

Journals/Monographs

Angeli, M.v., 'Ulm und Austerlitz,' *Österreichische Militärische Zeitschrift*, (Ulm), 1877–78, p.395–510 and *Mitteilungen des K.K. Kriegs Archivs*, (Austerlitz), III (1878), p.283–394.

Castle, Ian, 'The Battle of Dürnstein: A Defeat in Battle, A Victory of Words,' *Osprey Military Journal*, Vol.4, Issue 2, 2002.

Castle, Ian, 'The Rise of "the Unfortunate Mack,"' *Osprey Military Journal*, Vol.4, Issue 2, 2002.

Dalton, Lieutenant Colonel. J.C., R.A., *The Battle of Austerlitz Tactically Considered: Minutes of Proceedings of The Royal Artillery Institution*, 1896 (reprinted Cambridge 2003).

Mahler, Major, 'Tagebuchblatter aus dem Jahre 1805,' *Mitteilungen des K.K. Kriegs Archivs*, VI (1881) p.499–523.

Neuville, Henri de la, (trans. Edward Ryan), 'Karl Ludwig Schulmeister,' *Gazette: The Newsletter of the Napoleonic Alliance*, Vol. 2001, No.3.

Spring, Laurence (ed.), 'Russian Losses at the Battle of Austerlitz,' *The Kiwer: The Newsletter of the Russian Army Study Group*, Issue 29.

Thiébault, Baron, 'Bataille d'Austerlitz: Passage du Goldbach,' *Spectateur Militaire*, May 1847.

Thiébault, Baron, 'Role de la Brigade Thiébault a la Bataille d'Austerlitz,' *Spectateur Militaire*, June 1847.

Archives

National Archives, Kew, London.

Foreign Office papers: FO7/75 – Sir Arthur Paget Sept.-Dec. 1805.

FO7/79 – Sir Arthur Paget Jan.–Jun. 1806.

British Library Newspapers, Colindale, London.

The Times, Jun. 1805–Mar. 1806.

Internet

A number of Internet sites now offer online access to Napoleonic memoirs, mainly in French. I have used the following sites in the preparation of this book.

http://gallica.bnf.fr/
Mémoires du Général Rapp
Mémoires du Duc de Rovigo
Mémoires du général Baron Thiébault

http://www.napoleonic-literature.com/
Mémoires du Général Lejeune (English translation)

http://www.histoire-empire.org
Extracts from memoirs of:
Major Dumas, Chrurgien du batallion d'élite du 28ème Légère.
Colonel François Roch Ledru des Essarts, 55ème Ligne.
Jean-Baptiste Barrès, Garde Impériale.
Colonel Lataye, 10ème Cuirassier.
Colonel François-René Calloux (Pouget), 26ème Légère.
Général Philippe-Paul Ségur, ADC.

Index